TransBuddhism

TransBuddhism

Transmission,
Translation,
Transformation

EDITED BY

NALINI BHUSHAN, JAY L. GARFIELD,
AND ABRAHAM ZABLOCKI

University of Massachusetts Press · Amherst

in association with the
Kahn Liberal Arts Institute of Smith College · Northampton

This is the second volume of the Collaborations series—an occasional series of books initiated by the Kahn Liberal Arts Institute of Smith College and published by the University of Massachusetts Press in association with the Institute.

LC 2009034571
ISBN 978-1-55849-708-5 (paper); 707-8 (library cloth)

Designed by Steve Dyer
Set in Adobe Garamond by Westchester Book Group
Printed and bound by Thomson-Shore, Inc.

Library of Congress Cataloging-in-Publication Data

TransBuddhism: transmission, translation, transformation / edited by Nalini Bhushan, Jay L. Garfield, and Abraham Zablocki.
    p. cm.—(Collaborations)
  Includes bibliographical references and index.
  ISBN 978-1-55849-708-5 (pbk. : alk. paper)—ISBN 978-1-55849-707-8 (library cloth : alk. paper)
  1. Buddhism—Social aspects.   2. Buddhism and culture.   3. Intercultural communication—Religious aspects—Buddhism.   4. Globalization—Regligious aspects—Buddhism.   I. Bhushan, Nalini.   II. Garfield, Jay L., 1955–   III. Zablocki, Abraham.
  BQ270.T73 2009
  294.3′37—dc22   2009034571

British Library Cataloguing in Publication data are available.

To our teachers

CONTENTS

All artwork, including the cover image *New Growth Tapestry* and the images
of oldest Vietnamese and American trees, of Thai ordained trees, and of
environmental monks in Chapter 11, by Meridel Rubenstein.

ACKNOWLEDGMENTS

The idea for this volume and for many of the essays collected in it arose from a year-long research seminar funded by the Henry and Louise Kahn Institute at Smith College. We gratefully acknowledge the support of the Kahn Institute and in particular the assistance and encouragement of Marjorie Senechal, then director of the institute, and Rick Fantasia, the current director. Peter Gregory was a co-convenor of this seminar, and we thank him for his leadership. We also thank our other faculty colleagues in the seminar, Andy Rotman and Ardith Spence for the insights they provided, and we acknowledge with gratitude the participation of the ten student members, two of whose essays appear in this volume.

We are especially grateful to two distinguished visiting Kahn fellows, the Ven. Prof. Geshe Ngawang Samten and Achan Sulak Sivaraksa. Each contributed enormously to the seminar and to the ideas represented in many of the essays in this volume. Bruce Wilcox of the University of Massachusetts Press has been very helpful in bringing this project to fruition, and we benefited from the advice of three anonymous reviewers for the Press.

Meridel Rubenstein created the images of the Thai trees and monks for the Kahn Project. Her other images of Vietnamese and American Trees (2000–2004) are part of the *Millennial Forest Project,* which previously appeared in her monograph *Belonging: Los Alamos to Vietnam* (Los Angeles: St. Ann's Press, 2004).

"Translation as Transmission and as Transformation" first appeared in the *APA Newsletter on Asian and Comparative Philosophy,* 2005.

"Toward an Anatomy of Mourning: Discipline, Devotion, and Liberation in a Freudian-Buddhist Framework" first appeared in *Sophia* 47 (2008): 57–69.

An earlier version of "The Transcendentalist Ghost in EcoBuddhism" appeared in *Bukkyō to Shizen* (Buddhism and Nature), Kyoto: Research Institute of Bukkyo University, 2005, under the title "Baptizing Nature: Environmentalism, Buddhism, and Transcendentalism."

The final preparation of this volume would have been impossible without the heroic efforts of Carol Betsch, Candace Akins, Mona Morgan, Caroline Sluyter, and Kolsang, to whom we are grateful.

TransBuddhism

TransBuddhism

Authenticity in the Context of Transformation

Nalini Bhushan
and Abraham Zablocki

The Global Proliferation of Buddhism

Buddhism is booming. In Western Europe, Australasia, and North America, Buddhism has attracted new converts not only in metropoles such as New York, San Francisco, London, and Paris but also in places such as Kansas and Ireland. In the former Soviet bloc, Buddhism has established a loyal following of new converts, while it is also undergoing a resurgence—after being suppressed for seven decades—in Mongolia and the Russian republics of Tuva, Kalmykia, and Buryatia. Buddhism is even growing in South and Central America, in Africa, and in Israel.

In the United States, this boom has taken many forms. Buddhist converts often exist side by side with Buddhist immigrant communities and, although the worlds of convert and migrant Buddhists were once separate, the borders between them are becoming blurred as the children and grandchildren of converts and immigrants find themselves participating in Buddhist practices and identities that are simultaneously ethnically specific and culturally universalized. Not only does American Buddhism comprise a variety of vibrant Buddhist communities, but Buddhism in America is also having an impact on the practice of other religions. For example, Buddhism has inspired a renewed interest in the contemplative dimensions of Christian practice, and, under the rubric of "interfaith dialogue," many of the techniques of Buddhist meditation practice are being incorporated into American lifestyles.

It is not only in Western convert and Asian immigrant communities that the effects of the global expansion of Buddhism on Buddhist culture are apparent. Throughout Asia, Buddhism is being revitalized through a variety of linkages. In Sri Lanka, Taiwan, Tibet, Mongolia, and the rest of the historically Buddhist world, new paradigms of Buddhist practice and identity are taking root. In some cases, this involves borrowing or communicating elements from other Buddhist societies, now newly in conversation with one another. As Karma Lekshe Tsomo points out in her chapter in this volume, Taiwanese nuns have played a central role in transmitting the full ordination lineage for nuns back to Sri Lanka, where it has been lost since the eleventh century. Globalized, American-inflected Zen has circulated back to Japan, sometimes mediated by Japanese teachers who have resided in the West, and sometimes by eagerly embraced Western *roshi*s. Western feminist converts have been influential in transforming the position of women in Tibetan Buddhist communities, affording these women new opportunities to study and practice Buddhism in ways that were historically limited primarily to men, including the opportunity to study the full monastic curriculum and to participate in monastic debate.

In India, the birthplace of Buddhism, ten-day *vipassanā* meditation courses, organized and taught by S. N. Goenka in a new modernist version of the Burmese forest tradition, have become popular, attracting middle-class Hindus, gaining a significant role in the Indian penal system, and even drawing Tibetan practitioners. In China there is a resurgence of interest in Tibetan Buddhism. Large crowds attend the Tibetan Buddhist Yonghegong Temple in Beijing. The fact that Chinese devotees come to study with charismatic Tibetan lamas has led the state to crack down, with limited success, on the participation of Han Chinese in Tibetan Buddhism. In Taiwan, the number of Buddhist nuns has exploded, and they now substantially outnumber monks. In India and Nepal, influential members of the Hindu elite may be found sitting at the feet of Tibetan exiles who had arrived destitute in South Asia only a few years before, while Indian and Nepali Buddhists from remote Himalayan communities have swelled the ranks of these exiles' newly (re-)established monasteries.

The transmission of Zen to the West—and the United States in particular—has been so successful that American Zen teachers are received in Japan with enthusiasm. In Southeast Asia political activists develop critiques of patterns of economic exploitation and social injustice by articulating modern visions of engaged Buddhism that reflect these activists' immersion and participation in larger global networks that adopt such Western ideologies as environmentalism or American Transcendentalism. On the one hand, these networks reflect Buddhist members' participation in a worldwide effort to engage religious institutions in struggles for social justice, such as the liberation theology movement in Christianity; on the other hand, these networks demonstrate the formation of global, pan-Buddhist identities that transcend particular national traditions. In the present volume, in their respective chapters, Susan Darlington and Mark Blum illustrate the interaction between Western ideologies about the environment and Buddhism.

Paradoxically, the internationalist desire of the American convert to Buddhism, Col. Henry Steele Olcott and his protégé, the Sri Lankan lay missionary Anagarika Dharmapala, in the late nineteenth century, to bring the diverse Asian national Buddhisms together under the framework of a shared Buddhist sensibility, has largely been fulfilled through the mediation of Western convert communities. Indeed, throughout Asia, Buddhists fly Olcott's Buddhist flag— invented by him in a self-conscious effort to construct a pan-Buddhist identity— and assert with complete confidence that it is an ancient Buddhist symbol.

The emergence of new Buddhist vernacular literature, especially in English, is also reshaping Buddhist sensibilities throughout Asia as some Buddhists— particularly the educated laity—increasingly find that English language presentations of Buddhist insight, or translations of these works into local languages, are more accessible than the older religious texts upon which they are based. This phenomenon is explored in the chapter by Jay Garfield. American publishing houses that were created to make Asian Buddhisms accessible to American audiences now find that their publications sell briskly in Asia, where some Asian practitioners find the American presentations more comprehensible and useful than indigenous texts, many of which were created specifically for monastic and scholarly audiences.

Buddhism has acquired a peculiar position in transnational public culture. Its appeal is far out of proportion from many people's encounter with, or knowledge of, actual Buddhists or actual Buddhist doctrine or practice. Its mystique has been produced through the imagining and re-imagining of Buddhism, until it today exists as a floating signifier, a term with no determinate meaning but rather a set of flexible connotations. For example, Jon Stewart ends "The Daily Show" every night with a "Moment of Zen." The choices of what constitutes a moment of Zen on this comedic television show are, in fact, far removed from any historically informed understanding of Zen Buddhism, either as practiced in Japan, or as it is now being transposed to societies outside Asia. They do, however, reflect an increasingly common understanding of Zen as a mere pointer to anything whimsical, mysterious, vaguely exotic, or redolent with unstated meanings.

While the global appeal of Buddhism owes much to fascination with *imaginary* Buddhism, it is also due to the hard work of *real* Buddhists, many of whom have spent much of their lives traveling the world as missionaries and cultural ambassadors. The widespread interest in Buddhism owes much to the thoughtful propagation of the Buddhist diagnosis of the problem of human suffering and the means for its elimination by these Buddhist teachers. Their crossings of cultural, linguistic, and religious boundaries tap the power of human imagination. Contemporary transnational Buddhism is more than *virtual* Buddhism. Although the appeal indeed owes much to the popular imagination, it is also constituted by *genuine* engagement with the views, practices, and personalities of living Buddhists. These intersections of the real and the imagined, and of the Asian and the Western, generate what we refer to as *TransBuddhism*.

This volume examines the global expansion of Buddhism and the changes in Buddhist culture, both in the United States and in the Asian countries in which it developed over the past two and a half millennia. The authors of these chapters explore the impact of this growth both on its new American hosts and on historically Buddhist societies in the wake of the upheavals of modernity and postmodernity.[1] They examine the *transformation* of traditionally Buddhist as well as non-Buddhist cultures *by* Buddhism and ask how the many different national Buddhisms are being transformed *by* their new transnational constituencies. This volume also explores how the *transmission* of Buddhist insight and authority unfolds in light of these transformations, and how the terms, texts, and theories of Buddhism are being *translated*. The grand question to which this volume is addressed is hence this: To what extent do these changes collectively portend the emergence of a new Buddhism, a *TransBuddhism*?

What Happens When Tradition Meets Modernity?

Cultural encounter is always multifaceted, and each cultural encounter is so distinct from all others that generalization about cultural encounters may be false or vacuous. American TransBuddhism—the translation, transmission, and transformation of the religion to the United States in the nineteenth, twentieth, and twenty-first centuries—is paradigmatic of a particular historical and cultural moment. The TransBuddhist encounters captured by some of the chapters in this volume offer a glimpse of that multifaceted-ness and complexity. Others explore the encounter as it occurs on the other side of the Pacific. These are but instances of what happens when tradition meets modernity, and in particular, of what happens when a religious tradition confronts the distinctly secular version of modernity that exists in the West today. What, for example, are we to make of the eager adoption of Buddhist metaphysics and cosmology—with its hell-beings and hungry ghosts—in the lives of those who are otherwise shaped by the hyperrational and scientific worldview characteristic of Western modernity?

We find three axes of analysis to be useful in thematizing the issues raised by these encounters: (1) authenticity versus appropriation; (2) translation, transmission, and transformation; and (3) the import and export of Buddhism.

What counts as authentic within a tradition, who are its authenticators, and what mechanisms of authentication are effective? What motivates people from another culture to appropriate that authenticity? How do their own narratives of authenticity figure in that act of appropriation? These questions in turn raise psychological and moral issues concerning individual transformation and the appropriate relations between cultures.

The thoughtful connoisseur of culture—whether anthropologist or aesthete—is often alerted by his or her peers to ways in which people "appropriate" bits and pieces of others' cultures as and when it suits their interests, and asked to learn to distinguish "authentic" from "inauthentic" practices in representing such traditions. The two ideas are inversely related: the more authentic a person, culture, or practice, the less prone they are to being appropriative (although more prone to being appropriated, perhaps!). Thus the thoughtful and culturally enlightened among us imagine the authentic to be morally desirable, and at the same time take appropriation to be morally problematic.

The very desirability of the authentic can, however, result in the actual desire to appropriate it, for oneself or on behalf of ones' culture. Thus, from another perspective, authenticity and appropriation are two sides of the same coin, and the preservation of the authentic from appropriation may not even be a coherent goal despite the fact that at times this deeply paradoxical attitude is taken to be self-evidently the only reasonable one to adopt.

Among the things being bought and sold in the global market is culture itself. History is replete with examples of cultural and religious appropriation that are clearly, at least, disrespectful, at worst, immoral. In the American marketplace, authenticity sells, and many businesses devote considerable effort to working out how best to package and market it. And so an MP3 player is named "Zen." So is a coffee blend. And the box for Organic Optimum Zen cereal asserts that it "provides a serenity and calm for your busy world" and promises "cranberry and ginger for inner harmony." When the Zen signifier floats so completely free, at minimum, we do a disservice to its integrity.

The authentic is the subject of concern *within* historically Buddhist societies as well. If the issue for the marketers of Buddhism is how best to sell authenticity, the issue for many Buddhist practitioners is how best to protect it. For example, within all Buddhist traditions it is crucial to ascertain who is an authentic teacher; all Buddhists stress the importance of legitimacy and lineage and in fact strongly reject the idea that any innovation at all can be authentically Buddhist. This leads to interesting contests within Buddhist communities over the authentic. A case in point is discussed in Abraham

Zablocki's chapter: "Buddha Maitreya," a New-Age American religious teacher who claims to be, among other things, the reincarnation of the Buddhist teacher Padmasambhava (as well as King Arthur and Jesus Christ). Maitreya dresses his followers in Tibetan Buddhist monastic robes and instructs them to carry around special *dorjé*s, traditional Tibetan Buddhist ritual implements, that, while clearly modeled on the Tibetan article, incorporate Maitreya's own unusual design features, such as an enormous piece of crystal along the central axis, and are therefore rejected by Tibetans themselves for being inauthentic.

Maitreya and his followers have adopted some of the trappings of Buddhism, but no one except themselves considers them to be Buddhist. And yet, if somehow, over time, his following grows and acquires institutional longevity, at some point, as Mark Blum argues, even innovations like these could become part of Buddhism's global diversity. After all, many of the "new Buddhist schools" of Japan were of suspect authenticity at their inception. Thus, the whole history of change in Buddhism can be read through the lens of continual struggle over issues of authenticity and appropriation.

This gives reason to validate the resentment of those who feel their traditions have been appropriated. It also justifies the concern of those, both within and without traditional cultures, who are impelled to protect them. Authenticity can be both oppressive and exclusionary: oppressive of those who are regarded as authentic (and who have to remain pure, enacting an imagined unchanging identity), and exclusionary of those who would like to become part of a practice and who are forever excluded as inauthentic pretenders. By the same token, there are aspects to appropriation that can be creatively productive and liberating. The terms "authentic" and "appropriative" thus become contested terms in the discussion. The chapters in this volume demonstrate the need for fresh thinking on the following pairs of questions: What is authenticity, and why is it important? What is appropriation, and why is it so bad? These questions are raised and considered by Jane Stangl in her chapter.

The second axis of analysis that structures this book is that of translation, transmission, and transformation. One has to select carefully one's criteria for the translation of texts, especially when they belong to a very different tradition, as well as choosing mindfully the individuals to whom one should entrust this important task. This in turn raises the issue of distinguishing between better and worse ways of transmitting Buddhist ideas to the Western world, and of being in a position to anticipate some of the roadblocks to successful and accurate transmission. In addition, the issue of transmission reflects the reality of global transformation in Buddhism. It is important to ask not only how Western societies are transformed as Buddhist ideas become part of daily parlance but also how historically Buddhist societies are being transformed as a result of this interaction.

As Jay Garfield points out, questions about the nature of translation raise further questions about the intended audience of Buddhist translations. Scholarly translations always have a reader in mind. That reader has typically been clearly identifiable, with a narrow and quite specific range of interests with respect to the work on the docket for translation. She already understands in some depth the area within which the work to be translated is located; her interest is to broaden that knowledge by adding the work to the knowledge base and to engage in critical discussion about the relation of that work to the material that is already in translation. Often the scholarly reader is also familiar with the source language of the text and is in a position to judge whether or not the translation is competent.

The world of the contemporary translator of Buddhist texts in this regard is distinguished by the varied and eclectic character of her readers. It is not only Buddhist scholars who read scholarly translations of Buddhist texts. They are also, and in many cases, more frequently and seriously, read by graduate and undergraduate students, by lay practitioners, and by people whose mother tongue might be Tibetan, Thai, or Vietnamese, whose religion is Buddhist but whose primary textual access to Buddhist ideas are English translations! The issue of readership thus complicates the question of what makes for a good translation. When one considers the range in backgrounds, abilities, and interests of these readers, one can perhaps get a glimpse of the kinds of problems that face translation projects, for those translations will inevitably be part and parcel of religious practice and transmission.

Audience is not the only source of complication, for the translators themselves no longer constitute a small, select philological group defined by academic training, credentials, and affiliation. Increasingly, translators of Buddhist texts are scholars in other fields, such as philosophy, anthropology, or religious studies, who know the language of the text to be translated and translate with their own fields of expertise as the primary interpretive engine. Philological issues become relegated to a place of secondary concern. More significantly, important translation work is being undertaken by translators situated outside of the academy, as Buddhist practitioners themselves take a greater and greater role in the translating and re-presenting of their traditions.

This contemporary dimension of translation throws into stark relief its accountability to transmission, and, with this explosion of texts translated into English, its role in the radical transformation of Buddhism itself, as varieties of translations exist side by side, independent of the lineage that gave them birth. This last consequence takes us back to the first axis of analysis, as the issue of the authenticity of translations, translators, and audience comes into play.

The third axis of analysis that structures this text is that of import versus export. TransBuddhism involves a bidirectional flow of ideas, texts, and sensibilities between Asia and the West. While in the past this flow was primarily in one direction, from Asia to the West, what is striking about the flow of ideas, people, and texts in the last few decades is that it is more thoroughly interactive. Thus for instance, as Darlington and Blum argue in this volume, Western ideas about environmentalism, American Transcendentalism, and indeed, of Buddhism itself, in the form of convert Buddhists, have cycled back to Asia to be used productively either to justify or to condemn, on Buddhist grounds, current social and environmental practices.

The issue of *what* is being imported or exported, *by whom* and *to what end*, and even *whether* something counts as "imported" or "indigenous" in a particular context is important for a host of reasons. It is of course in many respects natural to speak of Asian Buddhisms as if they take place in Asia, and Western Buddhism as if it takes place in the West, when in fact both categories are thoroughly interpenetrating and have been deterritorialized.

Further complicating this picture, in the United States many Asian children and grandchildren of, to use Jan Nattier's evocative phrase, "baggage" Buddhists, continue to think of themselves as Buddhists (Nattier 1995). They are, nonetheless, simultaneously full participants in American modalities of identity and cultural expression: young Tibetans in Boston are as Buddhist as their parents and grandparents were, but that does not prevent them from wearing hip-hop clothes or adopting the latest American teen slang. Similarly, the children and grandchildren of Western converts are, themselves, not properly spoken of as convert Buddhists; they are the second and third generations of a new paradigm of *American* Buddhisms.

In this new TransBuddhist environment, these worlds often exist side by side. For example, the Peace Pagoda in Leverett, Massachusetts, was created by a transnational Japanese Buddhist organization that has worked to establish a global network of temples devoted to peace; it is staffed and administered by a mixture of convert Buddhists (both lay and monastic) and Japanese monks residing in the United States. Just below the pagoda, Cambodian immigrants to the area have established a Buddhist temple of their own, many of whose members are people of Cambodian descent born in the United States.

The ease of travel and the increasing hegemony of the English language further facilitate the circulation and interpenetration of Buddhist ideas. Although Buddhist ideas have always been translated from one language to another, never before has this taken place within the radically globalized space of what Arjun Appadurai calls the global ideoscape (1990). Many young Tibetan students at the Central University of Tibetan Studies in India, for example, use English-language translations and commentaries as study aids to help them comprehend the Tibetan canon. The result is a circulation of knowledge in which the ideas and products of Western scholars and translators of Buddhist thought, many of whom studied with Tibetan or other Asian scholars, reading and conversing in Asian languages, are now beginning to shape the way that Buddhist thought is learned and interpreted by Asian Buddhists.

This situation is ironic in part because the Central University's primary research mission is the translation into Sanskrit of Tibetan texts, which are themselves translations of ancient Sanskrit Buddhist texts that have long been lost in their original Sanskrit forms. Thus, the import–export axis of TransBuddhism speaks not only to the East–West dynamic of globalized Buddhism but also to its intra-Asian dimension. This global circulation of translators, texts, and technology has made possible radically new ways of working with Buddhist ideas. Nor is this phenomenon limited to translations. Many texts that express Buddhist ideas in English using specifically Western idioms of expression, meaning, and interpretation, such as Sogyal Rinpoche's *The Tibetan Book of Living and Dying* (1992) or Dan Goleman's *Emotional Intelligence* (1995), have enjoyed tremendous success in Asia, both in English and in Chinese translations.

Structure of the Book

This book explores the tension between a desire for the "authenticity" of normative Buddhism as it is sometimes imagined, and the cultural hybridity of contemporary Western Buddhism as it actually exists. In the chapters that follow, the contributors describe the transformation(s) of Buddhism that this hybridity has produced, and they demonstrate that the resulting transnational religion is neither aberrant nor marginal. It constitutes a new paradigm of Buddhist religiosity, one which incorporates both Asians and non-Asians, which is globally distributed, vividly exemplified in the North American context, and which continues to embody the philosophical, ritual, and meditative practices of historically Buddhist spiritualities, while also making possible new patterns of Buddhist economic organization, politics, institutional structure, and identity. In short, these chapters demonstrate that in a moment of great historical rupture, Buddhists have embraced change as a strategy for preservation.

The chapters constituting the Transmission section focus on the way in which Buddhism is taken up by the West and the ways in which that process rebounds in Asia. Judith Snodgrass investigates the early history of Buddhism's emergence as an object of knowledge in the West, with particular attention to the work of an anti-Buddhist missionary, the Reverend Robert Spence Hardy, whose polemics helped shape the early reception and understanding of Buddhism in Britain and the United States. Snodgrass shows how Spence Hardy fashioned an understanding of Buddhism built around a biographical narrative of Sakyamuni Buddha, and she argues that this had the effect of minimizing the importance of prior Buddhas. Hardy thus propagated a conception of Buddhism that could easily be juxtaposed with Christianity (and, for Spence Hardy at least, be found wanting).

This, in turn, helped lay the foundation for "modern" Buddhism's humanistic bent. Yet, Snodgrass vividly demonstrates that these early steps were taken not to fashion a humanistic Buddha that secular moderns would find appealing but as part of a systematic effort to rupture the British government's accommodations with the Buddhist sangha in Ceylon in order to facilitate Christian missionary efforts there. Thus, Snodgrass's investigation of how Buddhist ideas were first made available in the West in English reveals not only how this contributed to the later emergence of modern Buddhism but also how these representations were formed in a political context that consciously sought to undermine Buddhism's position. Her analysis of the oft-neglected history of Western influence on Asian Buddhism is reflected at the end of this collection in Mark Blum's discussion of the impact of American Transcendentalism on contemporary eco-Buddhism in Thailand.

Abraham Zablocki's essay weaves together the historical, the anthropological, the personal, and the fictional in order to analyze the creative appropriation of the Tibetan doctrine of "individual exceptionalism" by some non-Tibetans as they seek reincarnate lama status for their children or for themselves. Is this move, from wanting to celebrate and to practice Tibetan Buddhism to wanting to *become* Tibetan, simply another creative instance of appropriation that takes its place alongside other appropriative acts, or does it go too far? By analyzing the novel *Sherlock Holmes: The Missing Years* by the Tibetan author Jamyang Norbu, Zablocki shows how Tibetans also engage in their own acts of counterappropriation as a means of resisting and satirizing Western fascination with Buddhists that goes beyond a desire to participate in Buddhist philosophy or meditative practices to include even the appropriation of the body itself.

Constance Kassor complicates the question of what it means to be Buddhist as North American Buddhism moves from mainstream society into its prison system. She asks how, in the context of incarceration and prison culture, one can observe Buddhist precepts. She asks whether, given the realities of prison life, it is reasonable to view some Buddhist precepts (e.g., the prohibition on stealing) as less stringent than others (e.g., causing another individual serious bodily harm), without thereby ceasing to be a Buddhist practitioner.

Kassor's chapter asks whether such reinterpretations are best thought of as *deviations* from traditional Buddhist practice or rather as the natural consequence of *transmission* of this practice to the prison system. If the latter, we might have reason to worry about the dilution of Buddhism beyond recognition. Alternatively, we might find, in this adjustment to practice, cause to reaffirm once more the reality of what is at the center of Buddhist ontology—that everything is impermanent and subject to change, including what are traditionally taken to be accepted Buddhist moral precepts. Kassor provides the reader with a detailed description of daily prison life, the kinds of access inmates have to Buddhist literature and Buddhist teachers, and a careful case study of the experience of two incarcerated Buddhist practitioners. She both raises the questions and offers the beginnings of an answer to these difficult but fascinating concerns.

Elizabeth Eastman traces the rise and fall of a Buddhist temple in America. Given the intense attention paid to Buddhism's dramatic growth in the United States over the past century, it is instructive to follow the history of one Buddhist institution that, having once been well established here, eventually died out. Eastman shows that although her great-grandparents' temple appropriated elements of American religious culture, they were ultimately the wrong elements for the temple to survive. The "church," as they called it, needed to change its sense of what constituted authentic Buddhism in order to appeal to new generations of Japanese Americans, or to draw in, as some other immigrant Buddhist temples did, convert Buddhists. Instead, the institution remained faithful to its roots—an "authentic" Shingon temple in America—and lost its succeeding generations to aggressive Protestant proselytizing, intermarriage, and, perhaps most of all, the secularizing and de-culturing dynamics of the American melting pot.

The Oregon Koyasan Shinnoin Temple adopted the outward elements of American religious institutions, looking and feeling like a legitimate church—and these appropriative moves may well have made great sense to its parishioners in the wake of the World War II internment of Japanese Americans and the long history of anti–Asian American racism, especially on the Pacific coast where the temple was located. Nonetheless, in the end, other forms of appropriation might have been more strategically necessary for the temple's long-term survival. Although the temple was undoubtedly an *authentic* exemplar of Shingon Buddhism, authenticity, this case shows us, does not necessarily ensure successful transmission.

The section on Translation collects essays concerned both with the literal translation of Buddhist literature from Asian to Western languages and with the more metaphorical translation of Buddhism into popular culture representations. Jay Garfield explores the relationship between translators and readers, along with their respective, sometimes disparate commitments, and the nature of the craft of translation in contemporary TransBuddhism. He focuses on the particular case of the translation of Asian Buddhist texts in North America. Contemporary translators come equipped with vastly different kinds of expertise, as do their contemporary readers, and there is no easy way of sorting out translations based on clear principles of translation etiquette. Which translators are authentic? Which readers matter? Should we even care to ask these questions? Without resolving all of these issues, Garfield urges his own readers to think diligently about what matters most to them about being "loyal" to Buddhist precepts, whether they be translators or practitioners, in an era in which translations proliferate and inevitably transform Buddhist thought and practice in unpredictable ways.

Thomas Rohlich invites his North American audience to pay attention to the development of the idea of the "mountain village" in medieval Japan. He does so by means of an annotated translation of twenty poems, most of which have not been previously translated into English. This exchange between two poets who lived as semi-reclusive hermits in twelfth-century Japan describes the poetic ideal of the recluse in the mountain village, or *yamazato*, which for Rohlich is a key to understanding the aesthetics of medieval Japan. This chapter is a three-way conversation, rather than a dialogue, as it is not only an exploration of how two poets engaged in a conversation with one another but an exploration of what a twenty-first century American translator makes of that conversation. This chapter illustrates an indirect but powerful way in which Buddhism filters into Western consciousness.

Rohlich's twenty-first-century translation into English of a twelfth-century Japanese poetic exchange illuminates both the challenges of contemporary translation and the ways in which finding the right words to convey Buddhist ideas was *already* exacting to the two Japanese monks. We thus see that the demands inherent in Buddhist translation are not peculiar to the present moment in Buddhist history, but reflect a perennial struggle between Buddhism and language.

Mario D'Amato interprets Jim Jarmusch's film *Ghost Dog* to reveal how a popular American film can simultaneously appropriate and validate Buddhist ideas in an American context. The film's central character, an African American urban samurai, represents the transposition of Buddhist ideals into the familiar terrain of American action movies. This could easily lead, as American pop-cultural appropriations of Buddhism so often do, to an Orientalist reduction of Buddhist ideas to familiar American moral truisms or fortune cookie wisdom. D'Amato shows, however, that the film deftly weaves Buddhist ideas and symbolism into a thoroughly American idiom. The result is a meditation on the intersection of Buddhism and American pop culture that privileges neither, while showing how it is that an American TransBuddhism is being constituted even for those movie-goers who may never encounter a Buddhist text or teacher.

Jane Stangl's essay documents the explosion of books and journals in North America that are almost exclusively devoted to the business of marketing to interested consumers the allegedly intimate link between Buddhism and ideal sport practice, using golf as the central case study. She observes, for instance, that golf gurus stress that one should "be mindful" at all times, focus on the "process" rather than the outcome of each stroke, and view the game itself as ultimately a meditative or contemplative form of exercise. In addition, Stangl provides examples of comments by famous golfers such as Tiger Woods and Vijay Singh that capitalize on connections they see between their own daily practice and what they take to be Buddhist ideas.

This chapter addresses the relation between what one might think of as serious Buddhist methodology and practice and the kinds of Buddhist-inspired suggestions provided by sports writers and star athletes. We are left to ask whether it should matter *how* Buddhist ideas happen to be taken up, transmitted, and transformed in various historically non-Buddhist realms of activity, and, if so, whether the fact that it matters to us is more a reflection of our own sense of what constitutes the authentic practice of Buddhism rather than a principled concern that is reflected in the Buddhist texts themselves.

Together these chapters illustrate the challenges of *translation* in Buddhism, showing the ways in which meaning and interpretation are always constructed, impartially and imperfectly, and how this process of construction relies, critically, upon the mutual collaboration of writer, translator, and reader. Inevitably, the quest for an *authentic* rendering of meaning becomes an irresistible, yet ultimately elusive goal, as the translator struggles to capture the multiple valences of terms and adequately render them in ways that capture meaning, style, and tone.

The final section in this volume addresses the *transformation* of Buddhism as it is transmitted to the West and back to its home. Karma Lekshe Tsomo addresses the history of Sakyadhita, the international women's organization she founded, and its role in advancing women's involvement in lay and ordained Buddhist life. She explores the barriers that have restrained women from participation in the full range of spiritual activities and roles available to men. Her account of the struggle for the restoration of full ordination lineages for nuns in the Theravāda and Tibetan traditions is stirring and provides dramatic evidence of the collaboration between Western Buddhist feminists and Asian Buddhist women activists made possible precisely because Buddhism was transmitted to the West. This is one of the most important aspects of TransBuddhism—the fact that it facilitates the circulation of ideas and the transformation of Buddhist institutions in the East and the West.

Tsomo's account of the enhanced role of women in Buddhism is illustrated by the contents of this volume. In addition to Tsomo's own chapter, six other women authors and one woman artist complement the contributor list. Five of these chapters (Darlington, Eastman, Kassor, Snodgrass, and Stangl) adopt very different perspectives on Buddhist religious and cultural practice in the West; while the sixth (Bhushan) offers a distinctively feminist TransBuddhist framework on a subject with universal appeal, arguably of special interest to women.

Nalini Bhushan juxtaposes Freudian and Buddhist mourning practices through a close reading of a Buddhist folk tale. Bhushan's chapter is an instance of how an ancient story is translatable into psychological language and idiom and thereby transmittable to a contemporary Western audience; it is at the same time an instance of how Freudian ideas, read into a well-known Buddhist tale about human suffering, serve to overcome the narrow confines of Freud's thinking, broadening the reach of his ideas in the realm of human psychology.

Bhushan de-emphasizes what is culturally specific in mourning ritual and stresses the universality of that which produces those more specific rituals for cultures, namely, the suffering occasioned by grief. In this way, the concern about preserving or protecting rituals as belonging to one culture (for instance, by wanting to keep clear and unsullied the lesson taught by Buddhist folk tales about mourning, as *Buddhist*, or Freud's own specifically articulated views on the subject, for that matter, as *Freudian*) is obviated. At the same time, the appropriation from both traditions, of rituals as well as the ways to think about their function in society, is justified by the resonance of the hybrid model of mourning in the actual phenomenology of mourning. Here we have a different sort of case study of TransBuddhism, involving the translation, transmission, and transformation of both a Buddhist folk tale and a Freudian narrative.

Susan Darlington explores, by means of a powerful contemporary environmental example, the integration of traditional Asian Buddhist ideas with Western political ideas and modernity. She demonstrates that the new Buddhist paths that contemporary Thai environmentalist monks are charting are simultaneously rooted in Thai religious tradition and modern environmental principles. The result is a new paradigm of socially engaged Buddhism that uses Buddhist rituals and identifications in creative ways to resist the depredations of consumerism, globalization, and exploitation.

For example, the Thai eco-monks are performing ceremonies for trees that are reminiscent of monastic ordination as a way of fighting against the massive deforestation that has almost completely denuded Thailand in a single generation. Similarly, the monks are doing long-life ceremonies for rivers as a way of reinterpreting the pollution of rivers as not merely an environmental problem but also seating it within a religious context. Although this move is radical on many fronts—as Mark Blum shows, the environment has never been a matter of central concern for Buddhism in its 2500-year history—Darlington argues that in the eyes of the environmentalist monks they are in many ways continuous with traditional Buddhist values in that Thais have always respected the relation between humans and the environment. Darlington's chapter illustrates the way in which Buddhism provides a space for the contesting of economic and ecological struggles within Thailand. She argues that these monks appropriate environmentalist ideas and practices from the West in a creative way, which in the end is not alien to Buddhist practice.

Blum adopts a different perspective on Buddhist environmentalism. In tracing the history, or lack thereof, of the concept of nature in Buddhist scripture, Blum finds no evidence for the widespread assumption that Buddhism takes nature to be sacred. While Blum allows that contemporary Buddhists may well be in the process of inventing an eco-Buddhism, and that this is an entirely legitimate way of responding to genuine environmental crises, these Buddhists, he argues, are mistaken when they imagine their view as continuous with Buddhist doctrinal history. On the contrary, Blum argues that the understanding of nature as sacred in contemporary environmentalism owes much more to American Transcendentalists such as Emerson and Thoreau, who, although they saw themselves as influenced by Buddhism, were, Blum shows, in fact drawing upon a broad range of Hindu, Confucian, and Unitarian ideas to construct a sensibility that experienced nature as sacred.

Blum demonstrates that this move drew upon currents of Indian religious thought—particularly regarding the intrinsic sacredness of all phenomena—that were explicitly rejected in early Buddhism. Thus, he argues, some contemporary eco-Buddhists are misreading their own history in order to imagine that the lineage of eco-Buddhism goes back to canonical Buddhist figures, while Blum traces the same lineage back to Emerson and Thoreau and their idiosyncratic and selective appropriation of ideas from Eastern philosophy at a time when their understanding of the spectrum of Asian religious thought was very narrow. In this respect, Blum's analysis echoes, although in a different context, Snodgrass's discussion of the role of Western ideology in the construction of a model of Buddhism in the nineteenth century.

Throughout the volume, photographs by the noted American artist Meridel Rubenstein serve as a visual narrative complement to the essays. Rather than exploring the nature of TransBuddhist encounters through text, as the other contributors have done, Rubenstein has created photographic images that reflect her own encounter with, and interpretation of, Buddhism and the cross-cultural understanding it facilitates. Her work stands as an example of TransBuddhism.

Buddhism and Change

There is nothing surprising or controversial about the fact that Buddhism is changing in America during our century. Buddhism has been changing since its very inception, and given the centrality of the doctrine of impermanence to Buddhism, this should be no surprise to Buddhists. This volume addresses the *kinds* of changes happening now, in and to Buddhism. The current situation differs from those of past transmissions by virtue of the speed of transmission, the multiplicity of languages and cultures involved, and the reciprocal relation between the source and target of the transmission.

These factors have led to a penchant for blending different kinds of Buddhist doctrine and practice, raising questions about authenticity and appropriation, the role of lineage, and the selectivity of one's chosen beliefs. These questions force us to ask how we are to view the practices and beliefs that are the result of those changes: Are they in some important sense linked to the earlier practices and beliefs, or do they represent a radical disjuncture from them? If the latter, might the changes we are seeing in our century in Buddhism be responsible for its erasure? That is, does the radical transformation of Buddhism coincide with the end of Buddhism? Or can a system be radically transformed and still be in some meaningful way continuous with an older version of itself? The concerns and arguments raised in the chapters in this volume lead the reader to consider anew what it means to be Buddhist, whatever the persuasion, in our times, and what it is for a tradition to propagate itself in the context of postmodernity and globalization.

Note

1. Of course, as already mentioned above, Buddhism is currently taking root in many new places aside from the United States. For the purposes of this volume, however, we are focusing on the growth of Buddhism in North America and its connections to Buddhist revitalization in Asia.

PART I

Transmission

THE CHALLENGE OF PRESERVING the intact, pure transmission of authority, lineage, and insight has preoccupied practitioners throughout Buddhist history. Buddhist institutional structure is intended to ensure that Buddhist teachers derive their authority from the validation of their own masters to reinforce existing practices, and to reassure successive generations that the Buddhism they practice is in all important respects identical with the original doctrines, practices, and realizations taught by the Buddha himself.

Nevertheless, as the Buddha taught, all phenomena are impermanent and, as the chapters in this book demonstrate, this has been true for the structure of Buddhism itself. As Buddhism has crossed national, ethnic, linguistic, and cultural borders it has generated radically different forms of itself, often in syncretic dialogue with the religious ideas of its new host societies. Making certain that Buddhism has been properly and *purely* transmitted in ways that ensure its inward continuity—even as outwardly transformations, sometimes dramatic ones, are taking place—has been a particular concern for contemporary Buddhists.

The chapters in this section demonstrate the complexity of these issues of transmission as Buddhism is moving to the West. Judith Snodgrass shows that Buddhism's initial presentation in the West was strongly influenced by the political and religious agendas of its English interpreters and translators. Abraham Zablocki demonstrates that the transmission of Buddhism does not only occur in the context of doctrines and institutionalized authorities, but sometimes is quite literally embodied in its practitioners. Constance Kassor explores the challenges to Buddhist transmission faced by prisoners in the American penal system. Her analysis shows how, even in a social context pervaded by violence and other constraints, Buddhists in the United States are working to transmit authentic lineages of practice and insight. As Elizabeth Eastman's history reveals, not all cases of transmission are successful. In her highly personal account of how one Buddhist temple was established in Oregon and then eventually failed, we see another face of transmission, one that reveals that the failure to adapt may be just as fatal to Buddhism as the impulse to transform.

CHAPTER 1

Discourse, Authority, Demand

The Politics of Early English Publications on Buddhism

JUDITH SNODGRASS

> Until Europeans wrote about them, the "Buddhists" were happily unaware that they were "Buddhists." What they were preaching, practising, and meditating about was not Buddhism but the "holy dharma" . . . Buddhism was an abstraction, coined by unbelievers for their own convenience.
>
> CONZE, "Problems of Buddhist History"

A DEFINING FEATURE of Buddhism in its modern Asian and Western transformations—indeed, its very name—is the centrality of the Buddha Sakyamuni and the assumption that he was the founder of the religion. Many of the key features of transnational, translated modern Buddhisms depend on it. It is the premise that enabled the nineteenth-century definition of "real" Buddhism as a rational, humanist philosophy. It justified the dismissal by early scholars of traditional ritual practices and the trappings of institutional religion, the stripping away of two thousand years of "cultural accretions" and "priestcraft," to create Buddhism as a universal teaching that transcended cultural, geographic, and chronological differences (Lopez 2002, xiv, xxxvii).[1] The image of the Buddha seated in meditation beneath a tree provides the model for modern Buddhism's disproportionate emphasis on meditation (ibid., xxxxvii–xxxxviii) and the basis for a certain arrogance among some Western Buddhists who feel that the Buddhism of their practice is closer to Sakyamuni's teachings than that of traditional Asian practitioners.

I have elsewhere described the role of T. W. (Thomas William) Rhys Davids and the founding scholars of the Pāli Text Society in establishing the academic credibility of the fundamental principles of modern humanist Buddhism (Snodgrass 2007, 186–202); but as I commented then, beginnings are always problematic. The features of Buddhism that these scholars legitimated by their editing, translation, and presentation of the Pāli canon were already circulating in the discourses over the future of Christianity in an age of science, several decades before the society was formed in 1881. In this chapter I propose to pursue in more detail the writings of the Reverend Robert Spence Hardy, Wesleyan missionary to Ceylon from 1825 to 1847, whose two books *Eastern Monachism* (1850) and *Manual of Budhism* [*sic*] (1853) were among the sources quoted by Rhys Davids in his first book, *Buddhism: A Sketch of the Life and Teachings of Gautama the Buddha* (Rhys Davids 1878). They were the first books published in English on Buddhism, and though they sank into obscurity after the appearance of the more academically accepted work of Rhys Davids and the Pāli Text Society, they circulated as the authority on Theravāda Buddhism for the crucial thirty years of growing Western interest that preceded them. Hardy's books were therefore extremely influential, disproportionately so given their extremely unsympathetic origins. Their publication and circulation also point to another of the key features of modern Buddhism: the importance of publications—books, magazines, and now electronic media—in its formation. The teachings of the various schools of traditional Asian Buddhisms were authenticated by the lineage of their patriarchs, the truth preserved and protected as it passed in direct line of transmission from master to pupil. The teachings of modern Buddhism, however, circulate freely, their meanings uncontrolled, open to the readings of anyone able to access them, their truth determined not by tradition but by the dynamics of discourse.

The Buddha and Buddhism

While no Buddhist doubts the historical existence of the Buddha Sakyamuni—pilgrimage sites marking the locations of the pivotal events in his life in India have been honored for 2,500 years—until the emergence of modern Buddhism in the mid-nineteenth century, no Asian Buddhists regarded him as the founder of the religion or as the only Buddha. Sakyamuni was understood to be but one of a series of Buddhas born into the world to teach the eternal dharma (Snellgrove 1978, 7–10). The earliest records stress his position in a recurring pattern. The bas-reliefs of Bharhut that date from about the second century B.C.E., for example, depict differently named Buddhas, each sitting in meditation under a tree, and each tree has markedly different leaves. Sculpture on the gateways of the Sanchi stupas from a similar period show seven previous Buddhas. The earliest Pāli texts also convey the existence of prior Buddhas. Traditional tellings of the life of the Buddha constitute what John Strong has called a "bio-blueprint," a pattern of actions on how to identify a Buddha (Strong 2001,

10–14). That Sakyamuni's life conforms to the pattern is proof, like the thirty-two signs on the Buddha's body, that he is indeed a Buddha. Even Rhys Davids, whose work did much to document Sakyamuni's humanity, confirms that the word *Tathāgata*, one of the most commonly used titles of the Buddha, was interpreted by Buddhaghosa to mean "that he came to earth for the same purposes, having passed through the same training in former births, as all the supposed former Buddhas; and that, when he had so come, all his actions corresponded with theirs" (Rhys Davids 1881, 147). Traditional sources went to some trouble to make it clear that Sakyamuni was not the founder of the teaching.

Early Western scholars seeking a life narrative were frustrated to discover that although the texts contain a great deal of information on incidents in the life of the Buddha, nowhere did the texts offer what could be recognized as a biography: the life of the man from his birth to his death. The importance of this to scholars of the time was apparent in an article in April 1854 by the eminent Sanskritist, H. H. Wilson, then Director of the Royal Asiatic Society, in which he announced the start of Buddhist studies (Wilson 1854, 229–65). The article was inspired by the publication of Hardy's books, the particular value of which, in Wilson's view, was that it filled this gap; they contained a complete and consistent history of the Buddha beginning with accounts of the previous Buddhas, through to the distribution of the relics of his body after his cremation (ibid., 245–46). But even as he recognized the value of Hardy's work in providing a framework on which to hang the casual observations of travelers and the fragmentary information of early translations, and in providing a base against which cross-cultural comparisons could be made that would reveal the essence of the religion, he himself was not convinced of the historical reality of the Buddha. On the basis of the evidence, Wilson concluded, it was by no means certain that such a person actually existed. After comparing the various texts on the life of the Buddha available to him, and "laying aside the miraculous portions," Wilson decided that while it was not improbable that Buddhism began from the teachings of one man, "various considerations throw suspicion upon the narrative and render it very problematic whether any such person as Sakya Muni ever lived" (ibid., 247). He pointed to the wide discrepancy within the tradition on the date of his birth, which ranges from 2420 B.C.E.—a time well beyond that of historical conjecture—to 453 B.C.E., and to the lack of historical evidence at the time Wilson wrote of the existence of the Sakya clan or the city of Kapilavastu where he was said to have lived in his youth. Most important for Wilson, as one who understood Sanskrit, were the names of people and places in the narrative, which strongly suggested an allegorical significance. The Buddha's given name, Siddhartha, means "he by whom the end is accomplished." The name of the Buddha's mother is Māyādevi. Māyā is the divine illusion that creates the reality of men. According to Wilson, the narrative is "all very much in the style of Pilgrim's Progress. . . . it seems possible, after all, that Sakya Muni is an unreal being, and all that is related of him is as much fiction as is that of his preceding migrations, and the miracles that attended his birth, his life, and his departure" (ibid., 247–48). Why then was Hardy so determined that Sakyamuni was an actual historical person?

The Buddha of Spence Hardy's Mission

Although Hardy's work was a landmark in documenting and publishing on the historical humanity of the Buddha, he did not invent the idea. It was "in the air," a consequence in large part of a Christocentric gaze making sense out of the unfamiliar by imposing its own presuppositions upon it: in this case, by jumping to conclusions based on the parallels between the life of Jesus and the life of Sakyamuni as religious teachers. Just as Jesus, the Christ, was the Founder of Christianity, Gotama was assumed to be the Founder of Buddhism. That the Buddha—usually referred to in English writing of this period as Gotama, his personal name, rather than his title "Buddha," which honors his achievement of attaining awakening—taught an atheistic, or at least agnostic, system was also already widely known (Almond 1985; Droit 2003). Indeed, as I will show, it was a crucial factor in Western interest in Buddhism. Hardy's contribution was getting the ideas into print so they could circulate. There was already such a demand for information on Buddhism when he published that it overrode the shortcomings of his work and his anti-Buddhist agenda, but a demand which in turn welcomed and reinforced his premise of the strictly human nature of the Buddha.

Hardy was quite explicit about his antipathy to his subject. As a Wesleyan missionary, he studied Singhalese to more efficiently know the religion he aimed to supplant. His first publication, a pamphlet called *British Government and the Idolatry of Ceylon* (available first in Colombo in 1839, then in London in 1841), was overtly political, a savage attack on Buddhism aimed at undermining the British Government's patronage of the undefined "religion of Ceylon," (a condition stipulated in the Kandyan Convention of 1815 [De Silva 1965, 290–92].) Briefly, Ceylon had not been conquered by Britain but had been ceded to it by the combined authority of the Buddhist sangha and the Kandyan chiefs on the stipulation that the British government would, in return, maintain and protect their religion. The agreement was, in effect, that the British government would fulfill the traditional role of the king in a Buddhist polity. The mutually supportive roles of the king as patron of religion, and the

Buddhist sangha as generators of dharma for the protection of the state, were signified by the ritual presentation of the Sacred Tooth Relic of the Buddha to the British. Possession of the Tooth Relic, the palladium of the state ritually housed in the former capital of Kandy, bestowed the authority to rule, and certain associated obligations toward the sangha. The actual demands on the government were not onerous. It was required to validate appointments of *bhikkhus* (monks) to positions within the sangha, to supply small amounts of money for temple upkeep and ceremonial purposes, and to preside at certain ceremonies such as those associated with the Tooth Relic. The cost for the Kandy Perahera, the principal ritual associated with the relic, was, in 1840, £15. 19. 9.1/2 (Hardy 1841, 25). The total cost to the government in temple support was about £150 annually (De Silva 1965, 69). It was a connection so undemanding that the British government and the missionaries could not understand why it was so important to the Kandyans (ibid., 104).

Even such minimal honoring of the Kandyan Treaty, however, offended the missionaries. Hardy's pamphlet called for an end to the "unnatural, sinful, and pernicious connection between the British Government of Ceylon and idolatry" (Hardy 1841, 10). Arguing from the premise that the world moved according to the design of God, Hardy derived great significance from a comparison of the great extent of the Roman Empire at the time of the birth of Christ with the spread of British power in the nineteenth century. The wide influence of the Roman Empire had been instrumental in the initial propagation of Christianity, so Hardy believed, and it was clear that God had placed nations under British authority to facilitate the conversion of the world. The purpose of Empire, as he saw it, was Christian conversion. It was time to inquire, he declared, "whether our authorities in the east were carrying into effect the intention for which they have been raised by God to their present anomalous position" (ibid., 8).

As this quote suggests, Hardy's campaign was motivated at least in part by the lack of success of Christian missions in Ceylon. Conversion was not making much headway, and Hardy believed one reason for this was that the treaty gave the people the impression that the government approved of Buddhism. He made this point on the first page of his pamphlet by presenting an image of a British soldier "wearing the uniform of our most gracious Queen" standing guard at a Buddhist temple to the "constant roll of the tomton." This is, he wrote, an image "most disturbing to the mind of thoughtful Christians," because "instruction by example is the most powerful method of impressing the mind" (ibid., 3–4). If government support were removed, he believed, Buddhism would collapse. Hardy's concern was not simply that the people of Ceylon showed little interest in becoming Christians, but that the majority who did, joined the Anglicans. The state-supported Anglican Church enjoyed considerable advantages over the non-conformist missions such as his. The Colonial Office regarded the Anglican Church as the Established Church of Ceylon. Consequently, the Anglican Establishment controlled the Central School Commission, and thereby one of the chief means of propagating Christianity and weakening indigenous religions (De Silva 1965, 143–44). Of perhaps even greater importance was the Anglican monopoly over the registration of births, marriages, and deaths, and therefore of the legal documentation that was invaluable in deciding matters of property and inheritance (ibid., 51–56). As missionaries were aware, many people converted simply to receive the benefits of being on the register, and even Wesleyan converts were won over to Anglicanism because of it (ibid., 55). Hardy's pamphlet appeared in Ceylon in 1839, initiating public contention over the relationship between the Anglican Church and the Government of Ceylon (ibid., 58).

By midcentury when his books appeared, the issue of the relationship between the British Government and Buddhism in Ceylon was further complicated by economic considerations. Civil servants and missionaries had invested in plantations and wanted access to the rich Hill Country, much of which was under control of the Buddhist sangha. The process that began in 1839 with Hardy's pamphlet reached a peak in 1846, when the government, under the influence of expatriate pressure groups, moved to sever the relationship. The Tooth Relic was returned in 1847; in 1848 there was an anti-British rebellion in Kandy, and although the immediate cause was newly imposed and unfair taxes, it seems likely that the betrayal of the Convention added to the discontent (ibid., 11).

A deciding factor in the timing of Hardy's pamphlet was the success of the campaign by Christian missionaries in India to dissociate British rule from similar obligations to Hindu temples. In the opening pages of his pamphlet, Hardy reproduced key passages of a letter to the governor in India from the court at Leadenhall Street of August 8, 1838, that ordered these changes (Hardy 1841, 8–9). The republication of Hardy's pamphlet in London suggests that he too hoped to persuade missionary organizations there to use their influence at the Colonial Office to have the policy on Ceylon changed (De Silva 1965, 69).

Hardy's efforts to establish that Buddhism was idolatrous were central to the campaign, since it made continuing support "an offence in the sight of God" (Hardy 1841, 9). It was also the central rationale for missionary activity in Ceylon. Hardy and his colleagues recognized that native conversion to Christianity was slower than in India because of the nature of the religion they faced. Colonial Secretary Sir James Emerson Tennent made the point explicitly: "The Christian missionary of the South of Ceylon has a very different form of heathenism to overcome" than those who work among the Hindus of the North (Tennent 1850, 249). Missionaries in Hindu areas had found abundant material from which to construct their images of Hindu barbarity in the caste system, marriage customs, infanticide, and *sati*. By the time Hardy wrote, they had so successfully overturned the admiration for Indian thought and culture of the previous century of colonial scholarship, that, in Hardy's words, "it is now too well known to be contradicted, that a baser, more bloody, and more licentious system than Brahmanism never cursed the fair creation of God" (Hardy 1841, 8). Their colleagues in Ceylon, however, found it hard to justify conversion on social grounds alone. They readily noted the similarity between the Buddha and the Christ, and conceded that Buddhism's moral and ethical system was comparable with Christianity's own. Hardy advised his missionary colleagues against simply declaring Buddhism to be a false religion, since it undeniably had enough in common with Christianity to prompt the reply that if Buddhism is false, then Christianity must be, too. "It must rather be explained that Buddhism is *not divinely inspired* and Christianity alone is the revelation of an all-wise being" (Hardy 1850, 339). "I rest my argument for the necessity of [Buddhism's] destruction upon the simple fact that it is opposed to the truth—denies the existence of God—is ignorant of the only way to salvation, by faith in our Lord Jesus Christ—and is utterly impotent as a teacher of morals, or as a messenger of peace to the awakened consciousness of its deluded votaries" (Hardy 1841, 9). Christianity alone held the truth.

Hardy's books perpetuated and developed the image of Buddhism projected in his campaign to sever the treaty agreement of the Kandyan Convention. The opening line of *Eastern Monachism* is an unequivocal statement of his position:

> About two thousand years before the thunders of Wycliffe were rolled against the mendicant orders of the west, Gotama Buddha commenced his career as a mendicant in the east, and established a religious system that has exercised a mightier influence upon the world than the doctrines of any other *uninspired* teacher, in any age or country. (Hardy 1850, 1)

Hardy's opening reference to a fourteenth-century Christian reformer, John Wycliffe, immediately introduced two by now familiar features of modern Buddhism: the origin of Buddhism as a reaction against the priestcraft and ritual of institutionalized religion, and the role of the Buddha as a social reformer. The key word, however, is "uninspired." Hardy wrote on Buddhism to show its errors, and the master error (his words) from his perspective was that the Buddha was just a man, a great man, as was John Wycliffe, but nothing more than a man. Buddhism, his teachings, were therefore "uninspired," and left man "unaided." Without the Christian God and his threat of divine retribution, "the Lightening of the Divine Eye, the thunder of the Divine Voice . . . the principle for good in man will soon be overwhelmed." "With these radical defects," Hardy confidently concluded, "it is unnecessary to dwell on the lesser" (ibid., 339).

With Hardy's insistence that the Buddha was merely an uninspired mortal, Buddhism became in essence an atheistic system of ethics, and its practice—as observed by Hardy in Ceylon where rituals were performed and offerings made before images—idolatrous. The discrepancy between the purity of the ethics of the founder and the idolatrous practice of the people was proof for him of the inadequacy of an atheistic system to meet the needs of man, and consequently of the natives' need for Christianity. In *Manual of Budhism* [*sic*] we find: "From no part of heathenism do we see more clearly the necessity of a divine revelation than from the teachings of the Buddha. The moral code becomes comparatively powerless for good, as it is destitute of all real authority" (Hardy 1853, 506). The Buddha was a man; his teaching was "not divinely inspired" but "was formed by a man or men, who were liable to err, and have erred, in innumerable instances; consequently it cannot teach the way to purity or peace, or save from wrath and destruction" (Hardy 1850, 334). He stressed the greatness of the Buddha as a person to make his point of the necessity of the Divine, which was from his conservative monotheistic perspective, the exclusive preserve of Christianity.

His first book, *Eastern Monachism*, as the title implies, compared the sangha of Ceylon with the Roman Catholic clergy. It carried the message that the contemporary practice of Buddhism in Ceylon was as far removed from the teaching of the founder of Buddhism—as, in his Protestant view, and presumably in the view of Protestant mission supporters he was lobbying—the Church of Rome is from the teachings of Jesus. His criticisms of the Buddhist sangha seem chosen to invoke historical memories of the misdeeds of the Church of Rome that inspired the Reformation. Hardy began with a short account of the exemplary life and teachings of the Buddha (1–6), followed by chapters on the various precepts to be observed by members of the sangha. The chapter titled "Poverty" demonstrates his approach. He devoted considerable space to the misdeeds of the monastics of pre-Protestant England, a history familiar to his audience. He then outlined the Buddhist precepts on poverty and contrasted these with a detailed description of the extent and wealth of temple property in Ceylon, thereby establishing that, in spite of the vows of poverty, the sangha holds more land than the Crown. "The mendicants of Ceylon are in reality," he wrote, "the wealthiest and most honored class in the nation. . . . In no place can we find the *recluse of the primitive institution*" (Hardy

1850, 70, emphasis added). Along with this call for reform, he also managed in passing to address the concerns of the planters' lobby, noting that the monasteries hold the richest and most fertile parts of the country—precisely the land that they coveted—and to raise concerns about the severe impact of such land-holdings on Crown revenues.

The pattern of Hardy's argument throughout the book is to express admiration for the Buddha's teachings but to criticize the degradation of current practices. He posited a primitive ideal and showed how current practice failed to measure up. His ideal of Buddhism was shaped by a strong Protestant bias against ritual, ceremony, and monastic life, and he seldom failed to denigrate the Romish features he saw in contemporary Singhalese practice. He was, for example, critical of the ritual use of Pāli—the language of the ancient sacred texts—rather than the vernacular Singhalese: "In the midst of much that is superstitious in practice or utterly erroneous in doctrine, there are some advices of an excellent tendency; but the whole ceremony being conducted in a language the people do not understand, no beneficial result can be produced from its performance" (Hardy 1850, 242).

Eastern Monachism culminates in a joyous description of the Buddha's prediction of the end of the religion after 5,000 years, which for Hardy endorsed his missionary enterprise. On the evidence of corruption he presented in the book, he concluded that "the ancient fabric already totters; it will soon be swept from its base by the power that alone is resistless; and in its stead will be erected the temple of the Lord, in which all the earth will worship the Father Everlasting" (ibid., 431). *Eastern Monachism,* a book shaped by such prejudice, seems an unlikely candidate for a source of knowledge on Buddhism.

Hardy's second book, *Manual of Budhism,* is an account of the Buddhism of Ceylon compiled from Singhalese sources, and although it is also a vehicle for Hardy's mission to undermine Buddhism, there is, perhaps paradoxically, much of value in it (Hallisey 1995, 3–61). Precisely because of his desire to demonstrate what he saw as the irrationality of contemporary Buddhism, he presents us with a conscientiously detailed statement of Buddhist belief and practice in Ceylon that he had compiled with the assistance of scholarly Buddhist *bhikkhu*s. The book opens with an account of the Buddhist cosmology (1–35)—providing the essential navigational points without which the Buddhist worldview makes little sense—and moves through the various hierarchies of existence (36–61). This is followed by the book's principle concern: Buddhas. It deals with Buddhas of the past, the characteristics of Buddhas, the lives of previous Buddhas, the previous lives of the Buddha Sakyamuni, and culminates in the centerpiece, a 220-page chapter titled "The Legendary Life of Buddha." The book does not end there, going on to offer a chapter on "The Dignity,

Virtues, and Power of Buddha" and concludes with chapters on Buddhist ontology and ethics. There is a great deal in it beyond the life of the Buddha that captured Wilson's attention. *Manual of Budhism* was based on Singhalese sources, and offered a wealth of information about what people believed, reproducing all the mythological detail and richness of the traditional stories. Paradoxically, in spite of Hardy's scurrilous attempt to discredit "the heathen," the imperative of the missionary endeavor, the desire to know the enemy directed him to record an image of Buddhism closer to that understood by its practitioners than would the later work of T. W. Rhys Davids. As Charles Hallisey has observed, Hardy's was the "road not taken" by scholars at the time, but which now is not all that far from the desire to focus more on the life of Buddhism than on the life of the Buddha. Hardy's objective in writing *Manual of Budhism*, however, was as ungenerous as that of his previous book. He reproduced all this to document the fallibility of the Buddha from the texts themselves; to show how far the teachings of the Buddha depart from the truth of a Western, scientific worldview.

To achieve this, Hardy assumed a posture of objectivity; he was simply the translator; his aim "not to give expression to an opinion" but to "present an authority" (Hardy 1853, xii). His goal, he explained, was to answer the question: "What is Buddhism, as it is now professed by its myriads of votaries?" His plan was to let the texts speak for themselves, to illustrate with details from the Singhalese texts the superstitions and priestly elaborations that he had described in *Eastern Monachism*. He restricts his own contribution to the footnotes and a commentary at the end of chapters, clearly marked from the main text by a distinctive typeface. Taken in isolation, the footnotes appear as a conscientious attempt to inform by fixing mathematical values to cosmological units of time and distance, but their destructive purpose is revealed in the commentary. The value he assigns a *yojana*, for example, proves that Mount Meru is too vast to exist on the globe; the periods of time, translated into a modern idiom, are incompatible with modern knowledge, and so on. On such evidence he claims to establish the human fallibility of the Buddha:

> The whole of his [Gotama's] cosmogony, and of his astronomical revelation is erroneous, and there are statements in nearly every utterance attributed to him upon these subjects which prove that his mind was beclouded by like ignorances with other men; consequently, he cannot be, as he is designated by his disciples, "a sure guide to the city of peace." (Hardy 1853, 35)

Although Hardy is among the earliest to document it, he does not consider the consequences of the cosmology any more than the later Buddhist humanists who discarded it as cultural accretion. By beginning with a statement of the historical existence of a man named "Gotama Buddha," he had excluded the issue of the supramundane nature of the Buddha, the subject of the texts he translated. For Hardy, the Buddha was a man, and the divine aspects he observed in modern practices and beliefs—the worship of images of the Buddha—were simply evidence of the failure of his "uninspired" teaching. On the one hand he argued that the Buddha was a fallible guide, as all mere mortals must be; on the other he argued that Gotama taught a system of ethics so ideal that it is beyond the possibility of most men to live by and leaves them to fall back on idolatry to satisfy the innate craving for religion. "How could it be otherwise," he wrote, "when man is left to his unaided efforts in the great work of freeing himself from the defilements of evil!" (Hardy 1850, 344–45). Further ignoring the implications of Buddhist cosmology that he himself described as essential to understanding the system, Hardy equated the Buddha's attainment of nirvāna with annihilation. He was therefore able to dismiss the Triple Refuge (Trust in the Buddha, the dharma, and the sangha) as trust in a being who was annihilated (the Buddha), in a law without the sanction of revelation (the dharma), and in a community of "partakers of sin and sorrow" (the sangha) (Hardy 1850, 339).

I could continue but this is probably sufficient to characterize Hardy's work, and to show the reason, from his missionary imperative, for emphasizing that the Buddha was nothing more than a man. His emphasis on the historical reality of Sakyamuni was clearly strategic, and the Buddhism he created was, to use Conze's words from the chapter epigraph, a "matter of his own convenience." The question is why these books, books that are, by contemporary standards, so blatantly anti-Buddhist, were ever taken seriously as a source of knowledge on the subject.

Publication and Dissemination: The Colonial Imperative

The dates of the publication of Hardy's two books strongly suggests that a major factor in bringing his studies of Buddhism out of missionary circles and into the public domain was a continuation of the project that inspired his pamphlet on idolatry, the controversy over the treaty, which was to be voted on in the British Parliament in the early 1850s. A book by Sir James Emerson Tennent, *Christianity in Ceylon*, appeared at the same time, and in spite of its title, presented a considerable amount of information on Buddhism and other religious practices in Ceylon as it set out to explain the lack of success of the mission endeavor. While Hardy continued to argue against the treaty arrangement, Tennent's book offered an interpretation of Buddhism that supported the government's desire to uphold its treaty obligations.

Tennent was Colonial Secretary in Ceylon from 1845 to 1850. In 1847 Viscount Torrington was appointed governor of Ceylon with instructions to complete the separation of sangha and state as soon as possible. However, he quickly realized the difficulties this involved and advised that Britain should return to the original agreement. Though neither he nor Tennent were pro-Buddhist, they believed that Britain was bound to honor the terms of the convention. They attempted to circumvent the issues of religion and state by arguing instead that the government's obligation was not a religious question but rather a civil one, and that maintaining the agreement was to the state's advantage since it gave the government some control over the selection of suitable *bhikkhus* for appointment and reminded the members of the sangha of the government's power. The alternative to maintaining the treaty obligations would be to appoint a committee of prominent Kandyans to administer the sangha. This was not desirable, Torrington observed, because it would "create a 'state within a state'" and throw "a strong engine of political and social power into hands often unfaithful, always unsteady" (Torrington, Minute of October 13, 1847, quoted in De Silva 1965, 104). As he saw it, separation of the state and the sangha would increase Buddhist strength, not undermine it. By returning to the former relationship, he believed, Buddhism would "sink of itself" (ibid.). The debate over the government's obligation to honor the treaty versus the impropriety of its connection with a "heathen religion" continued unresolved with missionary attacks becoming increasingly bitter. At the center of the dispute was the definition of the religion of the country, Buddhism. What had previously been of interest only to religious specialists became a matter of more general interest by the middle of the century.

Hardy's view, as we have seen, was that the nature of Buddhism made the government's obligation to the treaty of 1815 "contrary to the laws of God," and therefore not binding on a Christian government. While Tennent's earnest desire was, like Hardy's, to see the citizens of Ceylon converted to Christianity, his definition of Buddhism supported the maintenance of the treaty. He also shared Hardy's assumption of the historical reality of the mortal Gotama, and his opinion that Buddhism as it was practiced in Ceylon was a degeneration from the Buddha's teachings. As he saw it, however, this had less to do with the failing of the teachings than with the racial inadequacy of the Singhalese. By confining his definition of Buddhism to the teachings of this historical philosopher—he excluded present Ceylonese practice as an aberration; it was simply not Buddhism—he argued that "Buddhism is properly speaking, less a form of religion than a school of philosophy" (Tennent 1850, 207), and that the Buddha is not worshipped as a deity but "reverenced merely as a glorified re-membrance" (ibid., 222). He thereby rescued Buddhism from the charge of idolatry. Tennent did not deny the evidence of rituals and worship in contem-porary practice, but he attributed this "demon worship" to Hindu influence and a return to a quite separate pre-Buddhist indigenous religion (ibid., 230–38). It was not part of his definition of Buddhism. The *bhikkhus* (he avoided calling them either priests or monks, terms that Hardy's *Eastern Monachism* had loaded with negative Christian connotations in this context) are "teachers of ethics" and the sangha "a clergy of reason" (ibid., 192). By claiming that Bud-dhism was a philosophical system, he undermined the argument of the im-propriety of a Christian government's connection with a heathen religion. By similar logic he defused protest over British support for the Kandy Perahera, the ritual procession of the Tooth Relic, the government's principal and most visible connection with Buddhism, which was, therefore, at the center of the debate over the validity of this relationship. The procession, he observed, is "less religious than secular." It was "introduced not in honour of Buddhu [*sic*], but as a tribute to the Kandyan kings as patrons and defenders of the faith" (ibid., 221).

There can be little doubt of Tennent's sincerity in dedicating his book to missionaries in the hope that it would aid them in their task. In 1847, not long after his arrival in Ceylon, he was emphatic that the dissociation of the state from Buddhism would lead to the decline of Buddhism and the triumph of Christianity (De Silva 1965, 105). Perhaps closer scrutiny of the situation, the Kandyan disturbances of 1848, or Torrington's position, altered his views of how best to achieve this end. Torrington and Tennent were recalled in 1850 but Tennent continued to advise the Colonial Office on Buddhism, presenting a memorandum on Buddhism to the parliamentary committee in 1852 (ibid., 116). He was instrumental in framing the legislation that was to form the basis of settlement, since it managed to reassure the sangha while at the same time appease the missionaries (ibid., 125).

Both Hardy and Tennent were accepted as authorities on Buddhism in the 1850s, but to different degrees. Tennent's work, although remarkably similar to what would become the dominant interpretation through the work of the Pāli Text Society, was regarded as the informed opinion of one who had firsthand experience, a subsidiary reference since it lacked the strict dependence on sa-cred texts, the protocol academic authority demanded. He did not undertake his own translations. Hardy's work was acclaimed by H. H. Wilson as "mate-rial of an authentic character" (Wilson 1854, 235) and became the basis not only of Theravāda studies but also of the academic study of "Buddhism," the principles underlying its diversity. Rhys Davids acknowledged it as a principal reference for his groundbreaking work in establishing humanist Buddhism: *Buddhism: A Sketch of the Life and Teachings of Gautama, the Buddha* (Snodgrass 2007). So prominent is Hardy's work in the history of Western Theravāda Buddhist scholarship that it is useful to remember that although Rhys Davids was a colonial officer in Ceylon for many years and began his study of Pāli while there, he did not write on Buddhism until after his return to England. A modest comment from him regarding his knowledge of Buddhism at that time suggests that he was invited to do so because of an already existing popular interest in the topic (Wickremaratne 1984, 145). That Rhys Davids's first book was commissioned by the Society for Promoting Christian Knowledge is also an indication of the growing public interest and, significantly, its direction.

Buddhism and Christian Crisis

The most important reason for the popularity of Hardy's books in the 1850s, the reason for so much interest in Buddhism in Christian countries in the second half of the nineteenth century, was the religious crisis at home. This was implicit in the preface to *Eastern Monachism* in which Hardy wrote: "I ask no higher reward than to be a humble instrument in assisting the ministers of the cross in their combats with this master error of the world, *and in preventing the spread of the same delusion, under another guise, in regions nearer home*" (Hardy 1850, ix; emphasis added). The "master error" as he saw it was atheism; the "other guise" was materialist philosophy, which, in a climate of crisis in the clash between traditional Christian teaching and new developments in science, was gathering interest in Europe. The inherent fallibility of such systems was the organizing theme of *Manual of Budhism*.

Hardy's position would be championed by Barthelemy Saint Hilaire whose book *The Buddha and His Religion* appeared in French and in English around 1860. In the opening line Saint Hilaire declared that his purpose in writing on Buddhism was to bring out in striking contrast the greater truth of Christianity. The preface describes Buddhism as a system in which "man is denied all hope of an immortal life, in which the immortality of the soul is replaced by the immortality of good works, and God is dethroned by man" (Saint-Hilaire 1860, 15). He wrote on Buddhism to warn of "the fate of man when he relies on self" (ibid., 16). Although part of the authority of Saint-Hilaire's work was that he had studied Sanskrit, he continued to rely on Hardy for information on Pāli Buddhism. Like Hardy, he too wrote admiringly of the Buddha: "with the sole exception of the Christ, there does not exist among all the founders of religions a purer and more touching figure than that of the Buddha" (ibid., 14).

This only served to emphasize that Buddhism—his godless teaching—was "a hideous system"; the master error which leads "to the abyss in which the Buddha has lost himself" (ibid., 16).

It is intriguing to consider to what extent Hardy also provided the information for those they opposed, the free thinkers and humanists who, like Rhys Davids, saw Buddhism as proof of the possibility of an ethical system that did not depend on an interventionist god. Though Rhys Davids would go on to document and thereby authenticate modern Buddhism through his translation and interpretation of the Pāli texts, the book where he first published these ideas, his *Buddhism,* published in 1878, was, as already mentioned, compiled from existing sources including Hardy's books. (Succeeding editions substitute references to the Pāli texts as he translated them, but as far as I could see, never to an extent that disrupted pagination or altered the argument.) Rhys Davids's Gotama was also very definitely nothing more than a man, the historical founder of this agnostic philosophy. Rhys Davids studied the texts to show the process whereby a great man had been deified by the well-meaning desire of his followers to express their devotion to him, the process that transformed Gotama into the Buddha. By revealing this "universal principle" he hoped to help Christians realize how the other great teacher, Jesus, had similarly been deified to become the Christ. His aim was to establish a liberal scientific Christian agnosticism—the "latest developments among ourselves," as he put it—as the pinnacle of evolution of Christian thought. The two sides of the argument are very close in terms of describing the Buddha and his teachings. In Saint-Hilaire we find: "In the whole of Buddhism there is not a trace of God. Man, completely isolated, is thrown upon his own resources" (Saint Hilaire 1860, 13). For Rhys Davids, Buddhism was an agnostic ethical discipline of self-reliance. One is critical, the other admiring, but both depend on the Buddha being nothing more than a man, the founder of an ethical system independent of an interventionist God

From Hardy to Rhys Davids: Thirty Years in the Discursive Domain

Tennent's interpretation of Buddhism foreshadowed that of Rhys Davids, but it was to Hardy that early writers on Buddhism referred. Tennent's insights remained concealed behind a title, *Christianity in Ceylon,* which suggests it was chosen to target a different audience. Hardy's books, by contrast, circulated widely in the thirty years between the appearance of his books and the translations of the Buddhist texts in Max Muller's *Sacred Books of the East* and of Pāli Text Society publications. The popularity of his books was in part a consequence of the growing interest in the Orient at the time of their publication, stimulated by the increasing frequency and variety of colonial encounters. The early 1850s was a time of exhibitions, expositions—the Great Crystal Palace Exhibition in London opened in 1851—and popular writings about the East in general and on Eastern religions in particular (Almond 1985). Writing on Buddhism had begun in the early part of the century when the British and French empires expanded into Buddhist areas, but these early writings had not been readily available. The detailed bibliographies in Philip Almond's and Roger-Pol Droit's studies of early Western writings on Buddhism show just how much work was being done in these early years, but also how its circulation was confined to small groups of scholars and missionaries (Droit 2003). Missionaries such as Daniel Gogerly (1792–1862), one of the first Pāli scholars, published his translations in mission journals. Early Orientalists published in the journals of the Oriental societies. Hardy's books, bound and distributed through bookshops and libraries, were the first to be widely available, a readily accessible source of information on Buddhism, and they arrived at a time of high interest.

Hardy's books stood pretty much alone as a resource during the first decades of popular enthusiasm for knowledge of Buddhism, and many books and articles written between the 1850s and the 1880s obtained information from them. His work therefore had a secondary impact through the pages of intellectual journals such as the *Academy*, the *Edinburgh Review, London Quarterly Review,* and even the *Times.* Their impact was not confined to Britain. American historian Arthur Christy describes a copy of Hardy's *Eastern Monachism* that he found in the library of Boston transcendentalist Amos Bronson Alcott. It had originally belonged to H. D. Thoreau, and on his death, was delivered to Alcott by Ralph Waldo Emerson (Christy 1963, 292–96). The book had been marked in both red and black pencil, and while Christy admits it is impossible to be certain who did this, he makes a convincing case that those passages marked in red—passages on diet, ascetic attitudes to eating only out of necessity, and such concerns, every one of which dealt with the subject of food or its excretion—were made by the vegetarian Alcott (who marked his own manuscripts in red pencil) (ibid., 293); and that those in black pencil, which seem mainly related to the virtues of a celibate and frugal life unattached to material possessions, were most likely made by Thoreau. He also identifies a passage in Emerson's *Journals* (Vol. X, 234) as "an unmistakable echo, if not a direct paraphrase" of a passage from Hardy. (Christy 1963, 296). Christy concluded that "this book was probably one of the most influential in disseminating Buddhist lore in Concord" (ibid., 296).

The ways in which the book was used by these prominent thinkers usefully illustrates discursive processes. As Christy observes, "there was far more of the partial partisan in Spence Hardy than in the Concord men. He wrote much in attempted disproof of the Oriental systems, but these pages seem to have been utterly ignored—at least they were never marked" (ibid., 296). The Concord men dismissed what was not relevant to them. If Christy and the Transcendentalists were aware of Hardy's bias, they did not share it. We can also see here the transmission of the information gleaned by them from Hardy's books, through to the readers of their own works, providing another loop in the discursive lineage of modern Buddhism.

Edwin Arnold's epic poem *Light of Asia* offers a further example of a selective reading of Hardy's work. Arnold, who acknowledges Hardy in his preface, based the narrative of his immensely popular work on the long chapter of the life of the Buddha compiled by Hardy in his *Manual of Budhism*. The secondary transmission in this case contributed strongly to the formation of general knowledge. First published in 1879, it went through more than thirty official editions in England by 1885. It was also published overseas in English and in translation; it is estimated to have sold up to one million copies in the United States alone. The book probably did more than any other to project in the West the image of the Buddha as a great humanist philosopher. Arnold wrote, "I have taken the imperfect Buddhistic citations much as they stand in Spence Hardy's work, and have also modified more than one passage in the received narrative" (Arnold 1906, xiii).

Hardy and the Birth of Modern Buddhist Studies

H. H. Wilson's announcement of the birth of Buddhist studies in 1852 was based on his perception of what Hardy's books contributed to the then meager field of scholarship. Providing the biography that so many sought was a start. Its comprehensive account of the Buddhist system provided the framework upon which the various isolated and fragmentary work done in previous years—that of Alexander Csoma, Eugene Burnouf, Brian Houghton Hodgson et al.—could be organized. Its information on Theravāda Buddhism, when juxtaposed with the information on Mahāyāna Buddhism from the Sanskrit texts previously translated by Burnouf, provided the basis for the cross-cultural comparisons that would reveal the essence of Buddhism, the "reality" concealed under the various local elaborations. The search for Buddhism, as opposed to the mission initiated studies of the religion of Burma, or Ceylon, or wherever could begin. There was now, as Wilson put it, sufficient material from diverse sources to provide "the means to form correct opinions of Buddhism, as to its doctrines and practices" (Wilson 1854, 35). That is, to begin to define the essence of Buddhism as a world religion.

Hardy's emphasis on the historical reality of the life of the Buddha from his birth to his death also provided the basic "hard evidence" for situating the Buddha in history. While the *Manual of Budhism* provided a full mythological account, the earlier book, *Eastern Monachism,* had included a brief rationalized account of the life that included information from the Mahāvamsa Chronicles, which located the transmission of the teachings to Ceylon in historical times. From this, and the accounts of the various Buddhist councils, the dates of the Buddha's life in India were determined. In keeping with his fundamental aim of undermining the credibility of Buddhism, Hardy's point in doing this had been to establish there had been ample time between the life of the Buddha and the production of the earliest texts for the invention of the absurd legends, "as we may learn from similar stories that were invented relative to the western saints in a period less extended" (Hardy 1850, 1). His separation of the Buddha as hero from the texts of Buddhism as the work of hero-worshipping followers set a model for the creation of the secular philosophy.

This separation of the Buddha from the texts of Buddhism, which were undisputedly written after his death, would continue to be a key feature in the formation of modern Buddhism. For Hardy, Buddhism was the religion that had developed out of the inadequacies of the atheistic teaching, of man fulfilling his need for the spiritual with idol worship. But Pāli scholars, led by T. W. Rhys Davids and following Tennent, also defined Buddhism as the actual teachings of the historical man, a premise that allowed them to strip away the mythological, the irrational, the metaphysical, and the spiritual to reveal these words of humanist wisdom. This approach had unfortunate consequences for practicing Asian Buddhists, particularly for Mahāyāna practitioners who found their religion, the texts of which are of an even later date, excluded from any serious consideration.[2]

Hardy produced two more books, *The Sacred Books of the Buddhists Compared with History and Modern Science* (1863) and *The Legends and Theories of the Buddhists Compared with History and Science* (1866). Both were too blatantly anti-Buddhist to be taken seriously. Both sank without a trace, perhaps pulling the earlier two with them, although it is more likely that the reason for their disappearance is simply that their authority on Theravāda Buddhism was superceded by the academically accredited translations of the Pāli canon that began to circulate from around 1880. Rhys Davids formed the Pāli Text Society in 1881, and it is apparent from the list of inaugural members (which included Pāli scholars Fausboll, Oldenberg, Senart, Lanham) and the speed with which publications appeared after this date, that much work on Pāli texts had been under way in the preceding decade. From that time, Rhys Davids and other dedicated scholars began the process of collecting, editing, collating, and translating the texts of the Pāli canon, working strictly within the academic paradigms of the time, the scientific study of religion. Buddhist studies gained academic recognition, installing the strictly human Gotama and his rational, humanist teachings as the truth of Buddhism.

The Discursive Lineage of Modern Buddhism

If one of the ruptures marking the modernity of Buddhism is the reduction of the Buddha to the merely human Gotama, then a second is the dissemination of knowledge of his teachings through modern modes of communication, most notably in this case, publicly available and readily accessible texts. Publication of the sacred texts in modern languages was, for a start, a move toward another important feature of modern Buddhism, secularization. Lay people, even non-Buddhists, could gain knowledge of Buddhism unmediated by the ordained clergy, the specialists in the ancient languages of the canon. As we have seen with Christy's account of the reception of Hardy's *Eastern Monachism* among American Transcendentalists, once in circulation, a text will be read according to the interests and context of the reader, and in some cases such as theirs, further disseminated in the shape that they have given it to a body of readers who may or may not be interested in what Buddhism is. In contrast, within the tradition of Buddhist institutions, the truth of Buddhism was guaranteed through long periods of disciplined training, processes of ordination, and most important through the direct lineage of transmission from master to disciple. With publication, the truth of Buddhism was shaped instead by the roles that it played in various discourses. In the case of Hardy's books, as we have seen, these roles included the missionary imperative to denigrate Buddhism, colonial disputes over the definition of treaty obligations and associated economic considerations, and the crisis of Christianity at that time. Embedded within these issues are others, such as the relative acceptability of Buddhism and Hinduism in colonial perspectives, apparent in the presentation of the Buddha as a social reformer (Gellner 2004, 155–60). Returning to the Transcendentalists, we see the text fulfilling other needs, circulating in discourses even more removed. Hardy's plan to denigrate Buddhism, though propagated further in traditional Christian circles through Saint Hilaire's use of his work,[3] was countered by Edwin Arnold's *The Light of Asia,* which created a receptive audience for Buddhist humanism.

Although it is impossible to say to what extent Hardy's books impacted on Asian Buddhists directly, the Western construct of Buddhism to which he contributed so substantially played an important role in creating modern Asian Buddhisms (Snodgrass 2007). Though they were not unaware of the deficiencies of the representation of their religion by Western scholars, modernizing Asians, particularly among the Western-educated elites who were leaders of the late nineteenth and early twentieth-century nationalist movements, found the work of the Pāli Text Society, for example, extremely useful in their nationalist and anticolonial campaigns. Its emphasis on the human historicity of the Buddha, Sakyamuni, might have been a distortion of tradition, but it fitted well with local movements toward the rationalization of the indigenous religion that had already begun with the momentum of creating modern Asian states. Perhaps even more important, the academically validated, rational, scientific philosophy created by Western scholars made Buddhism acceptable to the Western-educated Asian elites—people who defined themselves by rejecting the "superstitions" of the past—and with their support, the reform already initiated within certain clerical circles was brought into a more public arena. Later, the concept of an essence of Buddhism would enable the pan-Asian Buddhist movements and Asian Buddhist globalization.

A premise of Lopez's anthology of English language writings on Buddhism referred to above is that there is sufficient in common among the various manifestations of modern, transnational Buddhism to see them as a new school, with its own interpretations, practices, and its own lineage (Lopez 2002). An anthology is necessarily selective and the thread of personal connections among those in his lineage is sufficiently strong to suggest that it was a key factor in the selection. It seems to me, however, that to understand the lineage of modern Buddhism, and the place within it of dubious authorities such as Hardy, the overtly political interpretations, and the curious appropriations that have nevertheless had considerable impact,[4] we should focus instead on the role of publications, the discursive flows that control the publication and dissemination of knowledge and that, in this case, gave shape to the concept of Buddhism.

Notes

1. Lopez's introductory essay provides a thorough and insightful survey of the shared characteristics of the various forms of modern Buddhism in Asia and the West, and a gentle correction of many of the most widespread misconceptions.
2. See Ch. 9 "Defining Eastern Buddhism" in Snodgrass 2003, for a discussion on the difficulty this caused Japanese Buddhists wishing to have their religion taken seriously, and my "Publishing Eastern Buddhism: D. T. Suzuki's Journey to the West,"

in Thomas DuBois, ed., *Casting Faiths: Imperialism and the Transformation of Religion in East and Southeast Asia* (New York: Palgrave Macmillan, 2009), 46–72, for D. T. Suzuki's eventual success in overcoming this attitude.

3. Saint-Hilaire's book was reissued in 1996 (London: Bracken Books) as a "timely and insightful guide to one of the world's most vital religions" (back cover). Was the publisher simply trying to capitalize on the demand for books on Buddhism, or was it once again brought out in defense?

4. I have in mind here the immense impact of writings on Buddhism by such people as Henry Steele Olcott, who appropriated Buddhism for Theosophy and Paul Carus, who used it to promote Christian Monism.

CHAPTER 2

Transnational *Tulkus*

The Globalization of Tibetan Buddhist Reincarnation

ABRAHAM ZABLOCKI

T IBETANS AND their culture often seem to inspire fascination in their Others. Monks are used in advertising to signify otherworldliness, purity, or the simple life. Religious rituals are transformed into museum installations and concert recitals. Tibetan-inspired material culture is used to express certain kinds of subject positions, such as countercultural (through the deployment of Tibetan art), politically progressive (through the wearing of a Free Tibet T-shirt), or spiritual (by wearing the latest fashion accoutrement, the Tibetan rosary-as-bracelet).

In each of these instances, Westerners utilize and consume Tibetan culture in order to participate in, and establish affinity with, the special qualities which Tibetans are presumed to have: such as being holy, exotic, or premodern. In this chapter I focus on one quite distinctive object of appropriation, that of Tibetan identity itself. In the cases of *"tulku* envy" I describe below, the would-be reincarnates are not so much striving to establish their affinity and sympathy with Tibetan culture, as much as they want to *be* Tibetan. This raises challenging issues about the nature of cultural appropriation, cross-cultural borrowing, and religious change.

As Tibetan Buddhism has expanded beyond its historical boundaries to acquire new converts in the West, Taiwan, and elsewhere around the world, the issue of what constitutes "authentic" Tibetan Buddhism has become a matter of some dispute. New transnational organizations, dedicated to the spread of Tibetan religion, have each had to grapple with this tension. On one hand, for these groups to succeed in transmitting Tibetan Buddhist practice and doctrine into radically new sociocultural contexts, they have often needed to adapt, either by altering Tibetan forms to suit their new converts, or by creating entirely new practices and institutions. On the other hand, the requirement to preserve the unbroken Tibetan lineage of authentic Buddhist insight—already conceived of as seriously threatened by Chinese occupation—and which, in any case, is imagined to be independent of cultural values, presents a serious impediment to altering Tibetan Buddhism just because it happens to (now) exist among non-Tibetan populations. In short, contemporary transnational Tibetan Buddhism finds itself pulled between the need to adapt itself and the need to preserve itself.

Of course, the same dilemma has faced every missionary religion as it has crossed into new territories, but in the Tibetan case this tension is heightened by several factors. The impulse to preserve Tibetan Buddhism is strengthened by the Chinese control of Tibet, with the consequent loss of a locus of normative Tibetan religion, against which transnational adaptations, modifications, and aberrations could be measured, and resisted. The preservation impulse is further strengthened by the Shangri-La fantasies of Western patrons eager to engage in cultural salvage operations. On the other hand, the pressure to adapt is likewise more intense than perhaps has been the case in other missionary encounters. The sheer magnitude of differences between the culture that the Tibetan exiles carried into their diaspora, and the cultures into which they have now carried their religion, is surely greater than has been previously experienced in the history of Buddhist missionary activity. And, in contrast to, for example, Christian missionaries, who *have* made similarly great leaps across cultural universes, Tibetan missionary successes in the West have not been built through the exercise of political, economic, or military power. On the contrary, Tibetan missionaries, the vast majority of them refugees, have achieved their impressive success *despite* their relatively powerless position, and this may, at times, have presented pressure toward adaptation.

In this chapter I consider the question of how Tibetan religion is changing as a result of these developments, with particular attention to the Western fascination with the Tibetan institution of reincarnation and Tibetan attempts to recruit Western reincarnates. I also examine the historical constructions of "Tibet" that created the fertile ground for this interaction, as well as contemporary representations of Tibetan reincarnation that continue to sustain these imaginings. The *tulku (sprul sku)* system, whereby individuals are recognized, usually while very young, as the reincarnation of a deceased Buddhist master, and then raised to be masters themselves, has proven to be particularly attractive to Tibet's Western interlocutors. In particular, some Westerners seem highly drawn to the system's implications of an esoteric and exotic "secret identity," one which parallels heroic narratives found in Western pop culture but with a specifically Buddhist religious cast. Ironically, for some would-be *tulku*s, the system's prospect of a unique identity—one marked as culturally exotic (at least in Western terms) and indicative of personally exceptional qualities—can be highly ego-aggrandizing, despite Buddhism's own thorough-going rejection of egotism.

Tibetans themselves have many reasons for recruiting non-Tibetan *tulkus* and this has been an important element of Tibetan Buddhist missionary efforts since at least the sixteenth century, when the reincarnation of the third Dalai Lama was identified as the grandson of Altan Khan, the Mongol ruler who had originally dispensed the Dalai Lama title in the first place. By identifying the fourth Dalai Lama as a Mongol prince, the Tibetans helped foster the growing interest of the Mongols in Tibetan Buddhism and the budding political alliance between the Dalai Lamas and their Mongol patrons. Both of these factors contributed to Mongol involvement in Tibet's internal political struggles a century later when, with the military assistance of his Mongol allies, the fifth Dalai Lama—once again reincarnated in a Tibetan body—defeated his Tibetan rivals to establish the political rule of the Dalai Lama lineage over the Tibetan state.

More recently, as various Tibetan Buddhist lineages have spread around the world, a number of non-Tibetan *tulkus* have been identified (Mackenzie 1996). Some of these *tulkus*—such as Lama Osel, the Spanish reincarnation of Lama Yeshe, a major figure in the global spread of Tibetan Buddhism (Mackenzie 1988)—have been given more-or-less traditional monastic training in an effort to prepare them to be Tibetan Buddhist teachers in their own right. In other high-profile *tulku* cases, such as the American actor Steven Seagal (Penor Rinpoche 1999) or *Jetsunma* Catherine Burroughs (Sherrill 2000)—both of whom were, unusually, recognized as *tulku*s as adults—such traditional training has not taken place, with the result that although these *tulku*s have received considerable symbolic capital from their recognition, they operate only marginally within the established spectrum of Tibetan Buddhism.

Thus, the recruitment of non-Tibetan *tulku*s has a long-established history in Tibetan Buddhism's efforts to spread into new geographic, cultural, and national spaces. Nevertheless, Western desires to participate in the *tulku* system strike many Tibetans as funny or unseemly, and the chapter concludes with a discussion of one Tibetan's response to the phenomenon of Western *tulkus*. The literary efforts of the Tibetan author Jamyang Norbu to engage in counter-appropriation of a Western culture-hero, Sherlock Holmes, reveal a complex logic of cultural authenticity that both parodies and mimics Western longings to occupy Tibetan bodies.

Tulku Envy

Several years ago while conducting research in Taiwan on diasporic Tibetan Buddhism, I met another Western researcher, a woman I'll call Susan, who had been living in India for the past six years, ostensibly pursuing academic studies in Tibetan philosophy, but actually devoting herself to her personal meditation practice. Her money had run out and, like many of the Tibetan lamas with whom she studied, she had come to Taiwan to raise funds. Meanwhile, her fifteen-year-old son was back in North America being raised by his grandparents. She told me this story about her son:

> Two years ago, the "Mafia" from [such-and-such famous Gelukpa monastery] recognized my son as a *tulku*. But they just wanted to get money. It's an investment. They figure they'll get money from me, or from my family, or from people coming to see him. They said they would pay for the enthronement and everything, but they're just trying to make an investment. One monk came all the way to see me and complained that he had already spent 25,000 rupees . . . but anyway, I gave him 500 for his train fare so he would go away. . . . Later the Nyingmas also wanted to recognize my son as a *tulku*.

Although Susan resented the possibility that the monasteries were trying to manipulate her and her son for their own gain, she clearly believed that they were right to identify him as an exceptional boy. She confided:

> He has great gentleness. And a very special air about him. When he was young he would enter deep meditation during *puja*s [rituals] and initiations. He said he doesn't care about being a *tulku*. He just wants to meditate like me.

Although her son apparently didn't care whether he was identified as a reincarnate Tibetan lama or not, Susan seemed more ambivalent, saying,

> When he was young the Kagyus tested him as a *tulku*, but he failed the test. So I always tease him: "You failed your *tulku* test."

Susan, it seemed to me, was torn between her growing recognition of the ways in which the *tulku* system can be manipulated for financial or political ends and her attraction to the system's doctrine of exotic exceptionalism.

Over the next several years, as I continued my research on the globalization of Tibetan Buddhism, I frequently encountered non-Tibetans who were fascinated by the *tulku* system and filled with longing to participate in it. One Western woman, herself a member of her country's ruling elite, dressed her six-year-old son in Tibetan monastic robes—at his insistence, she said—and brought him to meet a high-ranking Tibetan lama. "Tell Rinpoche about your dream," she urged him, obviously hoping to set the machinery of institutional recognition and approval in motion. Indeed, as I did my fieldwork, it seemed that I was continually running into Western women and men who were convinced that their young sons were *tulku*s. Some of the time the Tibetans agreed with these assessments, sometimes they did not, and much time appeared to be spent trying to convince the relevant hierarchs to bestow recognition.

Interestingly, when I told Susan about a particular American New Age figure who had Tibetan pretensions and had identified his own son as the reincarnation of a particularly high Tibetan lama, with whom Susan had a close connection, she became incensed. "I have no faith in people who recognize their *own* children as *tulku*s," she exclaimed. This led her to an extended denunciation of the quality of the Buddha dharma as it is practiced in the West, which she saw as superficial and materialistic. Although this was a common complaint from almost all Tibetan Buddhists I met, whether they were ethnic Tibetan or not, it was striking coming from her given that she had previously told me all about her son in tones which suggested that if he wasn't a *tulku*, he was certainly "special." When I asked her whether she, too, was interpreting Tibetan Buddhism to suit her own cultural sensibility, and was thus not so different from the other Westerners of whom she was so critical, she strenuously denied it, pointing out that she had been living in Asia for several years, seeming to intimate that this meant that she had become, if not Tibetan, at least less tied to her Western sensibility. The notion that one could become less Western and more Tibetan was a recurring theme during my fieldwork. It is an interesting question why one should even desire this, to say nothing of thinking that it is possible. But it is also curious that so few of the Westerners I met who expressed such views recognized the culturally specific history of appropriation and fascination in which these desires were rooted. Yet it does not seem a huge stretch to see in this view—that one's Western identity may be shed like a set of clothes and exchanged for one more appealing—the root of the desire that culminates in the wish to actually *be* Tibetan, or at least to occupy a Tibetan body.

The ex-husband of an American woman who *had* been identified as a *tulku* by the Tibetan monastic establishment, told me bitterly that his ex-wife had known nothing about Buddhism and that he had done all the leg work that led to her recognition. Then, at the urging of her Tibetan advisors, she had thrown him out in the cold. But now, he told me with satisfaction and a slightly secretive air, other Tibetan lamas had informed him that he too was a *tulku*; they were just awaiting the proper moment to make his status public.

Others expressed similar desires for recognition for themselves rather than for their children. One English woman explained to me that "after the Chinese took over Tibet, thousands of Himalayan yogis incarnated in the West. They're suffering greatly because they're out of place." Her teacher, an American who himself claims to be the incarnation of the Buddha Maitreya, Lama Tsong Khapa, Christ, Krishna, and King Arthur, among others, is helping these lost *tulku*s to "recapitulate," or return to, their previous situation. He had told her that she was a *tulku* too, although he hadn't yet revealed of whom.

I never met Maitreya Buddha, as his followers call him, but they were a regular presence in the Boudhanath neighborhood of Kathmandu during my fieldwork. They were immediately recognizable because, in addition to wearing Tibetan monastic robes, they always bore enormous crystal *dorjés* (*rdo rje*). The *dorjé* is a well-known symbol in Tantric (Vajrayāna) Buddhism. Among other uses, it refers to a small metal implement used by Tibetans as part of religious practice. While there is some accepted variation in the artistic design of these implements, the *dorjés* borne by the Buddha Maitreya's followers were well outside these restrictions. At the center of the *dorjé* was a large piece of crystal, around which various pieces of copper wire were wrapped, usually with some other decorations. Each piece that I saw was unique, and impressively large, large enough to attract attention when they were carried out into the street, which they invariably were. The crystal *dorjés* were immediately recognizable to any Buddhist as *dorjés*, but they were also clearly nothing like the normal *dorjés* of Tibetan Buddhist ritual practice. As one of the Buddha Maitreya's followers put it to me, "the Buddhists developed *dorjés*, but *dorjés* aren't Buddhist. It is an ancient wisdom which they tapped into." This comment echoes a long tradition of Western engagement with Tibet in which Tibet is simultaneously seen as the repository of wisdom and a repository that invites, by Western lights, its own transcendence. This attitude is not shared by the Tibetans themselves. The followers of Buddha Maitreya, for example, rented a house in Boudhanath where they established a dharma center. Although they were tolerated by the residents of Boudhanath (who are particularly accustomed to all sorts of people coming and going, and who economically depend on this traffic), it seemed quite clear that few Tibetans took them seriously. Indeed, though some were amused or intrigued by the *dorjés* of crystal and copper, others clearly took offense at this appropriation (and alteration) of an important sacred ritual object. Thus, while Tibetans welcomed non-Tibetans to participate in the global mandala of Tibetan Buddhism, some also felt threatened and angry when non-Tibetans sought to refashion the practices or identities of Tibetan Buddhism in accord with their own aspirations. Certainly, Tibetans I spoke with found Buddha Maitreya's self-recognition of his *tulku* status, and his re-imagining of the *dorjé,* to be offensive, and his Western followers' willingness to believe in him absurd.

The Super-Heroic Tibetan Body

What is the architecture of this desire to participate in Tibetan Buddhist culture to such a degree that one's very identity, one's very body, holds—one hopes or imagines—a secret self, a Tibetan self, waiting to be discovered? To understand this fascination we must recall the ways in which Tibet has been represented by Westerners. In the nineteenth century, with the filling-in of uncharted areas on the global map, and with the increasing hegemony of European colonial domination, Tibet emerged in Western consciousness as the untamed space, par excellence, the place in which pre-scientific mystery still held sway. One of the first Westerners to popularize ideas about Tibet was the Russian mystic and founder of the influential Theosophical Society, Madame Helena Blavatsky. Blavatsky claimed there was a global order of initiated masters who possessed secret esoteric knowledge, but who were under pressure from the increasing magnetism associated with industrial society, and who therefore were taking refuge in remote locations, such as Tibet. It was from Tibet, she claimed, that she received transmissions from her master who was, it should be noted, not himself a Tibetan.

Over the following century, Tibet has become the preferred icon for expressing longing and fascination for the hidden, the mysterious, and the premodern. James Hilton's best-selling novel (and later film) *Lost Horizon* continued the theme of Tibet-as-utopia, suggesting that the best of human inspiration—which in his case was all European—had been stored away in a remote Himalayan valley to protect it from the ravages of twentieth-century history (Hilton 1933). For many in the West, their first encounter with the notion of Tibet came through the popular books by Lobsang Rampa, such as the *Third Eye*; the author of these books, Cyril Hoskin, claimed to be a Tibetan whose consciousness had been mysteriously transposed into an English body (Lopez 1998).

My own first encounters with notions of Tibetan exceptionalism occurred while reading comic books as a child. In one series, a group of superheroes lived in a hidden Himalayan vale, protected by a giant bubble that kept them invisible. From time to time events would call them out of their refuge to fight villains and save the world. Perhaps no series of comic books more vividly expresses the conflation in Western imaginations of the concept of the superhero and the concept of the *tulku,* than the *White Lama* series (Jodorowsky 2000). The series draws upon the life story of the Tibetan culture-hero, Milarepa, combining traditional Tibetan elements with odd pieces from Rampa's narratives, such as his not-very-Tibetan preoccupation with cats. The story's hero, the White Lama, is a white boy who becomes the *tulku* of a high lama when the lama and the boy's parents—who are proto-hippie "seekers" in Tibet—are slain by the forces of the evil (Tibetan) lama who has taken over the monastery. The White Lama is then raised as a Tibetan, unaware of his powers until, like Milarepa, the tremendous injustice passed on to his family inspires him to take revenge. Also like Milarepa, and many classic superheroes as well, the White Lama's vengeance fills him with disgust and remorse and he turns thereafter to the cause of good. Yet, just as Hilton's Shangri-La was positioned as a space in which European goodness could reach its true fulfillment, so too, in the White Lama comic books—although the pinnacle of mystical power initially resides with Tibetan lamas, eventually it is the White Lama, whose identity is both Tibetan and not Tibetan, who heroically defeats the magic of the evil Tibetan lama.

Tibetans Strike Back: Counter-Appropriation and the Seizing of Sherlock Holmes

Such narrative arcs leave many Tibetans shaking their heads in puzzlement and bemusement. I want to conclude this chapter by suggesting that a 1999 novel, *The Mandala of Sherlock Holmes* (later released with the alternative title *Sherlock Holmes: The Missing Years*) by Jamyang Norbu, a well-known Tibetan intellectual and critic of efforts to romanticize Tibetan culture, can be read as an effort at counter-appropriation (for an alternative reading see Venturino 2008). The novel recounts the story of Sherlock Holmes's two years in Tibet. Arthur Conan Doyle, it may be recalled, having grown sick of the famous detective, killed him off in a struggle with his archenemy, Moriarty, at Reichenbach Falls. Public outcry was intense and a few years later Doyle succumbed to the pressure and brought him back for further adventures. He explained his absence to Dr. Watson with these brief remarks in the story "The Adventure of the Empty House," published in the *Strand Magazine* in October 1903:

> I traveled for two years in Tibet, therefore, and amused myself by visiting Lhassa [*sic*], and spending some days with the head Lama. You may have read of the remarkable exploration of a Norwegian named Sigerson, but I am sure that it never occurred to you that you were receiving news of your friend. (Doyle 1984, 344)

Norbu's novel fills in the details of these two years with an adventure tale that takes Holmes from India to Thibet [*sic*] and "Beyond." In many respects the story is a classic Sherlock Holmes detective romp, yet as Holmes gets closer to Tibet, the logical analyses that are his hallmark give way to a more intuitive style of sleuthing. After preventing a murder, Holmes gives the following explanation to his sidekick, Hurree:

> "You would not call me an irrational man, would you, Hurree?"
> "Of course not, Sir. If I may say so you are the most rational, most scientific man I have ever had the privilege of meeting."
> "Yet reason or science had nothing to do with what I did last night."
> "Please?"

"I just *knew*. One moment I was smoking my last pipe for the night and thinking about our meeting with the Lama Yonten, and the next moment I knew for certain that a dangerous assassin was going to enter the Grand Lama's Summer Palace."

"Like a premonition, Sir?"

"There was nothing vague about it. The singular thing was the absolute assurance I felt about this startling revelation. Yet there was no way to explain it in logical terms. It was a most peculiar experience." (Norbu 1999, 191)

In the Holmes canon, of course, such a suggestion borders on the absurd: as a literary figure, Holmes is constructed to be nothing but the personification of rationality, empiricism, and logic. To suggest that the detective who symbolizes the capacity of science to discover almost *anything* through the powers of deductive reasoning would, instead, prevent a terrible crime through a *premonition,* is to turn the Holmes myth on its head.

By the time of the climactic battle in the Ice Temple of Shambhala, Holmes has fallen further under the sway of Tibet, so much so that, in their moment of desperation one of his Tibetan allies cries to him: "Listen to me! . . . You are not really English. You are one of us. You have the power too. . . . You are the renowned Gangsar *tulku*" (ibid., 242). His true identity rediscovered, Holmes also recovers his lost powers:

Sherlock Holmes raised his hands and—as if he had been doing it all his life (which, in a manner of speaking, he probably had)—moved his fingers in a strange manner to form tantric gestures (Skt. mudra). Immediately, a barely visible barrier, a kind of curtain of shimmering energy, seemed to form. . . . The force wave smashed into the psychic shield with the noise of a thunderclap. (ibid., 245)

In Norbu's hands, Sherlock Holmes, like every other Westerner touched by Tibet—at least in the domain of *tulku* envy that he is satirizing—is transformed. By making the journey to Tibet (and like so many other fantastic Tibet narratives, eventually *beyond* Tibet, in this case to the Ice Temple of Shambhala, thereby echoing Tibetan culture's own utopian dreamscape), Holmes discovers his *true* self. And his truest self, revealed by this journey of self-discovery, turns out to be Tibetan. And not just any Tibetan, but a Tibetan superhero, complete with esoteric hand gestures that produce waves of force. The Western superhero detective of Victorian rationality has found himself, and he is actually a Tibetan superhero sorcerer of Tibetan Buddhism.

While such a plot twist may seem outrageous, Norbu points out the many ways in which Holmes shares the ideal characteristics of a *tulku*:

Mr. Holmes a former lama? Why ever not? He was celibate, of noble mien and great wisdom. In accordance with the Mahayanic precepts of altruism and compassion he had devoted his life to aiding the weak, the poor and the helpless against the powers of evil. He fasted regularly to clear the vital channels and bring about clarity of insight; and he had powers of concentration that would make many a practicing yogi look like a rank novice. Never was an incarnate lama truer, or more deserving of his monastic robe and cap of office, than my dear friend. (ibid., 243–44)

Norbu concludes by deploying the familiar trope of Tibet-as-refuge for a secret community of esoteric knowledge that protects the world:

They have always watched over our world, and through a small community of fellow seekers in the remoteness of the Thibetan highlands, they have maintained a bond with humankind. (ibid., 255)

. . .

[Holmes] had decided to stay a year more in Thibet to complete his studies. But after that he would return to England to finish his task of destroying Moriarty's criminal empire and removing his baleful influence once and for all from the cities of Europe. Only on the conclusion of this task would he finally return to Thibet. "I have my orders," said Holmes, "and I must obey." He did not elaborate about who had given those orders, and I did not ask. (ibid., 259)

Thus, by the end of his novel, Norbu has appropriated—or perhaps counter-appropriated—one of the West's greatest literary superheroes and given him a new, higher, identity. Just as Madame Blavatsky, in real life, built her precursor of New Age spirituality on the foundation of a secret group of adepts living in Tibet, Norbu, in literature, builds his satire of Western *tulku* envy on the foundation of Holmes and his Tibetan brethren, hidden away in their Tibetan solitude but keeping a careful and watchful eye over the outside world. It would be easy to dismiss all of this as a too-bizarre transformation of Sherlock Holmes from the very icon of scientific materialism and logical empiricism to a comic book caricature of Tibetan exotic supernaturalism. But I think the book—which won India's highest award for English fiction, the Crossword Book Award, in 2000—is more subtle than that. Norbu clearly aims to satirize the phenomena of *tulku* envy, poking fun at the tendency of some non-Tibetans to discover Tibetan-ness within themselves.

I recognize it is a tremendous oversimplification to see all transnational *tulku*s as manifestations of *tulku* envy. As noted above, there are precedents for non-

Tibetan *tulku*s in Tibetan history. Most Tibetans regard non-Tibetan *tulku*s, particularly if their recognition has been validated by the Buddhist establishment and if they have received traditional religious training, as affirming and strengthening Tibetan Buddhism in its hour of great need. Indeed, most of the non-Tibetan *tulku*s who have been recognized during Tibetan Buddhism's current wave of global expansion have led fairly uncontroversial careers. Some have become Tibetan Buddhist teachers, while others have adopted more low-key ways of living their *tulku* status (and in this respect, their experiences mirror that of many Tibetan *tulku*s, some of whom decline to lead lives of religious leadership, at least overtly). And, in addition to and outnumbering non-Tibetan *tulku*s, there are now numerous Western (and other convert) Buddhist teachers in the global Buddhist landscape. In short, the striking thing about the phenomena of *tulku* envy is not the growing participation of non-Tibetans in the social and imagined worlds of Tibetan Buddhism as practitioners, patrons, teachers, and even reincarnated Tibetans; the existence of these roles for non-Tibetans in contemporary Tibetan Buddhism is simply a reflection of the religion's newly transnational character.

Rather, the phenomena of *tulku* envy points toward another parallel dynamic, whereby the reproduction of Tibetan Buddhist institutions in non-Tibetan spaces has been linked to the growing power of the Tibet-of-the-imagination. This imagined or fantasized Tibet is not new—as noted above it has a long pedigree in the history of the representation of Tibet—but it is as strong and powerful as ever. The longing for a Tibetan body, or more precisely, the longing to discover that one's Western body is actually a vessel holding a Tibetan identity, reveals something of the symbolic potency that Tibetan-ness continues to hold for so many in the West. In this sense, the desire for a Tibetan identity appears like the desire for so many other forms of symbolic capital, albeit that *tulku* status renders this capital in a unique way.

Against this dynamic, Norbu's satire is an act of counter-appropriation, responding to the appropriation of Tibetan culture heroes with a comparable theft of a Western mythic figure. And just as such an act calls our attention to the fact that Sherlock Holmes is, after all, just a storybook character, whose powers of deduction are perhaps an artistic expression of the spirit of the age of scientific materialism, but which are not meant to be taken literally, so too, perhaps, Norbu seeks to gently mock those in the West who wish to make Tibetan culture heroes *their* culture heroes, or perhaps even a constitutive part of their *identities*.

CHAPTER 3

Buddhism in American Prisons

CONSTANCE KASSOR

T HE RAPIDLY GROWING interest in Buddhism in the West has led to the emergence of Buddhist practices among diverse communities.[1] Notably, one community in which Buddhist practice is beginning to take root is the American prison system. An increasing number of inmates are working to overcome their often violent and seemingly hopeless situations by adopting the compassionate, nonviolent, and mindful ideals of Buddhist practice while incarcerated, thus transforming their own experiences as well as contributing to changes in the prison system as a whole.

It is difficult to characterize life within the prison system in comparison with life on the outside. Prisons and jails are operating well beyond their capacity,[2] and violence among both inmates and staff is commonplace (Sabol et al. 2007). Life within prisons is often brutal, and gang-related activities put many inmates in danger on a regular basis. Under these circumstances, it seems implausible that one can successfully engage in mindful practices, such as meditation, but many dedicated inmates are trying to accomplish exactly that. Because of the rigid structure of daily prison life, it is difficult for forms of deviant activity to emerge, even if such activities are religious in nature. The lack of tolerance for change within the prison system has forced Buddhist practices to undergo a number of extreme transformations in the ways in which it is taught, learned, and practiced by inmates.

The inmate population is steadily growing. As of June 30, 2006, there were 2,245,189 people in U.S. prisons and jails, equaling roughly 750 inmates per 100,000 citizens (Sabol et al. 2007). With this growing number of inmates, Buddhist teachers and practitioners are becoming more aware of the demand for information and instruction within prisons. The Engaged Buddhism movement (Jones 2003) as well as Mindfulness Based Stress Reduction (MBSR) programs, are working to train volunteers to teach meditation in prisons and jails. These meditation programs, in addition to reducing recidivism rates,[3] are contributing to reductions in drug use, violent offenses, and anxiety among inmate populations (Jeen-Fong 1998). The psychological and social benefits of Buddhist practice in American prisons appear to be significant, and they warrant careful investigation.

I do not have the resources to conduct such a full-blown investigation at this time; however, it is my aim in this chapter to identify characteristics of Buddhist practices that are widespread among American Buddhist inmate populations, and to determine whether and to what extent these practices can be distinguished from Buddhist practices in general. Based on this framework, it will be possible to conduct further research to determine the overall effectiveness of Buddhist practices in American prisons in greater detail. These distinguishing characteristics of American "prison dharma" are a direct result of the ways in which Buddhist thought is brought into prisons, the ways in which it is understood and practiced by inmates, and the overall structure of the American prison system.

Transmission of Buddhism into Prisons

For many inmates, the thought of engaging Buddhist meditation within the confines of a prison is daunting, but for others, prisons present themselves as the perfect places to practice; a primary tenet of Buddhism is the acknowledgment that all life involves suffering, and in few places is suffering more overtly present than in the prison system. A growing number of inmates, former inmates, and others are helping to perpetuate the spread of Buddhist practice into prisons, and its popularity is increasing as a result (Kabat-Zinn 1991; Lozoff 1985; Masters 1997; Whitney 2003). That said, the spread of Buddhist practices is occurring at a slower rate inside of prisons than outside due to the bureaucracy involved in the prison system and the restrictions placed on inmates. Because of these restrictions, the transmission of Buddhist thought into prisons is limited to four methods: (1) through books, (2) correspondence programs, (3) other inmates, and (4) outside volunteers, such as individual teachers and facilitators of meditation groups. Each of these methods proves effective in the transmission of Buddhist practices into prisons, but with varying degrees of efficiency and success.

1) By far, the most common method of transmission is through books. A number of Buddhist, non-Buddhist, and secular organizations send books about Buddhism and meditation free of charge to inmates who request them.[4] For many inmates who wish to learn about Buddhism, these written materials are their only source of information. When Buddhist practice is taught in this way, inmates have the ability to study and learn at their own pace, but they

must be their own teachers. They may have questions that cannot be answered by books, but because they may have no contact with other practitioners, they must resolve these questions entirely on their own.

2) Like those that distribute books, numerous groups exist that match interested prisoners with "dharma pen-pals," who can correspond with inmates, answer their questions, serve as a source of friendship, and help them overcome difficulties and obstacles that may arise in their meditative practices. This form of transmission, often accompanied by the distribution of Buddhist literature, allows inmates to ask questions of someone who may be able to provide some insight into their situations, or who may have access to a skilled practitioner or teacher who could provide insight. For many Buddhist inmates, written correspondence is the only form of contact they have with other Buddhist practitioners. While a pen-pal may be able to answer specific questions about Buddhism, other issues, such as the intricacies of a particular meditation technique, which are ordinarily explained through face-to-face meetings between teachers and students, must still be resolved by the inmate.

3) Sometimes Buddhist practices may be taught to inmates by other inmates who practice Buddhism. In a handful of prisons across the country, meditation and study groups that are organized by inmates themselves have been permitted. This method probably proves the most effective means of transmission, but it is not always available. In addition to difficulties in organizing such groups within the rigid structure of the prison system, many prisoners feel uncomfortable revealing a particular spiritual practice to their peers, especially something as seemingly foreign as Buddhism. In an environment where violence pervades, some inmates fear that their peers will perceive someone who meditates and practices nonviolence as having become weak (Whitney 2003, 40).

Even if two or more inmates discover a mutual desire to practice Buddhism, prison administrators have the ability to make this exceedingly difficult. In high-security prisons, inmates are constantly transferred from one area to another in attempts to deter gang-related violence. Even if a small group of inmates finds itself fortunate enough to be in a place where they can openly discuss their meditation practices, administrators frequently make it difficult for them to practice together. As one inmate explains,

> From time to time other inmates would observe me meditating or find out I was a Buddhist, and several expressed an interest in learning how to meditate. But my attempts to get permission from the prison administration to organize a group were simply ignored. Finally, after several years of trying,

I received a terse note from the prison chaplain, an ex-guard, who baldly stated that no such group would be permitted, and that any inmate wanting to meditate could jolly well do it in his cell. (Buddhist Peace Fellowship 1992, 32)

Western Buddhists outside of prisons generally have opportunities to find other practitioners with whom to sit on a regular basis, and this serves as one of the foundations of their practice. While Christian and Jewish services are almost universally permitted in prisons, a service in which a handful of inmates simply sit quietly in a room is rarely permitted. On the rare occasions when inmates are able to organize a sitting group, they are able to ask questions of each other and discuss issues that arise in their practice, but they still lack the formal guidance of a teacher, a resource that has historically been considered essential to traditional Buddhist practice (Wallace 2006).

4) Outside volunteers can bring Buddhist ideas into prisons by teaching meditation, yoga, nonviolent communication, or stress-reduction classes. The benefit of this method is the direct, in-person instruction that inmates are able to receive. Instead of learning from books and teaching themselves, inmates can spend time with volunteers who genuinely want to teach, and they can ask questions of people who have spent time practicing and have likely encountered similar difficulties themselves.

Unfortunately, organizing a sitting group or meditation class in a prison is a dauntingly difficult process. Prison administrators may immediately reject the idea of any Eastern religious practices being brought into a prison; as one inmate describes, "it is not uncommon to encounter prison chaplains who regard Buddhism as some kind of foreign and even dangerous cult" (Buddhist Peace Fellowship 1992, 20). One warden was apprehensive about meditation classes being taught because he "knew that [Buddhist ideas] were somehow vaguely connected with kung fu" (Whitney 2003, 67). Most administrators believe that it's safer to allow only the public practice of more familiar Western religions, such as Christianity, and that inmates can practice meditation independently if they so desire. It is also likely that the suspicion and hostility toward Buddhism are rooted in religious chauvinism, at least in some cases, despite the legal requirement that freedom of religious belief and practice extend even into the prison system.[5]

Given the difficulties that surround introducing Buddhism into prisons, many Buddhist volunteers succeed in getting meditation groups started under the auspices of a prison's mental health department, rather than through the chaplain. They market meditation as stress reduction or as a skill linked to non-

violent communication. Such terms aren't quite as loaded as "Buddhist meditation" and seem to have more success in passing under the radar of strict
administrators. When such classes are offered, the term "Buddhism" may never
be used at all, though the Buddhist principles of compassion and nonviolence
are nevertheless explained (Kassor 2003).

Even when administrators are willing to allow Buddhist meditation groups
to be formed within their prisons, volunteers are not always readily available.
As Fleet Maull, a Buddhist practitioner and former inmate recalls,

> the nearest Buddhist group or center able to provide some support to our
> group has been the Kansas City Dharma Study Group. They have only
> been able to visit us twice so far though, since it's a four- to five-hour drive
> each way and they are very involved in just keeping their own group going
> amidst the pressures of city life, jobs, and family responsibilities. (Buddhist
> Peace Fellowship 1992, 20)

Some groups that wish to teach classes lack the resources and time to travel to
prisons to instruct classes. As in the case of the Kansas City group, volunteers
are often willing, and prisons are accepting, but the simple fact of geographi-
cal distance is enough to prevent the transmission of Buddhism into some
prisons.

Even in instances where a group is able to visit the prison, a successful meeting is never guaranteed. Sometimes the problem is getting in; even after volunteers travel (sometimes for hours) to a prison, administrators may not let them
inside. This can be attributable to a variety of factors, such as lockdowns to
prevent potentially violent situations among the inmates. Other times the
challenge is prisoners getting there; guards may simply fail to inform inmates
that a meeting or class is scheduled. Prison administrators may impose strict
work schedules that conflict with a scheduled class, preventing some inmates
from attending.

Yet another difference in Buddhist practice inside prisons as compared with
practice on the outside concerns the relationship between a student and a teacher.
Such a relationship, if existent at all, must be transformed to accommodate the
rigid structure of the prison system. In Buddhist communities on the outside,
practitioners may attend weekly meditation groups, or have some sort of community or spiritual advisor to help them with their practice. Usually the teacher
is someone with years of experience who is specially trained to give teachings.
In prisons, however, if Buddhism is not self-taught through books, it is typically taught by volunteer lay practitioners, with whom inmates have restricted
and generally infrequent contact.

Although the above-mentioned four methods are ways of transmitting Buddhism into prisons, not all meditation classes are taught specifically with Buddhism in mind. Some groups have initiated meditation classes inside prisons that have no religious motivation whatsoever; their goals may be for neurological or psychological research,[6] or to introduce stress-reduction techniques into the lives of inmates to help them better serve their time. Because of the broad, generalized nature of "meditation," especially in the West, it is not always clear when specifically Buddhist practice is being taught and when it is not. Some groups unaffiliated with Buddhism still employ Buddhist techniques, and other Buddhist groups are forced to tone down the Buddhist aspects of their teachings so much that they are almost unrecognizable as such. In this respect, there is no clearly defined separation between Buddhist and non-Buddhist meditation practice as taught by volunteers within prisons.

This blurry distinction between Buddhist and non-Buddhist meditation, however, is common in the West outside of prisons as well. Texts such as Wallace's *The Attention Revolution* and Jon Kabat-Zinn's *Full Catastrophe Living*, for example, present a collection of ideas and meditation techniques from diverse Buddhist traditions, as well as some methods for meditation that do not appear in Buddhist textual traditions at all. It is actually very difficult to distinguish traditionally Buddhist meditative practices from non-Buddhist practices in the West, and the juxtaposition of such diverse methods for teaching meditation in American prisons only serves to highlight this ambiguity.

Transformative Adaptations of Buddhist Practice

One aspect of Buddhist practice in prisons that many inmates acknowledge is that a prison environment bears some remarkable similarities to a monastic environment. If an inmate is serious about his practice, he can view his time in prison as a "total practice situation" (Buddhist Peace Fellowship 1992, 19). Prisoners have little or no contact with the outside world; in many cases, they do not keep in touch with family members, and they have little reason to deal with anyone on the outside. Often Buddhist inmates remark that they have no obligations aside from a job they are required to perform and their practice.

Another similarity is that traditionally a monastic lives simply, and a prison cell is stripped to the bare necessities: a bed, a toilet, and a sink. When compared with the fast-paced, cluttered, hectic lifestyle on the outside, prisons could be almost ideal settings for practice—if it weren't for the violent, noisy, isolated, and degrading conditions in which prisoners live. And though many Buddhist inmates have compared prisons with monasteries, just as many have likened them to realms of hell.

Although meditative practice is difficult in prisons, when it is successful it can have tremendous results. "If one can practice under such difficult circumstances the potential for realization is greatly increased," claims Fleet Maull (Maull 2004, 70). Most inmates practice early in the morning, when the din of the televisions is quietest and most other inmates are still asleep. During the daytime, "usually it's too cacophonous for reflection or prayer" (Buddhist Peace Fellowship 1992, 28). Even if an inmate *can* handle the noise during the day, he still has to concern himself with being watched or disturbed by other prisoners or guards.

Many inmates notice a change in themselves once they become involved in a regular practice. As one man claims, "when I was practicing I felt much calmer and more able to cope with the stressful environment of prison" (ibid., 32). And another reflects, "practice has brought me no earth-shattering insights; I have experienced no *satori* at the sound of a key turning in a lock, yet over the years I have changed" (ibid., 32). They do not claim to be trying to become Buddhas, yet many inmates do experience insight into how to relieve the suffering that prison life entails. That is, while they may not be seeking to become enlightened, many inmates strive for and sometimes reach a sense of equanimity, and are more able to cope with their situations. Many of these inmates are looking to transform themselves in some way, whether by changing their outlook on the world or by improving the ways in which they deal with difficult people and situations.

Meditation may be the only quiet time that one can find inside a prison. Some inmates are able to attend retreats of some sort, and these become cherished opportunities. As Fleet Maull recalls,

> I was able to do a retreat each year. They give you a week's vacation from your prison job. So I'd buy a week's worth of food from the commissary, and I'd lock up in my cell and do a full retreat for nine or ten days, twelve hours of practice a day. (Maull 2004, 73)

Maull had the fortunate opportunity of having a single cell for his retreats; many inmates are crammed into tiny cubicles, with two or four people occupying a cell originally intended to house one. In some jails and minimum-security prisons, inmates are housed in large dormitories with dozens of other people crowded into a small space. These inmates have no personal space except for a bunk and occasionally a footlocker. Maull also had discipline; he had taken novice monastic vows while in prison and was determined to follow them. Other inmates may lack the ability or skills necessary to perform such a "retreat" on their own, but Maull's experience illustrates the commitment that some inmates have to their meditative practices.

Despite the general hostility that is occasionally displayed by prison administrators toward Buddhist practices, a number of prisons in America are beginning to organize *vipassanā* retreats. These ten-day prison retreats were first introduced in Jaipur, India, and eventually gained recognition as a successful tool for rehabilitation in other countries. In some American prisons, these retreats have yielded tremendous results. Prisoners claim the retreats are stricter than even the rigid structure of prison life, and for the first few days it can be an incredibly painful and frightening experience. As in the case of weekly meditation classes, the goal at these intensive retreats is not necessarily for the participating inmates to become enlightened, but rather to have experiences that can change their lives for the better. Inmates have noted that when they begin to meditate, they feel—often for the first time—the power to change themselves. Instead of blaming their situations on myriad outside factors, they realize they have the ability to change themselves, and that they must accept and endure consequences for their actions (David Donnenfield Productions and University of California 1998).

Although many meditation programs in prisons are geared toward simply helping inmates cope with their present situations, some inmate practitioners completely adhere to specifically Buddhist styles of practice, albeit with alterations to conform to the prison environment. Jarvis Masters, an inmate on Death Row in California's San Quentin Prison, follows a Tibetan tradition of Buddhism. When he first became serious about his practice, he arranged to receive an empowerment ceremony from his teacher Chagdud Rinpoche. In a traditional empowerment ceremony, the teacher makes physical contact with the student, and a number of ritual items are used. In the ceremony for Masters, Chagdud Rinpoche was not allowed to bring any of the necessary items into the prison, and he had to speak to Masters over a telephone while looking at him through a sheet of Plexiglas. Rinpoche was not fazed by these inconveniences, however; "It doesn't matter we can't touch," he reassured Masters. "The power of the ceremony is in your hearing the words" (Buddhist Peace Fellowship 1992, 26). Masters went through the ceremony that day and called himself a practicing Buddhist after that. In this case, although external conditions prevented the ritual from being performed in the traditional way, both Masters and his teacher, working within the limitations of the prison environment, were able to modify the ceremony in such a way that allowed Masters to be initiated into Buddhist practice according to tradition without expressly violating any parameters that either of the participants saw as crucial to the ritual.

Regardless of whether an inmate intends to practice to achieve some sort of spiritual awakening, or whether he practices to simply feel less stressed and more in control, research results show that regular meditative practices can improve the mental health of inmates. As previously mentioned in the introduction to this chapter, analysis from a preliminary study has shown that recidivism rates decreased substantially among inmates who participated in meditation programs, as compared with other rehabilitative programs. In a time when the general recidivism rate is well over 50 percent,[7] the prison system in America would benefit from more extensive studies on the benefits of meditation.

Presently, the effectiveness of specifically Buddhist meditative practices, as compared with secular forms of mindfulness practices in prisons, is unclear. Clinical studies have shown, however, that Mindfulness Based Stress Reduction (MBSR) programs have a high rate of success in improving mental health (Bishop 2002). This research suggests that meditation programs can be of great benefit to prison populations, reducing recidivism and violence within prisons, in addition to improving the mental health of individual inmates.

Transformative Adaptations of Buddhist Ethics

I have shown that meditation practices in prisons must be altered in significant ways due to the structure of the prison environment. In addition to these practical changes, significant transformations can be seen in the ways in which inmate practitioners understand ethics. Buddhist scriptures explain a number of clearly defined precepts that practitioners are to follow, but the nature of life in prison requires these precepts to be altered in creative ways. This creative interpretation of Buddhist ethics is explicit in prison environments, but it is not necessarily unique to inmate practitioners. I will begin to explain this creative re-interpretation of ethics by highlighting several specific examples cited by individual inmates.

One of the basic precepts that a Buddhist practitioner is required to follow is to refrain from stealing. Fleet Maull, however, writes of engaging in a form of stealing by participating in the black-market economy that pervades prison life:

> I try, but it's difficult to avoid participating in the black market completely. Like it or not, this convict world is my community, and I often find myself trying to balance my commitment to the precepts with the Mahāyāna vows I have taken to extend myself to others. Something as simple as a birthday party for a friend is bound to involve some black-market food. (Buddhist Peace Fellowship 1993, 24)

Inmates who work in the dining halls of prisons tend to steal food and supplies. In fact, "the staff expects the prisoners to steal and lets a certain amount of it go, in many cases, as a kind of job perk in order to keep good workers" (ibid., 24). The reasoning underlying this behavior is that if inmates are allowed to steal from their places of work, they are more likely to have a better rapport with prison staff and will be better workers. Inmates and staff agree that "hardly anyone sees stealing from the institution as immoral" (ibid., 24). It is commonly seen as just another part of the system, and many inmates consider stealing as necessary to get by on a daily basis. In this context, an inmate's taking supplies or food from his job is not considered stealing by virtually anyone in the prison system. Thus, Maull, although he participated in an action that can be technically classified as stealing, did not view his actions as immoral or as going against Buddhist ethics.

This description of stealing shows that Maull's participation in the prison black market was generally limited to instances in which he wanted to help his fellow inmates, whether it was for the purpose of throwing a birthday party or giving resources to friends. Might one argue that Maull turned the non-virtuous action of stealing into "right action"? Might one even go so far as to view his innovative methods of turning stealing into right livelihood as promising for other Buddhist practitioners on the inside? While these are provocative questions to raise in trying to get a sense of how far one could justifiably go in modifying the practice of basic Buddhist precepts based on the context of one's life, the fact is that in most cases these opportunities are rare. Most prisoners are just trying to get by, and, being paid literally pennies a day for their prison jobs,[8] it's nearly impossible to refrain from participating in the black market on a regular basis.

In his book *Finding Freedom*, Jarvis Masters justifies violating another precept—refraining from using harsh speech—in order to help a fellow inmate. He tells the story of a young man named Alex who attempted suicide one day in his cell. After he recovered, another inmate lectured him for four hours on the stupidity of his actions. The inmate calmly tried to explain to Alex that he didn't need to resort to suicide, since he only had a few months left of his sentence to serve. Alex didn't listen, and two weeks later tried to kill himself again. Seeing an opportunity to help Alex realize the importance of his life, Masters decided to scare him into wanting to live.

> "How 'bout them tennies you have on? You should at least let me have *them* [after you die]."
> "No way!" Alex stared down at his shoes. "I just got these Nikes last week. You can't have these for all the world."

"Those aren't Nikes. Let me see," I said, stepping toward him. "Wow, they *are* Nikes!" I snatched Alex by his coat and quickly pinned him to the fence. "Listen, you young chump." My eyes stared inches from the frightened kid's face. "You don't know nothin' 'bout this world. Trying to kill yourself—you don't know shit—and you know what? Since I got big plans for being on this here planet, dude, you going to give me those damn shoes." (Masters 1997, 92)

The exchange between the two inmates resulted in Alex becoming so angry that he vowed to live long enough to see Masters die. After another inmate had spent hours trying to gently dissuade Alex (to no avail), Masters was able to effectively communicate with the young man and prevent him from killing himself. Clearly, Masters had no intention of actually stealing Alex's shoes, but the empty threat and the harsh language were enough to get through to him.

In this example, Masters actually violated two Buddhist precepts: he was lying, and he was threatening to steal. But, because his intention was to save another man's life, his actions did not violate ethics according to Buddhism. Masters can be said to have used skillful means—the appropriate use of one's abilities relevant to a situation—in his harshness toward Alex. In a harsh environment, such as a prison, skillful means may necessitate acting with what might be considered unethical behavior in another circumstance.

In yet another illustration of the flexibility of Buddhist ethics in prison, Maull had a "strong desire to take the novice monastic vows" while he was in prison. Although he realized that, realistically, "it didn't seem reasonable to make a commitment beyond that point," he wanted to live his life following the dharma (Buddhist Peace Fellowship 1992, 19). He became ordained as a novice monk and tried to follow the novice monastic precepts as closely as possible.

Initially, Maull struggled just to be mindful of the fact that he had taken vows; "nothing in the environment recognized this major life change I had made," he recalled, "so it was a challenge to continually remind myself of it" (ibid., 23). He couldn't shave his head, and he certainly couldn't wear monastic robes. There was no sangha to support him; very few, if any, of his fellow inmates even knew that he had taken vows, let alone understood what that meant. After his ordination, he still lived in the same cell and performed the same daily routine.

Some of Maull's vows were easier to follow than others. One that gave him the most immediate trouble was the rule that monks are not allowed to take food after midday. Because the nutritional content of standard prison fare is so poor, skipping meals on a regular basis is not a healthy option. As a compromise, Maull refrained from solid foods in the evenings. He recalls, "I did take fruit juice in the evenings and even enjoyed a pint of ice cream at 5 pm on commissary night, our once-a-week night for shopping at the prison canteen. One shouldn't be too rigid in these matters after all" (ibid., 23). Maull reasoned that the difficulties of prison were intense, and when compounded with the rigidity of leading a monastic life, it seemed an almost crazy way to live one's life. But through his years as an incarcerated monk, Maull realized that it could be "a relief and at times even a great joy just to be alive and practicing dharma in prison" (ibid., 23). If he violated a few of his vows on the inside, he claimed that they were due to circumstance more than anything else, and he felt that his transgressions could be excused from time to time.

Adaptations of monastic laws to suit different environments are prevalent even in traditional Buddhist communities. Contrary to rules explicitly stated in monastic codes, a significant number of Asian monks and nuns no longer beg for alms on a daily basis and many regularly handle money. These transgressions of the textual tradition are overlooked by contemporary monastic and lay populations, because they are seen as necessary for survival.

In prisons, Buddhist practices must similarly be modified. Inmates rarely have a safe, quiet place to sit, let alone teachers or a community to turn to for support. Because of the harsh conditions inside, it is impossible for inmates to avoid reinterpreting concepts of right and wrong to suit the environment. The underlying common thread linking Buddhist ethics as practiced within prisons and elsewhere, however, is *intention*. According to Buddhist scriptures, when a person performs an action, if his intention is good, it is a good action, and if his intention is vengeful, greedy, or otherwise non-virtuous, then it is a bad action. This applies to all Buddhists, whether they are American inmates, Sri Lankan nuns, or Tibetan laypeople. Outside of a prison environment, intention is also important, but it is not so explicitly contrasted with harmful conditions as it is in prisons; generally, more traditional "right actions" correspond to traditional "right intentions."

What Can Buddhist Practices in American Prisons Teach Us about Buddhism?

Just as Buddhism was transmitted from India to China, and from Asia to the United States, Western Buddhist traditions are now moving from the free world into prisons. Because prisons are relatively self-contained environments, it is easy to see the rapid changes that Buddhist thought and practice have had to undergo as they have been transmitted from the outside to the inside. These changes are not unique to prison culture, they are simply more drastic, and therefore more easily noticeable when compared with other forms of Buddhism.

The ways in which Buddhist practice can be brought into prisons is comparatively limited, and as a result, certain types of meditation practiced in prisons might not be recognizable as explicitly Buddhist. When we consider the results of these practices, however, such as reduced recidivism rates and improved mental health, the question of whether these practices can actually be called "Buddhist" might not be significant. Research is inconclusive at this point as to whether more traditional Buddhist forms of meditation have a greater or lesser effect in achieving these end results as compared with more secular forms of meditation; nonetheless, meditative practice of some sort is undeniably beneficial for inmates as well as for the prison system as a whole.

Notes

1. Much of the information for this study came from a 2004 internship with the Buddhist Peace Fellowship Prison Project (now called the Transformative Justice Project) in Berkeley, California.
2. Inmate populations are growing at a faster rate than prisons and jails can be built to accommodate them. Between 2005 and 2006, the number of incarcerated people increased by 2.8 percent across the country. By the end of 2006, twenty-three state prison systems operated at above 100 percent capacity, and seventeen states operated at 90 to 99 percent capacity. The federal prison system was operating at 37 percent above its rated capacity.
3. Results from a study of more than one hundred maximum security inmates at the Massachusetts Correctional Institution showed that the recidivism rate for those who participated in regular meditation programs was 30 to 35 percent lower than for those who participated in other forms of rehabilitation programs.
4. The Buddhist Peace Fellowship, Human Kindness Foundation, and Prison Book Project are a few such organizations.
5. Notably, the 1972 case of *Cruz vs. Beto*, which went to the U.S. Supreme Court, involved a Buddhist inmate in a Texas prison who was not only denied use of the prison chapel but was placed in solitary confinement and fed a diet of bread and water for two weeks as a result of attempting to practice and teach Buddhism. The Supreme Court ruled that the prison had unjustly discriminated against Cruz on account of his faith.
6. Jon Kabat-Zinn at the University of Massachusetts, for example, has ongoing Mindfulness Based Stress Reduction (MBSR) courses in area prisons for medical research purposes.
7. According to the most current information available from the U.S. Bureau of Justice Statistics, the recidivism rate in fifteen states in 1994 was 67.5 percent, up from 62.5 percent in 1983.
8. "The actual wage of a California prisoner is a high $1.15 per hour. . . . Many prisoners make under $0.20 per hour, and some don't get paid at all." Source: Buddhist Peace Fellowship Prison Project, http://www.bpf.org/html/current_projects/prison_program/pdfs/StatsAboutPrisindcomplex.pdf (accessed September 28, 2008).

CHAPTER 4

Incense at a Funeral

The Rise and Fall of an American Shingon Temple

ELIZABETH EASTMAN

ONE OF MY earliest memories is of wandering the twisting paths in the overgrown garden behind my Watanabe great-grandparents' house.[1] I would meander over the fish pond's stone bridge, peering down through the tangle of weeds to catch a glimpse of fish darting in and out among the shadows. Then I would choose a path, turn a corner, and lose sight of the house behind me. One of these pathways, I knew, led to a church, though I couldn't remember ever having been there.

Although I didn't know it at the time, the church next door to my great-grandparents' house was a once-thriving Buddhist temple supported largely by my great-grandparents. I grew up calling them Ojichan and Obachan, the informal terms for grandfather and grandmother in Japanese. My great-grandfather's funeral is the first, and last, time I can remember entering the church—listening to the service but not understanding any of the words. In my child's mind, Buddhism was lighting a stick of incense after Watanabe Ojichan's funeral and leaving it smoking in the dish near his picture. It wasn't until years later that I learned how much more Buddhism once meant to my family. The temple was a vital part of my *issei* (first-generation Japanese immigrants) great-grandparents' lives, but I—three generations later—barely knew it existed.

I became truly interested in Buddhism when I spent a year as an exchange student in Thailand between high school and college. I went to Buddhist weddings and funerals with my host family. I visited temples, both the famous ones and the smaller, local variety. I bought incense, flowers, and candles to leave before the altar and had my fortune told by shaking a can of numbered sticks until one fell to the floor. I visited the Reclining Buddha and the Emerald Buddha. I studied meditation and learned about Theravāda Buddhism. I spent the year immersed in a world where I passed the Buddha every day at school and where my Thai host family placed incense before a miniature altar in the house each morning and evening. I had always considered myself Protestant in the tradition of my Caucasian father's family, though I wasn't raised in a particularly religious household. But in that year overseas, I gained a great respect for Buddhist values and lifestyle.

At Smith College I took classes in Japanese and Thai language and in Asian literature but didn't encounter Buddhism again until three years later when I heard about the TransBuddhism seminar being organized by Smith's Kahn Institute. I hoped the seminar would allow me not only to learn more about Buddhism as a religion but to create a stronger connection to my own religious heritage.

After reading the seminar's first few assignments I decided my project would focus on what Jan Nattier calls "baggage Buddhism." Nattier categorizes Buddhism in the West based on its method of transmission: "import" where Buddhism is "actively sought out by the recipient"; "export" involving active "'selling' by a Buddhist missionary"; or "baggage" brought by "Asian immigrants who came to North America in search of jobs, new opportunities, and a better future for their families." This third type of Buddhism is also termed "ethnic Buddhism" because its importance as a source of cultural identity in the new country means that these communities generally remain mono-ethnic at least initially (Nattier 1998, 183–95).

I wanted to choose a topic with personal significance to make my time spent researching more meaningful. I started by asking my mother about religion on her side of our family, thinking that my Japanese American relatives might once have practiced Buddhism. I was a bit surprised to find out that my great-grandparents, Watanabe Ojichan and Obachan, founded and helped build the church that was on their property in the small Portland, Oregon, suburb of Milwaukie. We spent so much time in the TransBuddhism seminar talking about the increasing interest in Buddhism in the United States that I expected the temple would be thriving like so many other Buddhist institutions. Because of this, I was startled to learn that in this climate of rising interest and acceptance, my own family's Buddhist community had dwindled and disappeared. I soon realized that the church's demise would make research more difficult. All of the church's old records were lost in the fire that destroyed the Watanabe house and most of the original congregation was long dead. Watanabe Ojichan had died when I was a young child and Watanabe Obachan when I was in high school. My other Japanese great-grandparents, Nakata Ojichan and Obachan, who had been dedicated members of the church, were also long gone. Their children, my grandparents, had witnessed their parents' experience but were more peripherally involved. It became apparent that my contribution to the TransBuddhism seminar wasn't going to be the straight-forward account of the transmission of ethnic Buddhism that I had initially anticipated. Rather, it would become a search to rediscover a lost community and to find out why it failed to flourish in America's inclusive religious environment.

My maternal grandparents, who still live in Portland, suggested that I con-tact Bishop Miyata at the head temple in Los Angeles in the hope that he might be able to give me some information about their parents' church. I was able to arrange a meeting with him and so I traveled from my college in Mas-sachusetts to meet him. I arrived early in the evening and spent some time exploring the area. The temple and my hotel were in the middle of the Little Tokyo district of Los Angeles. Having grown up in a white, middle-class town on the central Oregon coast, I was amazed to see an American neighborhood so remarkably Japanese.

In the morning I walked to the temple to meet with Bishop Miyata. I was shown to the back of the temple where the bishop had his office, and I was introduced to an older Japanese man dressed in traditional robes. We spent several hours talking about Shingon Buddhism, a form of esoteric Japa-nese Buddhism, in America; the Head Temple in L.A.; and the temple my great-grandparents founded, the Oregon Koyasan Shinnoin Temple. Through our conversation and from the head temple's fiftieth-anniversary commemora-tive publication, I learned how my family's religion had first come to America following the arrival of Japanese immigrants in the middle and late nineteenth century.

Unlike European immigrants, most immigrants from Japan never intended to stay permanently in the United States. They dreamed of making their for-tune and then returning to Japan, so long-term institutions—including Bud-dhist temples—weren't established until the early twentieth century, at which point the population of Japanese laborers in the United States had grown large enough that there was a mounting demand for religious establishments to serve them (Payne 2005).

In 1909, the Reverend Shutai Aoyama, former chief priest of Kakuganji Temple in Toyama-ken, left Japan for the United States with the blessings of his superiors in order "to observe the religious situation in North America, as well as propagate Shingon Buddhism" (*Koyasan Buddhist Temple, 1912–1962*, 115). Upon reaching the United States, he almost immediately fell ill and was delayed more than two years until he recovered both physically and finan-cially. In 1912, with support and encouragement from some of the Los Angeles Japanese community's leading citizens, he opened the first Shingon temple in

the United States in a house in Little Tokyo. Two decades later, the Los Angeles Daishi Church became Koyasan Beikoku Betsuin Temple, the U.S. headquarters for the Shingon mission, and a permanent temple building was
constructed (ibid., 116). During its first three decades, the temple membership
grew in strength, and the need to reach Shingon followers from outlying rural
areas prompted the establishment of *Daishi-ko* meetings—less formal gatherings for worship held outside the temple proper. During this period, temple
organizations such as a Women's Association, a Mutual Aid Association, and
Boy Scout Troop 379 were also founded. Koyasan Betsuin Temple thrived,
though it remained the only U.S. Shingon temple until after World War II
(Bishop Taiser Miyata interview).

The bombing of Pearl Harbor on December 7, 1941, forever changed the
Japanese American community. Anti-Japanese sentiment ran rampant. Within
a year the temple in Los Angeles was closed, its hall and basement piled to the
ceiling with members' possessions, and its membership, both U.S. citizens and
non-citizens alike, was relocated to internment camps throughout the West.
The same events were happening in Japanese American communities up and
down the West coast. My family and thousands like them spent the next three
years trying to create a sense of normalcy behind barbed wire fences.

Religion was a big part of this effort. Japanese Buddhists, facing the harsh
realities of internment, turned to religion for a source of strength and a sense
of identity. Faith flourished in the camps even without access to a proper
temple, religious texts, or ceremonial accoutrements and often without the
presence of a minister. Makeshift temples and *Daishi-ko* gatherings were established with church members stepping forward to lead the services. Religious writing became an important vehicle during this period. A Buddhist
periodical was published to provide guidance and inspiration to interned followers. At the same time, Buddhist leaders wrote sermons that were sent to
groups without a minister, creating an extended religious network based on
correspondence. One minister later described the situation: "Just like a candle
in darkness which can never be merged with the surrounding darkness however deep it may be, the light of their religious faith never went out despite the
hardships of camp life. On the contrary, the light glowed with an increasing
radiance" (*Koyasan Buddhist Temple, 1912–1962*, 179).

Eventually World War II drew to a close and Japanese Americans returned
to their Pacific coast communities or resettled farther east and began picking
up the pieces of their lives. Koyasan Buddhist Temple was reopened in Los
Angeles, serving also as a temporary hostel for its members, and *Daishi-ko* gatherings were reestablished. New temples began to appear, among them the Oregon Koyasan Shinnoin Temple that my great-grandparents helped establish.

Bishop Miyata and I concluded our interview late in the morning so that he could prepare for the afternoon ceremony. After lunch I returned to the temple to attend the special *goma* fire ceremony that was being held that day. It was a strange experience to sit in the hall watching the ceremony and feel a part of it—because it was a part of my history—and yet at the same time feel like an outsider. I watched the bishop prepare the ceremonial fire without really understanding the significance of the ritual. I recalled from the TransBuddhism seminar that many Buddhists in Japan, and elsewhere in Asia, also have little detailed understanding of the rituals performed at their behest; still, the unfamiliarity was unsettling.

After everyone in the hall had shared a meal of *mochi* soup, I flew to Portland, Oregon, to visit my grandparents. I spent two days talking with them and two of their friends who also remembered the temple. Mrs. Gimba is a *nisei* (second-generation Japanese American) woman whose parents and husband were very active in the temple. Mrs. Toma is a *kibei*, someone born in the United States but then sent to Japan to be educated. Their stories, along with the information I received from Bishop Miyata, began to bring the temple to life in my imagination.

Shingon followers founded Henjoji Temple in Portland in 1946, but by 1951 differences in ideology between that temple's leadership and some of its members caused a group to split from the temple (Miyata, n.d.). Led by my Watanabe great-grandparents and including my Nakata great-grandparents, this group, comprised primarily of Japanese immigrants from Okayama-ken, contacted Bishop Seytsu Takahashi, head of Koyasan Betsuin, in the hopes of establishing a new temple.

Watanabe Ojichan and Obachan owned a piece of property in the Portland suburb of Milwaukie that was originally purchased in the 1920s when U.S. law made it necessary to put the title under the name of Roy Yokota, an older *nisei* friend.[2] They renovated a former Japanese school on the property, which became the group's new temple building. The Oregon Shinnoin Temple's official opening on July 20, 1952, was marked by a ritual presided over by Abbot Shokai Wada from the headquarters at Koyasan, Japan, and by the Reverend Nakagawa, and supervised by Bishop Takahashi. Hundreds of Shingon Buddhists witnessed the rite. The Reverend Chigen Kimura was sent from Japan to become the temple's first minister. He was followed in 1954 by the Reverend Shoun Ishikawa, and in 1959, by the Reverend Shunyu Asahi who remained until 1971. During its prime, the 1950s, 1960s, and 1970s, Oregon Koyasan Shinnoin Temple had as many as a hundred people at its rituals and celebrations and was home to a vibrant community of faith (Frank and Ruth Nakata interview).

The services performed at the Shinnoin Temple were essentially identical to those performed at Shingon temples in Japan. Because ministers were sent directly from Japan and usually stayed for only a few years, it is not surprising that there was a great deal of continuity with traditional Shingon practices and norms as they existed in Japan. Small adaptations were introduced—the Christian practice of holding regular Sunday services, a pew-like seating arrangement, and the use of the terms "church," "minister," and "congregation" interchangeably with, or in substitution for, "temple," "priest," and "sangha"— but the temple's rituals remained essentially unchanged.

My grandparents, Mrs. Toma, and Mrs. Gimba described many of the ceremonies to me, illustrating the vibrant community that once existed around the church. One holiday, Hanamatsuri, on April 8, celebrated the Buddha's birthday with a house of flowers. My Nakata Ojichan always made the house covered with blooming flowers with help from some of the other church members. Mrs. Toma remembered everyone taking a turn pouring sweet tea on the Buddha placed in the center of the house and then praying together. June 15 of each year was Aobamatsuri, also known as the Green Leaf Festival, and it marked the birthday of Kobo Daishi, the founder of Shingon Buddhism. Green leaves were used in the celebration as an emblem of birth. Hoshimatsuri was always celebrated on a Sunday in February. In the weeks leading up to the ceremony, papers were sent out to local members and followers from the United States and Canada; these papers were sent back, inscribed with the names and ages of everyone in the family. People with health problems or specific wishes also included these prayers on the papers. It was believed especially important for individuals whose age was considered unlucky to return their completed paper. During the Hoshimatsuri ceremony, the minister built a *goma* fire in which he burned all of the papers collected in the previous year; the current year's slips were carefully saved until the following year. Every year there were also four days of spiritual observance during which members met at the temple and then visited the cemetery together. Spring Ohigan in March and Autumn Ohigan in September marked the change of seasons. Obon and Memorial Day, like Ohigan, were days to pray for and honor the dead.

The traditional event that I found the most intriguing was also the largest religious event for the temple, and seemingly one of the most memorable ones as well. The Osunafumi rite was held every June to honor Kobo Daishi, the ninth-century founder of the Shingon sect of Japanese Buddhism practiced by my great-grandparents. Commemoration involved a pilgrimage to eighty-eight Shikoku temples undertaken by Japanese Buddhists of various sects. When carried out in Japan, an individual might traditionally spend a month or more during any part of the year walking from temple to temple. With the advent of modern transportation and the increasing demand for efficiency of time, the pilgrimage is now completed much more quickly by car. At Oregon Shinnoin, the pilgrimage was completed symbolically once a year. Every June, eighty-eight bags filled with sand from Shikoku, each representing one of the eighty-eight temples, were arranged to form a path winding through and around the temple. Worshipers then walked barefoot along the path, stepping on each of the bags to symbolize visiting each of the Shikoku temples and offering tribute to its deity.

Osunafumi was also attended by Japanese Shingon Buddhists from as far away as Canada; *Daishi-ko* members from Seattle and Steveston, British Columbia, traveled by charter bus to attend the annual celebration. These visitors stayed with local members and, according to Mrs. Toma, guests always stayed with the same families, so over the years they became very good friends. The celebration was anticipated as a chance to renew these friendships. The ritual was first performed at the Shinnoin Temple in 1953 and continued until 1980 when the eruption of Mount Saint Helens prevented the ritual from taking place as usual. By this time the temple's membership had already begun its fatal decline, and in the years following this interruption the ceremony was never resumed. The end of the annual gathering eroded the formerly strong links among Shingon communities across the Northwest and further contributed to the isolation of the remaining members.

While most of the religious holidays attracted only the older members, the New Year celebration filled the temple with families. My grandfather told me, "They had a New Year's party with a lot of food and they invited the families—kids, grandkids, and whoever; they had a basement full of people. This was when most of the families came to church . . . when there was a party. Everyone had a good time. It was really wonderful" (Frank and Ruth Nakata, interview with author, January 2004). Every year the same group of women, Mrs. Gimba, Mrs. Tanabe, Watanabe Obachan, and Mrs. Ono, prepared food at the church. They made *mochi*, *sushi*, *onishime* (made from vegetables and chicken), shrimp for long life, black beans for good health, corn bread, *kamabako*, *kazunoko* (herring roll, until it got to be too expensive to serve), *sashimi*, and *chow mein*. The Shinnoin Temple used to give away raffle tickets, but rather than purchasing large expensive prizes, members donated many smaller prizes. The New Year celebration was relatively insignificant from a Buddhist spiritual perspective, but members and their families really looked forward to the food and entertainment.

The annual summer picnic was a similarly popular event. It was an opportunity for members and their families to gather socially. Like the New Year's party, the picnic was one of the few church events attended by the younger *nisei* and *sansei* (third-generation Japanese Americans) generations. Even my mother, a *sansei,* remembers the picnics.

These celebrations, although not particularly concerned with Buddhist doctrine or practice, used the church as a focal point for the maintenance of group solidarity and identity. Thus, the propagation of my great-grandparents' Buddhist community, in the radically new context of the United States, relied on seemingly mundane social and interpersonal interactions just as much as specifically Buddhist practices.

Although the congregation was small, Oregon Shinnoin had an active membership. Everyone helped to make *mochi* rice balls for the temple's *mochitsuki* fund-raising project. To pay for repairs to the temple building, local members donated money, and letters brought in donations from more distant Shingon followers. This support system gathered enough money to survive, though there was never any accumulated savings. This lack of a substantial church endowment contributed to the fragility of this particular community.

My great-grandparents also took responsibility for the care of the temple's resident minister. Watanabe Ojichan sponsored Rev. Asahi's immigration and helped him adjust to life in the United States. Each of the ministers who officiated at the temple, including Rev. Asahi, until he married and moved to an apartment, lived at the church and took their meals with the Watanabe family. Though my great-grandparents have all passed on, my family still offer their hospitality to the Shingon clergy. Bishop Miyata now stays with my grandparents when he visits Portland.

Though Watanabe Ojichan did most of the routine maintenance of the church building, once a year, usually in December, everyone gathered at the church to give the building a thorough cleaning. The women polished all the brass in the temple. Mrs. Ono always polished the lantern, and Mrs. Toma remembers Mrs. Ono telling everyone else not to touch it. While the women were doing the tedious cleaning, the men stayed in the basement. Though they weren't required to be there for the cleaning, they usually ended up there anyway, sometimes helping and sometimes talking over coffee.

The temple had a regular newsletter written by Mrs. Gimba's husband. He handwrote the publication and then mimeographed it. The newsletter was then distributed to both local and out of town members. Mrs. Gimba remembers him being a very dedicated member and a leader of the temple.

The two organizations established at the church were traditionally Japanese, unlike the Boy Scout troop at Koyasan Betsuin. The *fujinkai*, or women's auxiliary, was a smaller, dedicated group of women from the temple who performed services for the church community. They arranged for flowers to be sent for funerals and visited the sick. They ran the fund-raisers and ensured there was food available for functions.

The *goeika* was composed of women at the Shinnoin church although men could join. Its function was somewhat like that of a Christian choir; my mother described it as a choir that chants. The *goeika* sat at the front of the congregation during the service and performed chants specific to the particular ceremony or event. Mrs. Toma was in the *goeika* for a long time but says that she usually followed other people like Mrs. Ono and my Watanabe Obachan, who were very good. Even though she hasn't executed the chants for more than twenty years, Mrs. Toma is still able to perform one from the *goeika* book containing words to the chant written along with tones and marks for the bell and the chime.

In addition to formal groups, social gatherings were an important part of temple life. Because the temple was so far from the city, the worshipers would always bring food to share and eat together after the service. It was a time everyone enjoyed because it gave friends the chance to socialize. According to my grandfather, "these people were very close friends, all of them. [The membership was] not a very big group. Just like a family. So it would be fun to get together and talk [after the service]" (Frank and Ruth Nakata, interview with the author, January 2004).

Although the various Japanese Buddhist organizations in the Portland area were not officially affiliated, temple functions were often attended by friends from other Buddhist sects. Members of the Shinnoin Temple in particular, frequently attended events held by other temples. My grandfather recalls that his "mother used to go to all the other churches. She also had her own, but if someone was having a festival at their church, she'd go" (ibid.). In this way, the Japanese Buddhist temples functioned as informal community centers, a role that was very important for the *issei* but became progressively less important for the succeeding generations.

Remarkably, my grandparents have kept in touch with the last minister at the Shinnoin Temple who had gone back to Japan and taken over leadership of his father's temple. I wrote to Rev. Asahi and was able to arrange an interview with him in Japan over my college spring break.

I was met at the airport by an older Japanese gentleman in a gray suit. He was more like a retired American businessman than what I expected for a Japanese Buddhist priest. He introduced me to another couple who drove us to a nearby town in Mie Prefecture where I spent the night before my morning interview with Asahi Sensei. After a delicious Japanese breakfast, we sat down in the hotel lobby. With the help of a translator I learned a lot of about his time at the temple and about why he thought the temple had closed. By the end of our discussion I had a much more complete picture of the last decade at the temple.

As the 1980s continued, the membership of the temple began to experience a catastrophic decline. It is impossible, two decades later, to know with any certainty why the membership deteriorated so rapidly. Mrs. Toma, a *kibei*, is the only regular member still living. Even many of the *nisei*, second generation, the young people of earlier years, have passed on. For those who remain, memories may admittedly be vague and opinions, as always, vary. The most basic factor, however, is undisputed.

By the 1980s, the *issei*, who had formed the core membership of the temple, were rapidly aging. Many were deceased. Many others were either sick or essentially homebound. This aging of the *issei* generation caused a sudden loss of members. Although everyone I spoke with accepted that the Shinnoin Temple had failed to attract new, younger members to fill the void created by the loss of the *issei*, they didn't always agree on the reason for this breakdown. In reality it was probably not one cause but rather a combination of factors that led to the closing of the temple.

While the *issei* formed a dedicated membership, the *nisei*, who were born in the United States, had very little involvement in the temple. My grandfather spent more time at the temple than most *nisei*. He drove his mother, my Nakata Obachan, who was extremely dedicated to the church, into Milwaukie every Sunday, sometimes picking up her friends on the way. He had little personal commitment to the church, however, and would have preferred not to spend most of his day off there.

Though Mrs. Gimba's husband was a devoted member of the temple, she was only peripherally involved. Mrs. Gimba often spent days at the temple, but rarely as a worshiper. She was usually helping her mother in the kitchen, mostly washing dishes, when there was extra work during events or after services.

Most *nisei*, and later *sansei* and *yonsei*, the third and fourth generations, visited the temple only for special events. According to my grandfather, whenever there was a party the basement was full of people—members, their children and grandchildren. My mother, a *sansei*, says, "we went to Milwaukie some Sundays, but I never really went to church there, unless there was some special thing going on, mostly I remember funerals" (Janyce Eastman interview).

The language barrier was a major problem facing the temple. While the *issei* spoke primarily Japanese, the *nisei* spoke English. The *nisei* might have a basic knowledge of their parents' language, but they were generally not as fluent or as comfortable speaking Japanese as English. Ministers for the temple were always sent directly from Japan and spoke very little English, but since the majority of members were *issei* they didn't see this as a problem. According to Mrs. Toma, when her children attended the services they "didn't understand many things" (Michie Toma interview). Some implied that the ministers chosen were not ones who could be expected to successfully attract the younger members. The older *issei* Japanese got along very well with the resident ministers because they shared a common language and culture. For the younger generations who had been born in the United States and were culturally American, the minister, although closer to their age, was from their parents' world. As a *kibei*, someone who had gone back to Japan for her education, Mrs. Toma was fluent in Japanese and much more comfortable with Japanese culture so she interacted more easily with the *issei* and with the minister. That the *issei* members seemed to like the ministers suggests that the problems were primarily cultural and linguistic. Not surprisingly, Koyasan Betsuin has started offering ministerial training for Americans in order to bridge this gap.

Rev. Asahi, even with his limited knowledge of English, attempted to forge relationships with the *nisei* and *sansei*. He believes that even though he could not speak fluent English, he could still communicate and convey his feelings using gestures and broken English. He remembers that although the *sansei* and *yonsei* didn't understand any Japanese, they seemed to enjoy attending the annual picnic with him. While he might have been able to communicate his friendship without a common language, discussions about religion were much more problematic.

After the traditional service, Rev. Asahi read a sermon and explanation of the ceremony prepared in both English and Japanese by the headquarters. The sermon was intended to discuss the importance of Buddhism in the world for the benefit of both the English-speaking and Japanese-speaking members of his congregation. He wanted everyone to comprehend why they were coming to the temple by explaining the significance of the ceremony. It was apparent, however, that the young people still didn't understand.

In addition to the language problems, the Shinnoin Temple was not organized with families in mind. The temple had no nursery or children's programs, so children didn't grow up as part of a religious community as they do at many other temples and churches. My mother went to Sunday school at a Baptist church down the street from her house. She believes her parents would have taken her to Milwaukie every Sunday had she wanted to go. But most parents didn't push their children, and left on their own there was nothing to attract them to the church. The situation was essentially a vicious spiral in which there weren't enough youth to justify special programming and no special programming to interest youth.

When I asked Rev. Asahi to compare his American congregation with a Japanese one, I expected that the Japanese Americans might have lost their connection with Japanese traditions judging from the declining membership. So I was somewhat surprised to learn that Shinnoin's members were more devout than their Japanese counterparts. For the *issei* immigrants from Japan the temple provided something to depend on in a foreign country. Because of this, the temple community in the United States placed more importance on religion than did members of temples in Japan. Rev. Asahi observed that his *issei* followers were much more spiritual than either their contemporaries in Japan or, in his opinion, many Christian Americans. The *issei* established a much-needed connection to their home country through the familiar religious devotions.

Simple logistics also kept people from attending regularly. Milwaukie, a small suburb of Portland, had a relatively small local Japanese American population to draw from and was far enough from Portland that the drive to the temple was inconvenient for many. The young people, in particular, were too busy or preferred other activities. Even Mrs. Toma found the temple location too inconvenient to visit every week. Her home in Portland was almost an hour away, even longer before the freeway was built, so she usually went once a month. She admits, though, that as one of the youngest members she might not have attended more often even if the temple had been closer.

Rev. Asahi was the last of Oregon Shinnoin's resident ministers. He extended his term in the United States twice but was finally called back to Japan so that another minister could take his place. This new minister, however, was assigned to a temple in Seattle and visited Milwaukie for only a day or two at a time. Bishop Miyata and Rev. Asahi believe that this lack of a residential minister was a major reason for the demise of the temple. Bishop Miyata suggests lack of financial security and family ties to Japan as reasons for the difficulty of finding and maintaining residential ministers. Rev. Asahi theorizes that the three-year term of stay in the United States was too short to accomplish any large projects, and the diminishing congregation caused the priests to lose confidence and as a result the headquarters decided not to send another minister. He believes that the presence of a residential minister at the temple during this critical time might have given the temple a chance of surviving the shift in generations, but that without established leadership the temple had little hope of recovering.

Evangelism on the part of Protestant churches, coupled with lack of outreach on the part of the Buddhist religion, likely also contributed to the temple's inability to maintain adequate membership. Protestant churches, particularly Methodist, were very successful in converting Japanese Americans, both because of their active evangelism and because of Japanese efforts to assimilate (Payne 2005, 19). The Methodist church in Portland now has many Japanese members. Most Buddhist churches, however, do not attempt to recruit members from either the Asian or the Caucasian communities.

There were a few Caucasians who found their way to Rev. Asahi to ask about Buddhism or Japanese culture. Some of these individuals had even trained themselves in Zen meditation, and ten of them met with Rev. Asahi a couple of times a month for meditation practice.[3] They seemed to find these practices rewarding and might have been encouraged to attend a service had the temple been of that mindset. In contrast to other Buddhist communities in America, however, which found success by cultivating new American constituencies, the Shinnoin church seems to have had little interest in this sort of outreach. Thus, in the end, the church's strength—its close-knit web of "family" ties—also proved to be a major weakness.

Moreover, in the Shingon church, membership was left to the individual and was normally transmitted from one generation to another. This method of transmission had been very successful in Japan where the majority of the population is a combination of Shinto and Buddhist, but at the Shinnoin Temple the Americanized generations wanted a more American church. Yet, Oregon Shinnoin remained in many ways a traditional Japanese temple, albeit transplanted into an American context. While this familiarity was very important to the *issei* it seemed very foreign to the *nisei* and especially the *sansei*. The younger generations which had been born, raised, and educated in the United States identified with mainstream American culture. The services themselves and the attitudes of the ministers seemed foreign and old world.

For example, there was one minister in particular with whom my grandfather always argued. My grandfather described him as "a real [Japanese] minister. He had his head shaved and had his gown on all the time where the rest of the guys had suits or slacks and shirts" (Frank and Ruth Nakata interview). This traditional minister asked my grandfather why he didn't want to be a member of the church. My grandfather didn't agree with the church's attitude toward its sick and elderly and compared its practices with those of the Christian churches. An increasingly large portion of the church's members were confined in nursing homes or hospitalized, but, unlike Christian ministers, the Shinnoin ministers never went to see them. He explained his belief that a minister should visit those who could no longer attend services. The minister, however, maintained the traditional stance, born of a Japan rich in local temples, that those who wished to worship would find a way to reach the temple. My grandfather often picked up his mother and other elderly members to take them to Milwaukie on Sundays, and he believes that the ministers should have taken a more Christian approach of visiting the sick and elderly in their homes to offer comfort and spiritual advice. Mrs. Toma agreed: "When my husband was in the hospital sick, [the minister] never came to see him" (Michie Toma interview). This is a striking instance of dissonance in changing attitudes toward the old and the sick. While the church membership appears to have been strongly influenced by the American religious traditions of social work and community-based care that they saw around them, the church ministers appear not to have recognized the challenge Christian norms posed for their own approach. Continuing to minister to their community as they would have in Japan, they failed to recognize their community's shift from being strictly Japanese toward a new composite Japanese American identity.

Many other Buddhist sects, and even some Shingon temples, in the United States have adapted to their new cultural context by using a Protestant service format, singing Buddhist "hymns," or emphasizing the importance of lay religious practice. Buddhism has also been adopted by many Americans, of all ethnicities, who are drawn to its teachings on meditation, for example. In contrast, the Shinnoin temple remained relatively unaffected by American culture other than the adoption of a regular Sunday service and the use of Protestant terms. These forms of appropriation represented a genuine accommodation to American religion. Nevertheless, they were insufficient to maintain the long-term viability of the church. In this sense, the problem was not that the Shinnoin Church did not adapt at all, but that its adaptive choices were circumscribed by an overly narrow notion of what Buddhism is. The church and its practices gave excessive weight to specifically Japanese cultural traits that did not transpose well into a new American context.

The internment during World War II probably also widened the generation gap. Not only in the camps, where cafeteria-style feeding caused a breakdown in family unity, but also in significantly far-reaching ways. After the war, members of my *issei* great-grandparents' generation wanted to cling to their Japanese identity in an America that had ostracized and dehumanized them, denying them the possibility of citizenship while condemning them for not denouncing the emperor, and in effect leaving them stateless. The *nisei*, in contrast, wanted to be "normal," to be seen not as the "other," but as the everyday American citizens they believed themselves to be. The experience of internment made assimilation a greater cultural imperative for the Japanese. In this case the cultural and generational divides created a situation in which my great-grandparents' temple wasn't what my grandparents' generation needed. It is rather ironic that when the United States was, on the whole, becoming much more open to Buddhism, these ethnic Buddhists felt so disconnected from it.

After the interview, Asahi Sensei took me to visit his temple. It sat at the top of a steep hill, at the end of a road so narrow our small car could barely make the passage. It was a beautiful temple with a sunny garden, a giant bell near the gate, and a sort of rectory off to the side. Seeing it I could almost imagine what the Shinnoin Temple might have been like: a place of tradition, peace, and worship.

Before I left Japan I wanted to visit the Shingon sect's headquarters at Koyasan, or Mount Koya. I took two trains, a cable car, and a bus before I reached the remote town late in the evening. I spent the following day hiking around the town and visiting a number of the community's many temples and shrines. My first destination was the Okunoin where the bones of Kobo Daishi are interred. The long approach to the temple was like entering another world far removed from the bustle of modern Japan. I passed thousands of gravestones and bibbed figures on the misty forest path before I reached the mausoleum where Kobo Daishi entered eternal meditation.

My next major stop was a visit to the Shingon sect's main temple, Kongobuji. I toured the many rooms with their painted screens and sat quietly admiring Japan's largest rock garden before heading for my final destination.

My last stop was the Shinnoin Temple for which my family's temple in Oregon was named (Miyata, n.d.). The Reverend Zenkyo Nakagawa, chief priest of the temple at Koyasan, dedicated and sent the central deity Kobo Daishi statue to the temple in Oregon. I felt like a white American interloper walking across the gravel courtyard to the temple, knowing that my upbringing was culturally mainstream American, and that, unlike most Americans who seemed to instantly identify the Asian "other" in my features, most Japanese did not see my Asian ancestry. After I managed an awkward explanation in less-than-perfect schoolroom Japanese of why I was visiting Japan, one of the caretakers showed me around the small temple. Walking through the living shrine, it was almost impossible not to see the shadow of my family's temple. I couldn't help wondering how a tradition as vibrant as the one on display at the shrine at Koyasan could have disappeared so completely from my family's church in Oregon.

So, the demise of the church may have been due to a failure to sufficiently adapt to this new American environment and to its Americanizing younger generation, or the simple logistical problem of an inconvenient location, or the floundering of a leaderless congregation. Most likely it was actually a combination of all these factors. Regardless, by the end of the 1980s the once thriving congregation was reduced to a small handful of elderly Japanese.

It was very difficult for my great-grandparents and their friends to watch the temple that had been so important to them simply fade away. They agonized over the imminent closing but felt helpless to prevent it. My grandfather described the situation: "Oh yeah, they talked about it. They were quite concerned. But there was nothing they could do. It was beyond their control. They didn't have a minister. They had to send the minister back to Japan, so it was quite a concern, but they just couldn't do anything about it" (Frank and Ruth Nakata interview). The temple officially closed in a ceremony presided over by Bishop Miyata on March 11, 1991, after only thirty-nine years. In 1992, the main deity statue and other important ceremonial instruments were transferred to Koyasan Betsuin in Los Angeles. The temple building, which had never been officially registered for religious use, was returned to my family and is now a private residence.

Some of the remaining members attended services at the Nichiren Buddhist temple in Portland. Mrs. Toma started going because she "didn't have anywhere else to go." Though her husband was Shingon, her parents had been Nichiren Buddhists so she returned to their church, though she never officially joined (Michie Toma interview).

When I was very young, I remember my Watanabe Obachan as a little Japanese woman stooped over by age, pushing a cart in front of her like a walker as she shuffled around the house. By the time I was in middle school, she could no longer walk and spent most of her time sitting in a recliner in the main room. I barely spoke to her. We were separated by more than just three generations. We were divided by language and by culture. I wish now that I had been able to talk to her before she died, to hear about her life and about my history. I find it amazing how little I really know about my own family. The older generations don't tell their stories and so a great deal of the history dies with them. Maybe they don't want to relive it, or maybe they think no one is interested. There are so many things that I want to know about but don't ask because I don't want to be intrusive. My grandparents and their friends were willing to talk with me about the temple, but I don't think they felt their history and memories were important enough to record. Perhaps one of the reasons that institutions like my family's church die out is this failure to share stories and heritage from one generation to the next.

The stories and the pictures of the church and its members that I collected give me a brief glimpse into our history; but they leave me feeling a great sense of loss. In the end my project became so much more than I ever could have imagined. As much as I am fascinated by all that I've learned, I am even more saddened that there are so many experiences I will never share with my great-grandparents. At times, I feel that a part of my life and my history is gone forever. In four generations we went from intense devotion to benign neglect to, now with me, rediscovery of our tradition, yet as an outsider. Although it was a foundation of my great-grandparents' lives, over the years my family's religious tradition has faded to the point where I learn about it in school just as I might study Judaism or Islam.

I set out to learn how, in an increasingly Buddhist United States, a Shingon Buddhist Temple could have vanished. I discovered a rich cultural tradition that had traveled from Japan to Oregon, but it was perhaps too true to its origins and too tied to one-dimensional understandings of Buddhist identity and practice to survive in the American melting pot. Now I know at least some of the story, and as I sit with the old pictures and my Obachan's beads and *goeika* set scattered around me on the floor, I know that this might have been my church, too.

Notes

1. Much of this chapter is based on interviews that were conducted in January and March 2004 with Ruth and Frank Nakata, Mrs. Kina Gimba, Mrs. Michie Toma, Bishop Taisen Miyata, Rev. Shunyu Asahi, and Janyce Eastman. Special thanks to all of them.
2. At that time immigrants from Japan could not own property, so land was often purchased in the name of *nisei* children or friends who were U.S. citizens.
3. *Ajikan*, Shingon meditation, is not the same as *zazen*, Zen meditation, though they are similar. However, since Westerners rarely distinguished between sects they referred to their meditation practice using the popular term, and Rev. Asahi wasn't able to explain the difference with his limited English.

PART II

Translation

TRANSLATION HAS ALWAYS BEEN (deliberately) integral to the transmission of Buddhism and (inadvertently) integral to its transformation. The initial codification of the canon in Pāli at the First Council probably already represented a translation of the Buddha's talks from one or more vernacular languages to a common tongue. As Buddhism was transmitted throughout Asia, the developing Buddhist canon was translated into many languages. These translations followed different patterns. The translation into Tibetan, for instance, was highly systematic, and involved the close collaboration of teams of Indian and Tibetan scholars, issuing in the creation of virtually a new language whose vocabulary and syntax are redolent with Sanskrit. The translation into Chinese, by contrast, was haphazard, usually accomplished by individual monks, using a classical language already inflected by Chinese philosophy. Japan and Korea received their canons by translation primarily from Chinese, not from Pāli or Sanskrit texts originating in India, an intriguing precedent for some translation practices in the contemporary West.

As Buddhism moves West, translation again mediates its transmission, and once again we see multiple models, each generating its own kinds of intentional or inadvertent transformations. English is the most common Western target language and, like Chinese, is a language in which much of the vocabulary is already pregnant with philosophical and religious meaning. As English locutions are recruited for Buddhist ends, these semantic penumbrae necessarily inform Buddhist ideas.

Jay Garfield and Thomas Rohlich, each experienced translators of Buddhist literature, explore the craft of translation in its current form, along with its implications for the transmission of Buddhism to the West and its transformation in this new context. Mario D'Amato and Jane Stangl address the translation of Buddhist ideas into popular culture through film and sports media. The representation of Buddhism in action film or in sport literature and ideology may be jarring, demonstrating the extent to which translation inevitably transforms, but at the same time providing a useful lens through which to magnify and examine this process in its contemporary context.

CHAPTER 5

Translation as Transmission and Transformation

JAY L. GARFIELD

THIS IS NOT a general chapter on the craft and institution of translation, though some of the claims and arguments I proffer here might generalize. I am concerned in particular with the activity of the translation of Asian Buddhist texts into English in the context of the current extensive transmission of Buddhism to the West, in the context of the absorption of cultural influences of the West by Asian Buddhist cultures, and in the context of the increased interaction between Buddhist practitioner communities and academics in Buddhist Studies. These three phenomena and their synergy are very much phenomena of the late twentieth and early twenty-first centuries, so I am talking about a particular scholarly activity engaging with a particular literature and extended community at a very particular time.

Each of the phenomena to which I advert requires a bit of comment, and each has a role in determining the nature of the activity of translation as it is undertaken at this moment in intellectual space-time. First, it is important to note that we are the midst of a massive missionary religious transmission that carries with it a great deal of not specifically religious cultural baggage (including secular philosophy, medicine, art, music, literature, food, and so forth). Buddhist religious teachers and texts are being exported from Burma, India, Tibet, China, Japan, Korea, Sri Lanka, and Thailand and are eagerly being imported by denizens of North and South America, Europe, Australasia, and Africa (Baumann 2002; Wallace 2002). Buddhism is making significant inroads in these new cultural milieus, both in immigrant Buddhist communities and in so-called convert communities (Clasquin 2002; Matthews 2002; Spuler 2002). Often multiple traditions are adopted in the same region simultaneously, and they find syncretic adherents (Prebish 2002; Seager 2002). In every case, we find that the imported Buddhist teachings are adapted as much as they are adopted, and that host cultural forms and ideologies function as a matrix that determines the nature of these transformations and selections (Gregory and Weaver 2004; Harris 2002; Hayes 1999; McMahan 2002; Metcalf 2002; Padgett 2002; Snodgrass 2003; Tsomo 2002; Wetzel 2002).

Unlike past intra-Asian transmissions of Buddhism, the present transmission is very much a two-way street. At the same time that Buddhism is transforming Western culture in countless subtle and not-so-subtle ways, Asian cultures, through the global information economy, tourism, education, and migration, are being dramatically transformed by ideas and cultural forms deriving from the West (Keown, Prebish, and Husted 1998; Loy 2003; Sivaraksa 2004). Many of these ideas and practices are, at least prima facie, in serious tension with the ideologies and practices central to traditional Buddhist life. Among these we might count cosmological views, the rejection of rebirth, consumer capitalism, liberal democratic theory, and permissive attitudes toward sexuality. Others may at first seem peripheral to the religious and philosophical concerns of Buddhism, but on reflection touch on areas of life hitherto dominated by traditions grounded in Buddhism. Among these we might count traditions of medicine, theater, music, dance, and the academic curriculum itself.

While some might regard this cultural globalization as in effect destroying the Asian Buddhist cultures with which it interacts, this is surely incorrect. On the one hand, Buddhist cultures, like all cultures, evolve, and there is no more essential conflict between Buddhism and modernity than there was between Buddhism and medieval Chinese culture, or between Christian culture and modernity. On the other hand, the effect of Western influence in Buddhist Asia is not negligible: it is issuing in the dramatic, rapid transformation of those cultures. Asian Buddhist cultures are not only absorbing Western technologies and popular culture but also Western approaches to Buddhism itself, and this is often mediated by Western Buddhist texts and Western translations of Asian Buddhist texts. Dharma centers in Asia offer teachings modeled on those of Western dharma centers, at which not only Western dharma pilgrims are found in the audience but also Asian students eager for a more modern religious pedagogy. One often also finds in these dharma centers Western teachers teaching in English to Indian, Nepali, Thai, or Japanese citizens. The intra-Buddhist multi-traditional syncretism that so often characterizes Western Buddhism is finding its way into Asia, and interpretations of Buddhist doctrine and scripture mediated by Western science, political theory, popular psychology, and philosophy are increasingly familiar to Asian Buddhist scholars, monastics, and lay practitioners.

There was a time not so very long ago that the communities of Western Buddhist practitioners and of Western Buddhologists were nearly completely disjoint. Where they overlapped, we often found "closet practitioners" among the academics who dared not confess their religious proclivities for fear of losing professional standing. It was a common view that to confess a Buddhist religious practice would be to be regarded as a missionary, not a teacher or a scholar; or at least as one who could no longer pretend to the scholarly distance and objectivity requisite for serious academic work or teaching. So for those for whom scholarship and teaching in Western academia was at the center of their lives, the closet was the only option.

Members of the community of practitioners, on the other hand, were concerned to obtain liberation from cyclic existence for themselves or for all sentient beings, and often pursued that goal through devotional practices and recitations of whose content and philosophical underpinnings they had little real understanding. To be sure, there have always been those practitioners for whom developing a deep understanding of the texts and doctrines of Buddhism was a central concern. The point is that this was far from universal. Indeed it appears that this academic approach to Buddhism in the dharma center has been growing dramatically in recent years, largely because of the interaction to which I refer here. Nonetheless, it remains true that at least in the earlier years of Buddhist transmission to the West, for many Buddhist practitioners in the West, just as for many of their coreligionists in Asia, their practice involved a set of actions and recitations taken to be soteriologically efficacious, independent of any cognitive grasp of their significance. (Of course, this is not a uniquely Western phenomenon: the practice of mantra recitation, or of the ritual recitation of sutras by those oblivious to their meanings, is and always has been a part of Asian Buddhist practice.) Study of doctrine, philosophy, or language was not always a salient feature of Western dharma centers.

All of this has changed dramatically over the past few decades. Dharma centers of all Buddhist sects and lineages host teachers, offer classes in Buddhist philosophy, canonical languages, and ritual arts and generally take their mission to involve educating their membership in order to facilitate spiritual transformation. Often the speakers and teachers at these centers are in fact academic specialists in Buddhist studies; and a very large proportion of the texts studied in these contexts are translations or textbooks prepared by such academics. On campus more and more Buddhist Studies scholars who happen also to be Buddhist have come out of the spiritual closet. No longer are those who profess faith immediately suspect as scholars, just as Christians are free to teach Christian religion or philosophy without a presupposition of a failure of objectivity. Not surprisingly, we also see increasing collaboration between campus-based and dharma center–based academic programs, with teaching burdens shared and students receiving credit for studies in Dharma centers. (I find myself invited with increasing frequency to teach Buddhist philosophy at dharma centers in the West and in India, and informal conversations with colleagues suggest that I am far from alone in the academic community in this respect.)

Why is this relevant to translation? For precisely this reason: translations are not merely completed by translators. They are read; they are read by particular readers; they are read for specific reasons; they have determinate effects on their readers; they are often chosen because of (possibly incorrect) views about what those readers want or need to read, and about the probable effects of those texts on those readers. In the present context we must then ask: Who is reading the texts we translators are producing, and what effects are these texts having on the transmission of Buddhism to the West and on the Asian cultures into which they inevitably percolate?

Who Is Translating? What Is Being Translated?

The translation of Buddhist texts was once the exclusive province of academic philologists. Translations were almost always complex affairs, involving critical editing of original material, the comparison of multiple editions of the source text, compilation of extensive lexicons, and were texts aimed almost exclusively at other academics, and indeed at other translators.[1] To translate was principally to participate in a dialogue with other translators about translation. The result is that the present community of translators benefits from rich philological scholarship, extensive discussion about how to render particular terms and locutions, as well as a healthy diet of success and failure from which to learn. Texts chosen for translation were texts deemed important objects of study by philologists, that is, typically texts thought to be historically significant for the development of Buddhist literature. This is a reasonable criterion given the role that these translations played in the nascent scholarly enterprise of Buddhist studies. But it is orthogonal to criteria such as philosophical depth, poetic beauty, frequency of study in a home tradition, and importance for spiritual practice, to name just a few.

The community of translators of Buddhist texts is now much broader, with a correspondingly broader set of agendas and intended target audience. The academic philologists are still at it, and are still producing a substantial set of important scholarly editions. But texts are being translated by scholars who think of themselves very differently as well—philosophers, or religious studies specialists, who are not so much concerned with specifically linguistic or text-historical and text-critical issues as they are with the philosophical or religious content of these texts, their cogency, spiritual significance, and so on (Blumenthal 2002; Garfield 1995; Thurman 1994; or Wallace and Wallace 1997, for instance). These texts may be presented with less scholarly apparatus than those of the professional philologists, but often with substantial essays on the texts or issues they raise. Their audience is typically broader, comprising not only other academics but undergraduate or postgraduate students, and an interested, educated nonacademic audience, prominently, and significantly, including Buddhist practitioners for whom these texts might have religious significance and use.

This is significant precisely because it is at this point that translation becomes most clearly implicated in transmission. Scholars who are producing these texts are no longer engaged only, or even primarily, in a professional conversation with one another, though to be sure this is still very much an aspect of their activity. They are now producing the body of texts taken as canonical by the current generation of students and practitioners of Buddhism in the West.

We have been considering the *scholarly* interlopers in the philologists' preserve. But there are other interlopers as well. Buddhist societies or individual practitioners are producing their own translations. Many of these appear with no scholarly apparatus at all, and even with no attribution to particular translators.[2] Their audience is certainly not the scholarly world, but rather practitioners. When these translators produce texts they are self-consciously *transmitting* Buddhism to their intended audience. Translation has always been an inextricable part of the transmission of Buddhism. (Organized translation was integral to the propagation of Buddhism in Tibet; the shape of Buddhism in China was determined in large part by the often haphazard selection of texts to be translated, with major schools developing around small sets of texts that happened to be available in Chinese.) So, we should not be surprised to see the activity undertaken in this way in the present context. But it also forces us to ask just how much the translation by scholars of Buddhism is also part and parcel of the transmission process, whether or not this is the intent of these translators.

When we ask what is being translated by these translators, the kind of answer we find will be different. Texts are chosen here for their soteriological efficacy, for their importance for rituals in the traditions in which these translators practice, or because of their role in the relevant teaching lineage. We thus see bookshelves filling with a disparate set of Buddhist texts, translated using a disparate set of methodologies, aimed at a variety of audiences, translated in pursuit of a variety of agendas.

All of this has implications for the nature of the current transmission, inasmuch as transmission, as we have noted, is always dependent on and deeply influenced by translation. The heterogeneous set of texts translated and the heterogeneous lexicons and methodologies of translation encourage both an intra-traditional syncretism and a robust sense of the autonomy of the translated texts from their source material. Syncretism is encouraged by the sheer appearance at the same time of texts from so many different traditions, and the voracious appetite for texts of any kind among the Buddhist readership. It is simply inevitable that the interested practitioner will be reading Theravāda, Dzogchen, Gelukpa Madhyamaka, Zen, and Pure Land Buddhism within a short span, and blending the insights and views of these traditions in creative ways. Autonomy is encouraged by the fact that the language and methodology through which texts are presented often renders them clearly as Western objects of study, while nonetheless canonical Buddhist objects. The result of these two kinds of influence is inevitably the emergence of a new Western Buddhism with multiple roots, and the acceptance of a Western Buddhism as an authentic continuation of the Buddhist tradition. More of this below.

Translation as Transformation

Some naïve readers might read a translation and believe that they are thereby reading the text that was translated. But nobody involved in the translation business could ever take this view seriously. When we read a translation, we are reading a text in a target language composed by a translator or a team of translators who were reading in the source language. To be sure, different translators call the reader's attention to their presence and agency to different degrees, some occluding their presence in a presentation that suggests the presence of the source text, others calling constant attention to their choices and methodology. But whether or not the translator acknowledges this act of transformation, translation is always an act of this kind.

When we translate, we transform in all of the following ways: we replace terms and phrases with particular sets of resonances in their source language with terms and phrases with very different resonances in the target language; we disambiguate ambiguous terms and introduce new ambiguities; we interpret, or fix particular interpretations of texts in virtue of the use of theoretically loaded expressions in our target language; we take a text that is to some extent esoteric and render it exoteric simply by freeing the target language reader to approach the text without a teacher; we shift the context in which a text is read and used. No text survives this transformation unscathed (Gómez 1999). Let us consider each transformation in turn.

In many respects the task of the translator is not to succeed but to fail in as few or in as minimally egregious ways as possible (Bar-On 1993). When we take a term from a canonical Buddhist text, it will inevitably bear lexical and meta-phorical relations to a host of other terms in its home language—whether that be Pāli, Sanskrit, Tibetan, or Chinese. It will also have what we might, for lack of a better term, call its "core meaning" in the context in which it occurs—the center of semantic gravity we need to preserve in translation. In general, it is impossible to preserve both this semantic core and the complex set of peripheral semantic relationships borne by the term in question when we choose a term in our target language.

Let me take an example, chosen almost at random, only because it oc-curred in a translation I read today. The Sanskrit term *prapañca* has a root that connotes multiplicity, variation, and so forth. As it is used in Buddhist psychology and philosophy of mind, it denotes the mind's tendency to create ideas and experiences that have nothing to do with reality, to spin out of con-trol, to fantasize, to superimpose its own fantasies on reality. We have chosen to translate this as *fabrication*, which does a good job of capturing the core idea of creating a falsehood, of making things up (Tsong khapa 2005). Most other translators (including the one I was reading this morning) translate this as *proliferation*. This does a good job of capturing the meaning of the root of the term, as well as the metaphor it involves, but in English provides little of the core. And, of course, there is no English term that captures both components of the meaning of this term. So, we are forced to a choice. We can betray the core or betray the root and connections to other terms in the language. To translate a text of any scope is to agonize over countless such decisions.

The important point here is that in either case, when we render the term in English we have *transformed* the text. For the question we are addressing is not, "is the meaning of *prapañca fabrication* or *proliferation*?" We know at the outset that in Sanskrit it is *both*, and that anyone reading the text in Sanskrit receives this full range of resonances. That is what word meaning is like. It is never discrete, and for that reason, never fully translatable. This is the phe-nomenon of *différence*, the fact that we can never specify the meaning of any one word without specifying the meanings of all of the words to which it is semantically related, and so on ad infinitum (Derrida 1982). The consequence is both that translation is always *possible*, but always also *partial* (Bar-On 1993). We can always find a term or a circumlocutory phrase that captures a great deal in the target language of the source term, but there will never be a term that shares *all* of the relevant semantic connections. Hence, we make difficult choices, always betraying something important in the original text in order to produce *something* in the target language. *Tradittori Traduitori.* My colleague who chooses *proliferation* has transformed this text from one that is about the fabrication of a false reality to one that is just about the mind spinning out of control. I who choose *fabrication* have transformed the text from one that is about the mind spinning out of control and drawing distinctions and imposing a range of categories that have no basis in reality to one that is just about falsification.

The converse is also true. Proliferation and fabrication have their own core meanings and sets of lexical and metaphorical resonances that take them each even further from those of *prapañca.* The former recalls reproduction, fecundity, elaboration; the second mendacity but also construction. Any reader of either English text that results, whether she or he is reading for scholarly or religious purposes, is reading a specific, new text, that bears only an etiological relation to a text that once contained the word *prapañca.* Multiply this by the tens of thousands of such decisions that determine the content of a complete translation, and we see that the texts read in translation are distant indeed from those composed in their source languages.

This can have surprising consequences in a global academic community. For many of our Asian colleagues, and many of the lay students of Buddhism in Asian countries, are fluent readers of English. Often the source texts we choose to translate are forbidding technical documents in their source languages, replete with technical terms and archaic constructions and terminology. Often those source languages are nearly as opaque to the scholarly or lay Asian reader as they are, respectively, to the scholarly or lay Western reader. A text written in Sanskrit or in Chinese in the sixth century was no more intended for a contemporary Indian or Chinese reader than it was for a contemporary Canadian, after all, and even classical Tibetan is a difficult language for contemporary Tibetans. But when we translate, we aim for clarity, and for a readable modern idiom. That idiom will often be more accessible to our Asian colleagues and student readers than is the original text, and so we find that contemporary Asian Buddhist readers are reading a great deal of Buddhist doctrine in English. I was interested, for instance, to see a Tibetan colleague preparing to teach a class on the Tibetan and Sanskrit editions of *Mūlamadhyamakakārikā* and its canonical commentaries by reading an English translation and commentary on that text. "It's so much clearer in English," he said to me. And I noted that many young Tibetans at a recent Kalachakra tantric initiation in India were reading from the English translation of the rite of initiation because the Tibetan was incomprehensible to them. Hence the new "Western Buddhism" emerging on a platform of Western translations is being re-exported into Asia.

Many terms that occur in Buddhist texts are ambiguous, and these ambiguities are often critical to the way they function in the source texts. When we translate into English we may not have terms available that preserve these ambiguities, and perforce disambiguate. Let me choose again one among thousands of good examples: the word *dharma* can mean in Sanskrit *doctrine, truth, virtue,* or *phenomenon.* Just what term in English can convey *that* semantic range? And this is not a case of simply homonymy, as that between *bank* (financial institution), *bank* (riverside) and *bank* (a pool shot). In this case, the root is one (meaning "to hold"*)* and this is properly regarded as a single lexical item, with all of these uses recognizably connected. When we translate into English we disambiguate. We choose one of these target English terms, thereby occluding the others that may well be in play. It is no longer obvious that something is *dharma* (*virtuous*—holding one to the right way) precisely because it is in accord with *dharma* (*doctrine*—that to which one should hold on) and the *dharma* (*truth*—that which holds reality in the mind) about *dharma* (the *phenomena*—that which are *held* together, and which *hold* properties). When we choose, we have transformed a text, disambiguating the original, and introducing an entirely new range of determinate meaning.

Sometimes our translation choices amplify these effects because the terms we choose are theoretically loaded in particular ways. For sometimes we are translating highly theoretical texts, using technical terms. Translation demands that we translate these into technical terms in our target languages. But as any student of the philosophy of science is aware, technical terms derive their meanings from the theories in which they are embedded. The Buddhist technical terms we find in our source text thus have their meanings determined by the ambience of a Buddhist theory of mind or of the external world, or ethics; the meanings of the Western technical terms we have at our disposal are determined by their own very different theoretical ambience. For example, when we translate the Sanskrit term *ākara* as *representation,* we do a pretty good job. But not a perfect job. For the Sanskrit has a very imagistic component to its meaning, while *representation* is deliberately neutral between imagistic and verbal connotations. *Representation* involves *re-presentation,* and hence suggests something standing in for something else. *Ākara* might be present even though there is no object for which it stands. And so on. A text so translated has been transformed and is now read alongside other Western discussions of representation, such as those of Kant, Schopenhauer, or contemporary cognitive scientists.

A Tibetan colleague once told me that he finds the Western approach to texts quite bizarre for the following reason: In the Tibetan tradition, a text is conceived as a support for an oral tradition. One reads a text with a teacher;

the text is an occasion for the transmission of an oral lineage, and most of what is important, what is to be learned, is in that oral transmission. He compares the Western reader fixated on the written object and reading it alone with someone who goes into a library, sees books on tables, and studies the grain of the wood in the tables. Importantly, Buddhist texts are composed with this model of reading, transmission and study in mind. Translations of Buddhist texts, however, are aimed at Western readers. When we produce such a text, a condition on its success is that a reader can pick it up, read it, and, if suitably qualified by intelligence and relevant background, understand it. Alone. A text that fails this test is not a candidate for publication, and if the text we produced unadorned does not accomplish it, we festoon it with introductory essays, running commentary, copious footnotes, and so forth in order to bring it into line with the expectations of a Western reader. And as we have seen, this may have unintended consequences even back in the Tibetan community, where reading and study practices are altered by the availability of these more transparent, albeit somewhat different, texts.

This is a further transformation and in a different hermeneutical dimension. We have taken a source object designed to be understood only in the context of an extensive oral commentary imparted by a highly qualified teacher to a selected student and transformed it into a target object designed to be accessible to any educated reader. Note that this transformation is not simply textual. In translating in this way, we are creating a new Buddhist textual culture. In particular, we are making it possible for students or practitioners of Buddhism to engage with its literary tradition independently of a teacher or an authority—to choose what to read, and, in bringing these texts into Western literary practice, to choose how to read, how to interpret, and what of each text to accept or to reject. This is a profound transformation not only of these texts but of the engagement with the textual tradition that is so central to Buddhist culture. We are creating, in the act of translation, a new Buddhism, both in the West and in traditionally Buddhist Asian cultures.

So, What Are Translators Doing?

Translators of Buddhist texts are hence not merely involved in an innocent process of passing texts from one hand to another. We cannot pretend that translation is an activity independent of transmission, or that the transmission in which we are implicated is one in which what is received is identical with that which is given. Instead we are creating a set of texts that will be foundational to the emergence of Western Buddhism. These texts will be recognizable descendants of Indian, Tibetan, and Chinese texts, but they are Western texts in Western languages. This set of texts is strangely heterogeneous and disjoint, and so will be the Buddhism constructed upon this foundation. That is, we are not seeing all of the texts of any one tradition, or by any one author, or in any one genre translated. Decisions about what to translate, and when, are made according to the whims of translators, dissertation directors, dharma centers, a variety of teachers, and even movie actors.[3]

As we translate, not only is a new Western Buddhist canon appearing but a complex negotiation of terminology is occurring, as a cacophony of translators proposes alternative approaches and terminologies. In this sense the current wave of translation is very different indeed from previous waves of translation in the history of Buddhist transmissions: the Tibetan translation effort was highly organized and regimented, governed, and systematized by a royal translation council, with carefully vetted teams of Indian and Tibetan translators, and all translations carefully edited for uniformity and conformity to official norms by committees of scholars. The result is a highly uniform canon written in a kind of code for Sanskrit. The Chinese translation effort was, like the current case, a more individual and disorganized affair. But it differs in that only Mahāyāna texts were translated, and we do not see the kind of efforts to provide critical editions, introductory essays, and so forth that we do in the West, and so there is not the same kind of ongoing debate among translators. As we have seen, this cacophony is more than a war of words, for each word we choose comes with a theoretical background, a set of lexical kin, and a new context in which to set the Buddhist texts a reader assimilates. So, translators are also choosing the theoretical matrices that will determine the way Buddhism is understood and adopted in the West.

Translation and the Trope of Authenticity

In any discussion of the transmission of Buddhism it is impossible to avoid a discourse about "authenticity," and what it means for a formulation of Buddhist doctrine or a practice to be authentic. Often this trope is simply a cover for sectarian wrangling, a way of valorizing a particular, typically conservative, policy, or for settling intramural quarrels. But at certain times questions about authenticity become interesting, and a time when such radical change is occurring so quickly and on so many fronts is surely one such time.

It is tempting to think that the translation activity I have been canvassing is new, or revolutionary, or involves a kind of betrayal of "authentic" Buddhism. For authenticity is often understood as involving the "purity" of a lineage, unadulterated by extraneous material, or the preservation of the *identity* of texts or meanings across time and mind. If this is true, so-called authentic Buddhism has been betrayed from the beginning, for translation has been part of the transmission of Buddhism from the beginning, and it is impossible to translate without transforming. A central doctrine of Buddhism is the impermanence of all phenomena, and impermanence must be understood as a middle path: no phenomenon is immutable; but no continuum terminates. Instead, any extended phenomenon is a constantly changing continuum of causally connected but distinct events. Buddhism is not immune from its own ontology. Authenticity can be understood only in these terms, and the transformation through translational transmission is part and parcel of maintaining the longevity of the continuum, not in spite of, but because of its constant change and adaptation.

How, then, should we understand authenticity in a sense relevant to the transformative transmission of Buddhism to the West and relevant to a consideration of the authenticity of the translations that underwrite that transmission and that catalyze that transformation? There are different understandings of authenticity to which we might turn. *Mahāyānasūtrālaṃkāra,* for instance, suggests that we treat as authentic any teaching that leads to the alleviation of primal ignorance. This is problematic in at least two ways. First, it relies on the effect on the recipient of the teaching as a criterion of authenticity: If I fail to be awakened despite hearing a sutra spoken by Sakyamuni Buddha himself, does this undermine the authenticity of that teaching? Second, it is either overbroad or circular: surely remarks made by those with no relation to the Buddhist tradition can assist in the alleviation of ignorance. These should not thereby constitute Buddhist teachings, unless one takes their soteriological efficacy as evidence that they must have been inspired by the Buddha, in which case the circularity is uncomfortable.

Others insist on a direct lineage from the words of the Buddha—*Buddhavaccana*—leaving open two important questions: Just what constitutes *Buddhavaccana*, and what kind of lineage is relevant? For a practitioner in the Theravāda tradition, for instance, only suttas held to be directly spoken by, or in the presence of and with the approval of the Buddha constitute *Buddhavaccana*. For a Mahāyāna practitioner, on the other hand, the characterization of *Buddhavaccana* in the *8000 Line Perfection of Wisdom Sūtra,* according to which anything in accordance with what the Buddha said, anything that conduces to realization or to liberation is also *Buddhavaccana*—a characterization perhaps instrumental in the authentication of the controversial Mahāyāna sutras appearing half a millennium after the death of the historical Buddha who figures as a central character in them. Is a teaching or a transmission authentic only if it is represented in an unbroken oral chain leading back to the author of the text in question, as some would have it? Or is it sufficient that the transmission be in perfect accord with such a lineage, as others would have it? Do visions authenticate interpretations, or can they be only authenticated by senior teachers?

Although these problems are notoriously troubling, I think that we can gain some purchase on the question here. First, it is important that we rethink the proper subject of authenticity. It is tempting to think about authenticity principally in terms of texts, teachings, or explicit discursive or ritual practices, but this is the wrong place to focus, both on general hermeneutical grounds and from the standpoint of the specifically Buddhist hermeneutical doctrine of the four reliances. For one thing, many of the texts we are considering are composed not by Sakyamuni, but by later Indian, Tibetan, or Chinese scholars. It is more appropriate, and more faithful to Buddhist hermeneutical practice, to focus on insights, on realizations. We might imagine a lineage stretching to the historical Buddha; but only if we are relaxed about the notion of lineage. It is unlikely that all lineages involve unbroken personal transmission, though many surely do. It would be unreasonable, though, to stake the authenticity of a teaching on the question of whether there was a resurrection of interest in a text that had lapsed for, say, a generation. Transmission can, after all, be textual as well as personal, if appropriately supported.

There are two approaches possible here. We could, as we are wont to do in Western literary and scholastic traditions, treat *texts* as that which is to be transmitted. To the extent that we do so, it is our canons of textual criticism and of translation that determine the authenticity of the texts we produce and transmit, perhaps tempered by the overlapping markets of scholars and practitioners. To do this is fine, but to the extent that we adopt such a position, we must also acknowledge a higher-level transformation induced in Buddhism through translation and transmission—the very criterion of authenticity valorized by the tradition is supplanted with one from the Western scholarly tradition. This is indeed a transformation, but one that also occurs in the context of a richly constrained continuum of textual practices, a continuum neither disrupted nor one whose every stage reveals a transcendent essence; one neither permanent nor terminated. In short, a continuum that has conventional but not ultimate identity, just like every other phenomenon recognized as real in a Buddhist context.

On the other hand, we might take the insights and realizations these texts may facilitate to be the proper objects of transmission, and to urge that these should be regarded as authentically Buddhist to the degree that they derive from a lineage of textual or oral transmission that has its ground in the insights and realizations of the Buddha. This is to take the more traditional criterion seriously, and perhaps as a consequence, to rule out much contemporary Buddhist textual practices as participatory in transmission.

One can quickly develop arguments for either understanding of authentic transmission. In the end, I think that both processes, both criteria, are at work in assessing the current complex interaction between Buddhism and Western culture. But on either understanding of authenticity in the Buddhist tradition and of the nature of Buddhist transmission, it is important to see that authenticity denotes not the *identity* of a view, text, or formulation with something the Buddha or an appropriate acārya *said*, but rather the fact that an insight is salutary, soteriologically efficacious, or *causally grounded* in a transmission originating with the Buddha, or perhaps with another Buddhist authority. In either case, the continua in question are just like the continuum of self—impermanent in virtue of constant transformation, identified only by causal and conceptual relations among stages, and never ending.

So, while it is tempting to think of translators as traitors, on either account, we turn out, for the most part, to be loyal after all, and loyal to what counts most. We are traitors only to a mythical original, mythical because its originality is cast as permanence and immutability. But this treason is nothing but the embrace of the heart of Buddhism—impermanence, essenceless-ness, and dependent origination, and the recognition that reality makes sense only in the context of these three characteristics. We have an enormous responsibility as transmitters of Buddhism, a responsibility that forces a certain care and reflection in our practice. But we must remember that this responsibility is the responsibility not to preserve a permanent past but to manage transformation in a productive way. We need to be facilitating change that we can only hope follows a trajectory that, because of the effects these texts and the practices they engender have on future students and practitioners of Buddhism, is recognizably as authentic as were any of the past trajectories followed by the transformation of Buddhism.

Notes

1. See, for instance, any of the great works by de Jong, May, Frauenwallner, Steinkellner, or Le Valle de Poussin.

2. See, for instance, the editions prepared by the Padmakara translation group, including their translation of Candrakīrti's *Madhyamakāvatāra* with Mipham's commentary (2002) and their translation of Śāntideva's *Bodhicāryāvatāra* 1997).

3. My colleague and I were recently informed by a leading translator of Tibetan texts that whether it would be considered appropriate for us to translate a particular text we intended to translate would depend on a decision by Richard Gere!

CHAPTER 6

Two Monks and the Mountain Village Ideal

Thomas H. Rohlich

A T SOME POINT in the middle of the twelfth century, two monks in Japan exchanged a series of ten poems each, matching one for one. Here is the first of the ten exchanges, as recorded in the personal poetry collection (*Sankashū*) of Saigyō, one of the poets (Gotō 1982, 342–46):

> 1a. *yamafukami / sa koso arame to / kikoetsutsu / oto aware naru / tani no kawamizu*
>
> The mountains are so deep and yours perhaps the same, I hear, the sorrowful sound of the river in the valley. (Saigyō)
>
> 1b. *awaresa wa / kōya to kimi mo / omoiyare / akikuregata no / ōhara no sato*
>
> Do consider that the sorrow here may be much the same, autumn evening in the Ōhara village. (Jakuzen)

The poets are in different locations, Saigyō in the mountainous area of Kōyasan, the center of Esoteric Buddhism in Japan, and Jakuzen in the village of Ōhara, north of the capital of Heiankyō, present-day Kyoto. In this exchange, each poet imagines what the other's location is like, and concludes that while they are in very different spaces, one in the mountains, the other in a village, they share something in common. That experience is identified by the only affective word in the poems, *aware*, which appears as an adjective in the first poem translated as "sorrowful," and a noun in the second, "sorrow."

This expression of shared sorrow is a familiar trope in poetry exchanges in Japan, and it alone would not likely draw our attention to this sequence. What is more arresting is the discovery, as we continue with the exchange, that each poem by Saigyō begins with the word *yama* (mountain) and each poem by Jakuzen ends in the word *sato* (village). Combined into one, these words form the compound *yamazato*, or "mountain village." As I described in an earlier essay on the use of *yamazato* in Murasaki Shikibu's eleventh-century masterpiece *The Tale of Genji*, this word is somewhat of an oxymoron, composed of the Chinese characters suggesting both isolation (the mountain) and socialization (the village) (Rohlich 2003, 122). But the simplicity of the language belies the depth of the poetic expression and the rich overtones each of these words evokes. Just as the words enclose each pair of poems from beginning to end, the complete exchange embraces a shared experience of two recluses who have found in the concept of *yamazato*, mountain village, an ideal locus for the life of a Buddhist recluse in twelfth-century Japan. Embedded within the simple image of a reclusive life in a mountain village is a profound expression of medieval Japanese Buddhist perspectives on attachment, renunciation, reclusion, and living in relationship to nature and other human beings.

What does such an exchange mean in the context of an investigation into the dynamics of TransBuddhism, incorporating the transmission, translation, and transformation of Buddhism across national and cultural boundaries throughout its history? Japan's acceptance of Buddhism began in the sixth century with its adoption by aristocratic elites who valued it as much for its presumed magical powers as for its central role in the highly refined and materially far-superior culture of China that they eagerly embraced. Having recently emerged from a preliterate past, they were dazzled by its intellectually sophisticated literary texts and awed by the artistic and engineering culture that came with Buddhism in the form of temples and temple art. Centuries passed before Buddhism spread to the vast majority of the population, but over time the Japanese did with Buddhism what they have done so well with foreign influence throughout their history, beginning with all aspects of Chinese culture. A period of indiscriminate adoption was followed in time with a fine-tuning of the foreign import to their own liking, preserving and emphasizing that which best suited their tastes, and quietly letting go that which did not interest them. The poetic exchange examined below represents one small expression of that transmission. By the time this exchange took place, Japan was a thoroughly Buddhist country, and the poets were comfortable using *waka* poetry to express an approach to living that was informed by a Buddhist sensibility. Buddhist ideas took many forms as the religion moved from India throughout East Asia, and for these two monks the most comfortable mode of expression was their native poetry using familiar natural images.

By the twelfth century the changes wrought by the transmission, translation, and transformation of Buddhist ideas in Japan were considerable. Buddhism was said to have been introduced into Japan in the year 552 C.E. by Koreans, and while the precision of the date is suspect, it is clear that by the time Buddhism reached Japan it was close to a thousand years old. Its original texts and teachings had undergone centuries of development within India and had also been refracted through the lens of translation into Chinese language and thought. At the time Saigyō and Jakuzen exchanged their poems, Buddhism had existed in Japan for more than five hundred years and had reached a comfortable if occasionally contradictory co-existence with native Shinto beliefs in a syncretism known as *honji suijaku*, in which *kami* (gods) of Shinto belief were taken to be manifestations of bodhisattvas (DeBary 2001, 338). The transformation of Shinto *kami* into the Buddhist pantheon was a major step in the acceptance of the religion by both elites and common people. By the twelfth century, Buddhism was already well-established as the formal religion of the elites, and it was beginning to work its way into the belief system of common people over the next two centuries.

The twelfth century was also a time of major change for ruling elites and the political structure of Japan, marked by the rise of the samurai warriors and the irreversible decline of aristocratic rule. The period witnessed a gradual change in the familiar forms of literature, sometimes characterized as movement from the Literature of Court Ladies (*nyōbō bungaku*) to the Literature of the Recluse (*inja bungaku*), with its strong emphasis on Buddhist themes. As one of the most prominent practitioners of this newly emerging Literature of the Recluse, Saigyō lived and wrote at a time of transition in Japan, from the court-centered aristocratic culture exemplified most famously by *The Tale of Genji*, to one where the vanguard of literary arts rested primarily in the hands of Buddhist monks who deliberately shunned the urban life of the court, as exemplified by the exchange between Saigyō and Jakuzen.

The poems in this exchange all take the thirty-one syllable form commonly known as *waka*, the favorite poetic form in Japan from the sixth through the sixteenth century, and one that remains popular even today. The *waka* is short and deceptively simple, uncomplicated in syntax, and brief enough to generally be understood without much difficulty, even though the language is as distant from modern Japanese as Chaucer's English is from contemporary American speech. Perhaps because of the relative simplicity of the poems, it was a favorite means of communication among family, friends, and lovers, and it was not uncommon for two monks such as Saigyō and Jakuzen to engage in an exchange such as this one.

The simplicity of the original form does not mean it is easily translated into contemporary English. The poems that opened this chapter reveal some of the challenges the translator faces and the choices one must make. The thirty-one syllables of a *waka* poem are separable into five distinct syntactic units of 5-7-5-7-7 syllables, and some translators render it as five lines of English. Others make them into couplets, sometimes with thirty-one syllables, while many others do as I have done here, basically make them into one-line free verse poems.

Jay Garfield's chapter in this volume describes the difficult choices facing the translator of Buddhist texts, and the transformations these texts undergo as they move through very different cultural settings over centuries of time. The challenges facing a translator of poetry are no less daunting, although the stakes are perhaps lower, since the texts are not canonical. Modesty becomes the reclusive monk (and his translator), and it is unlikely that Saigyō and Jakuzen would think of their poems as part of the Buddhist teaching canon, except perhaps in the context of Po Chü-i's famous phrase discussed below on transforming "indiscriminate words and ornate language" into "an instrument for praise of the Buddha's teachings" (McCullough and McCullough 1980, 506–7). In this context, the "mountain village" found in these poems may be read as descriptive of an ascetic location peculiarly suited to Japanese aesthetics and culture, in which the recluse's transitory, remote abode in the ever-changing natural world is reflective of the human condition.

Looking at specific difficulties of translation, the final two sections of each poem above consist of two seven-syllable units, the first of which modifies the second, which in each poem is a noun phrase. In the first poem, *oto aware naru* (sorrowful sound) modifies *tani no kawamizu* (the valley's river water); in the second poem, *akikuregata no* (autumn evening) modifies *ōhara no sato* (the Ōhara village). In normal Japanese syntax, the predicate, usually in the form of a verb, comes at the end of the sentence, but both of these poems end in nouns, as if they were sentence fragments rather than full sentences. In addition, in each poem the middle unit, consisting of five syllables, *kikoetsutsu* (I hear) in the first poem and *omoiyare* (do consider) in the second, is a verbal expression that serves as a kind of fulcrum balancing the first two units with the second two units in each poem. In the first poem I am able to set off "I hear" with commas in an attempt to suggest that this phrase may go with either what comes before or afterward; that is, what is heard may be news of the companion's home, or the sound of the water, although the Japanese syntax puts it with the first half, and the English syntax is admittedly awkward in relation to the second half. The clear sharp images of nature expressed in the second half of each poem contrast with the uncertain and conjectural thoughts in the first half. Because Japanese and English are syntactically very different languages, it is all but impossible to structure a translation so as to capture the effect the original conveys with its parallel or juxtaposed syntax.

The difficulty in translating these poems lies in choosing what must be transformed from the original to the translation so as to preserve a semblance of meaning with poetic value. In most attempts, the poetry is lost in translation, sacrificed for meaning. The challenges with *waka* are formidable. In many instances, a *waka* in Japanese might comfortably be a sentence fragment without appearing at all fragmentary in concept or image. But too often a fragmented English translation carries the faint odor of a kind of exoticism or preciousness not present in the original. I chose this exchange to translate because I see it as important for the way in which it encompasses the idea of the mountain village. One manifestation of this is the fact that all of the poems by Saigyō start with the same five syllables, and all by Jakuzen end with the same seven syllables. For this reason I felt it critical to maintain the words "The mountains are so deep" at the beginning of each Saigyō poem and "the Ōhara village" at the end of each Jakuzen poem. Were I to translate one of the poems separate from this exchange, I would not feel bound to maintain the same words in the same positions. Since the poets speak freely of the flora and fauna that surround them, a second challenge is finding appropriate words for common Japanese plants or animals that are not common in English. But the most difficult aspect of the translation is attempting to achieve the appropriate tone that comes with the sense of companionship that the two poets feel as friends sharing a vision of the reclusive life.

> 2a. *yamafukami / makinoha wakuru / tsukikage wa / hageshiki mono no / sugokinarikeri*
> The mountains are so deep, moonlight parts the needles of black pines, striking and yet so chilling. (Saigyō)
> 2b. *hitori sumu / orobo no shimizu / tomo tote wa / tsuki o zo sumasu / ōhara no sato*
> Alone like the cloudy waters harboring the clear moon I invite into the Ōhara village. (Jakuzen)

In the second exchange of poems, moonlight is introduced as a key image. As in so many literatures, images of nature were central to Japanese poetry from the very beginning, and the moon was a favorite topic. The aesthetic sensibility to appreciate the beauty of the moon was long the mark of a cultured person in the Heian period (794–1185). For Japanese sensibilities of the twelfth century, moonlight had come to represent a spiritual companion and a means of attaining enlightenment (Kamens 1990, 41). In the exchange above, we see two poets who recognize the companionship offered by the moon, and this was easily transformed into an appreciation of the moon as a symbol of enlightenment. But whereas one might expect the Buddhist recluse to struggle to gain separation from the world as a first step in attaining enlightenment, Saigyō and Jakuzen, although separated and living alone, share a sensibility through their love of the beauty of the moon. And yet, their shared aesthetic takes place within the boundaries of a poetic exchange encompassed within the mountain village—although they share something, it remains within the confines of their poetic exchange, which both structures and defines their relationship. In a sense then, their shared exploration of the moon's ineffability, through poetry, enables the two recluses to be together while they are alone.

Buddhist images are taken up by Jakuzen in 2b and given clever treatment with the reference to a specific spring of water, the Oboro Spring, which is in the vicinity of a famous temple, Ōhara Jakkōin, and presumably near his hut. The word *oboro* suggests cloudy or misty and contrasts with the clarity suggested by the word *sumu*, which can be read with two meanings, either "live," as in "I live alone," or "clear," as in "clear the water," or by extension "clear one's heart" to receive the moonlight—Buddhist enlightenment.

Since all of Jakuzen's poems end in a noun, and a grammatical Japanese sentence must end in a predicate, except in cases of inversion, one could argue that none of Jakuzen's poems are sentences. To translate all as word phrases would be awkward, but in this case I have chosen to leave the poem as a phrase, not a complete sentence.

> 3a. *yamafukami / mado no tsurezure / toumono wa / irozukisomuru / haji no tachieda*
> The mountains are so deep, the sad visitor to my window is only the autumn tinged branch of sumac. (Saigyō)
> 3b. *sumigama no / tanabiku keburi / hitosuji ni / kokorobosoki wa / ōhara no sato*
> A wisp of smoke trails out from the charcoal kilns, lonely as the Ōhara village. (Jakuzen)

In the third sequence, Saigyō presents the image of the branch of a sumac tree scratching at the window of his hut, while Jakuzen draws on the familiar metaphor of a line of smoke from charcoal kilns, a product of the Ōhara area, to represent the lingering loneliness a poet feels upon seeing trails of smoke.

> 4a. *yamafukami / koke no mushiro no / ueni ite / nanigokoronaku / naku mashira kana*
> The mountains are so deep, sitting atop the moss carpet a monkey cries out heartlessly. (Saigyō)
> 4b. *nanitonaku / tsuyu zo koboruru / aki no ta ni / hita hikinarasu / ōhara no sato*
> Clappers ring out in autumn fields where weeping dew trickles down in the Ōhara village. (Jakuzen)

The fourth exchange returns to sounds, but this time the sounds are the cries of a monkey in the first poem and the sound of the clappers in the second. Saigyō's poem has an unusual repetition of the sound *naku* between the fourth and fifth units, which conveys the negative meaning in "without heart/heartlessly" but also serves as the verb "cry," which can be the sound of the monkey or the weeping of a human being. Since "moss carpet" is a trope for the bed of a recluse living in the mountains, Saigyō may be comparing himself to the monkey, especially with his use of the phrase "heartlessly," which in this case means "detached" rather than "coldly" or "cruelly." The monkey may be crying without conscious understanding, and Saigyō may view himself as wanting to become "heartless," free from emotional attachment. In response, Jakuzen's poem begins with a similar sounding phrase in which the dew in the village is like tears, and the sounds are of the village clapper, which serves as a kind of scarecrow.

While Saigyō and his contemporaries were still closely tied to the courtly tradition characterized by ideals of the so-called Cult of Beauty, they also longed for quiet escape into a natural setting conducive to meditative literature and practice, a turning away from luxury to an ascetic aestheticism and the ideals of *sabi* (loneliness), an austere, even astringent, beauty. The ascetic ideal represents severe self-denial and rejection of luxury, which contrasts sharply with the love of luxury, beauty, and worldly goods characteristic of the court culture. We must bear in mind, however, that the courtly love of luxury was by no means gross indulgence, since an absolute concomitant of the cult of beauty was the rule of taste, courtly elegance, and decorum, known by the phrase *miyabi*.

For many monks, and particularly for Saigyō, the place to find escape from the world was in the mountain village. As we read these poems, we can see that Saigyō and Jakuzen are poetically defining a Japanese version of the essence of the reclusive life of a monk. Central to their definition of this life is literature, particularly the familiar poetry of the court. In choosing poetry to express the life of a recluse, the two poets contribute to the development of a new literary consciousness, but one that had a split personality, a combination of a love of literature and especially nature in literature, the aesthetic, and a devotion to austere Buddhist practices, the ascetic. The austere life is accentuated by the sounds of nature as they gather food and water for a simple mountain village life.

> 5a. *yamafukami / iwa ni shidaruru / mizu tamen / katsugatsu otsuru / tochi hirou hodo*
> The mountains are so deep, I'll collect water dripping from the rocks as I gather chestnuts here about. (Saigyō)
> 5b. *mizu no oto wa / makura ni otsuru / kokochi shite / nezamegachi naru / ōhara no sato*
> I seem to hear the sound of water dripping on my pillow, sleepless nights in the Ōhara village. (Jakuzen)

In poem 5a we see Saigyō gathering chestnuts, presumably for food, but finding the going difficult. The dripping water serves as the link Jakuzen picks up, which becomes a sound he senses near his pillow as he finds sleep difficult in his Ōhara village. Both of these poems emphasize the lonely, austere life of the recluse.

> 6a. *yamafukami / kejikaki tori no / oto wa sezu / mono osoroshiki / fukurō no koe*
> The mountains are so deep, no sounds of familiar birds, only the frightful voice of the owl. (Saigyō)
> 6b. *adani fuku / kusa no iori no / aware yori / sode ni tsuyu oku / ōhara no sato*
> With the wretchedness of the roughly grass-covered hut comes dew-drenched sleeves in the Ōhara village. (Jakuzen)

While Jakuzen's poem in 5b above identifies the familiar sound of water, Saigyō's poem 6a emphasizes that his home is so deep in the mountains it lacks the cries of familiar birds, with only the frightening sounds of an owl. Jakuzen answers in 6b with the image of dew on sleeves in a grass hut barely covered at all. The grass hut and dew are favorite metaphors in Japanese Buddhist poetry, emphasizing the transience and fragility of life in this world. The first condition of *yamazato* life is to be separated from, to escape from, human pains and suffering, but to do so also means to be in a world of loneliness separated from one's dear friends. Many of Saigyō's poems address his wish for a friend in loneliness. This desire for a friend to share the loneliness is one way in which Saigyō's renunciation differs from the more familiar wandering ascetic, who would shun a companion. But while he longed for a friend, the condition was that the friend be someone who could understand the heart of the situation. Saigyō disdained the troublesome visitor who might disturb the stillness of the flowers in the *yamazato* but welcomed a visitor with the same heart.

Beyond his love of nature, Saigyō had a great love of people, and this led to a tension in his *yamazato* life. One important tradition of the *yamazato* life is that the essence of mountain village life is loneliness, which leads to a purer life due to a greater understanding of *mujō*, transciency, the idea of a constantly changing world in which it is foolish to try to find happiness or stability. Indeed, the loneliness of the mountain village provides salvation for the soul. But while it is loneliness one seeks in the *yamazato* life, it is loneliness one would like to share with a friend.

> 7a. *yamafukami / koguraki mine no / kozue yori / monomonoshiku mo / wataru arashi kana*
> The mountains are so deep, from the branches on peaks darkened with trees, the awesome storm blows down. (Saigyō)

7b. *yamakaze ni / mine no sasakuri / harahara to / niwa ni ochishiku /
ōhara no sato*
The mountain wind blows the chestnut leaves from the peaks to
cover the garden of the Ōhara village. (Jakuzen)

Poem 7a by Saigyō makes use of the Chinese character for *arashi* (storm), a
single graph but one made up of two components consisting of the character
for mountain (*yama*) resting atop the character for wind (*kaze*). Jakuzen picks
this up, using the two constituent elements separately, as *yama* (mountain)
and *kaze* (wind) to begin his poem. This clever conceit with the writing system
appeared earlier in the poetic tradition and shows here how familiar the two
poets were with the tradition, and how comfortable they were writing in it.
This can be taken as another sign that the space they inhabit, the *yamazato*, is
enriched by the literary tradition. Although spatially they may be set off from
Japanese society in the *yamazato*, the two poets, in their sophisticated engagement with Japan's literary forms, are nonetheless active agents in the transmission and creation of a new paradigm of Buddhist literature. English orthography
does not allow the translator a means to show this visual relationship, so it
must be left to footnotes or an explanatory essay, if dealt with at all.

The new literary paradigm was not without its difficulties, since Saigyō and
his contemporaries were very much aware that literature, particularly prose
literature, was viewed by many as a dangerous distraction for devout Buddhists, especially for those who had dedicated their lives to the austerities of
a recluse. Inasmuch as poetry was the favorite vehicle for communication between lovers, it too was potentially suspect, but it was never scorned as severely
as the "profane literature" of court fiction, where even a work such as *The Tale
of Genji* was viewed by many as the source of sin for its readers, mainly women,
and the reason why the author, also a woman, was suffering punishment in a
Buddhist hell of hot blades (Rohlich 1997, 186–88). *Waka* poetry, and particularly the poetry of monks such as Saigyō and Jakuzen, escaped such condemnation. In an important example of the transmission of Buddhist ideas from
China to Japan, the precedent for this is found in a phrase from a famous
poem by Po Chü-i, the favorite Chinese poet of Heian courtiers. This became
the guiding principle for the defense of literature in a Buddhist world.

In this world profane literature has been my occupation.
I have followed the mistaken path
Of indiscriminate words and ornate language.
My desire is to transform my faulty writing
And make it in this world and the next
An instrument for praise of the Buddha's teachings,

A vehicle for exposition of the dharma. (McCullough and
McCullough 1980, 506–7)

Saigyō seems to have learned the lesson well. According to a story told in
the *Biography of the Priest Myōe*, Saigyō is said to have told Myōe that he was
able to master the dharma by reciting a *waka* poem or meditating on a poem
(Pandey 1998, 47–48).

8a. *yamafukami / hodakiru nari to / kikoetsutsu / tokoro nigiwau / ono
no oto kana*
The mountains are so deep, one hears the chopping of firewood,
the woodcutter's lively sound. (Saigyō)
8b. *masurao ga / tsumagi ni akebi / sashisoete / kurureba kaeru / ōhara
no sato*
Lumberjacks carry branches of the *akebi* tree along with firewood
as they return in the evening to the Ōhara village. (Jakuzen)

Poem 8a brings people, or at least the sound of people, back into the exchange. Both poems deal with woodcutters, although Saigyō's is based on just
sound, perhaps accentuating the isolation of his village. Loneliness is the main
mood of the recluse, but this does not deny the presence of others in the area.
The only people he sees, however, are those who come briefly into the woods to
gather firewood and then retreat back to their humble villages. The wretched-
ness of the courtier turned recluse is accentuated by the humble status of these
occasional visitors.

Although Saigyō is revered today in Japan as one of the country's cultural
heroes, the contemporary Western reader may view some of his behavior with
skepticism. Based on generally reliable records we are fairly certain that he became a monk at the age of twenty-three, in 1140. Apparently a man of some
wealth and talent, we do not know why he took vows at such a young age. In
the elite society to which Saigyō belonged, most young men were raised to
become monks from childhood, or they entered during old age or after a particularly traumatic event. There is some inconclusive evidence that he married
and had a family of one or more daughters before he took vows. There is nothing certain we can say about his motivation for renouncing the world, except
what can be gathered from his remaining writings, which certainly point to a
mind deeply devoted to the religious life.

From our contemporary point of view, it is striking how little is said in historical records about what must have been abandonment of his family. A work
known as the *Tale of Saigyō*, written less than a hundred years after his death in
1190 and translated into English by Meredith McKinney, presents him as a family

man with a charming four-year-old daughter (27). Although we cannot be certain of the historical accuracy of the events portrayed in this story, one of the most compelling scenes depicts him kicking his daughter off the veranda as she comes out to greet him returning from work, "I'm so happy you've come home, Papa" (27). The rationalization is that an evil god appears as a loving wife and child precisely to hinder his pursuit of the true path (27–28). We don't know for certain Saigyō had a wife and family, but given his social position and family status, it is reasonable to assume he did. We do not know if he provided for them while in the priesthood, and while there are additional stories associated with his family that are part of the hagiographic tradition that soon sprang up around the Saigyō legend, for all the hundreds of poems he wrote there is nothing in the headnotes or poems themselves that points to the existence of a family, much less any affection he might have had for them. Perhaps it is not surprising, since attachment and affection are precisely what the devout recluse must avoid. It is another challenge to the contemporary translation and understanding of Saigyō's life and poetry that he may have willfully abandoned a family to partake in his reclusive life. Significantly, this story parallels the Buddha's own biography, in which he abandons his loving wife and infant son to pursue the path of asceticism. Whether or not the story of Saigyō abandoning his family is true, it is likely intended to create a metaphorical resonance with the Buddha, and, indeed, with many other such stories of Buddhist renunciates turning their backs on family life to pursue religious goals.

> 9a. *yamafukami / irite mitomiru / mono wa mina / aware moyoosu / keshiki naru kana*
> The mountains are so deep, entering to look and look about, the
>   sight is all so moving. (Saigyō)
> 9b. *mugura hau / kado wa konoha ni / uzumorete / hito mo sashikonu / ōhara no sato*
> Overgrown with twisting vines the gate is buried in leaves where
>   no one comes to the Ōhara village. (Jakuzen)

Poem 9a brings back the adjective *aware*, translated as "sad" in exchange 1a and 1b, but rendered as "moving" in this poem. The word is a capacious one in classical Japanese, able to encompass even more than the meanings shown here, and once the translator makes a choice, much is necessarily lost. The challenge faced here is precisely the one Garfield spoke of in his chapter when he discusses the possible translations of the Sanskrit term *prapañca*, translated as "fabrication" or "proliferation" among several possibilities. And his general comments in his section on Translation as Transformation hold true for translating Saigyō's poetry: we make choices that create or occlude ambiguities, fix meaning, create resonances of differing magnitude, and transform the text.

With poetry we face the added risk of losing much that is aesthetically pleasing in the original, the sounds and rhythms that are inseparable from the original language. Ultimately we hope it "works" at some level, conveying a part that is essential to the original, and hoping that our inadequate target language rendition does not do more harm that good. It is not an easy task.

> 10a. *yamafukami / naruru kasegi no / kejikasa ni / yo ni toozakaru / hodo zo shiraruru*
> The mountains are so deep when the deer come close I know how
>   far I am from the world. (Saigyō)
> 10b. *morotomo ni / aki mo yamaji mo / fukakereba / shika zo kanashiki / ōhara no sato*
> Deep in autumn and its mountain paths the deer cry out sadly in
>   the Ōhara village. (Jakuzen)

In 10a Saigyō brings the image of a deer near at hand to emphasize how distant they are from the world. Jakuzen, in a fitting ending, takes up Saigyō's words *yama* and *fuka-kereba* (deep), with the adjective giving depth to both autumn and the mountain path. He also uses *shika* as a *kakekotoba* (zeugma) meaning both "as you say" and "deer." It is also possible to read this as an allusion to the Buddha's first sermon in Deer Park.

What sort of audience might we expect for translations of these poems? To the extent that these translations are successful in capturing the description of the formation of the "mountain village" concept, they might appeal to a scholarly audience. They might also be attractive to a more general audience interested in Buddhist recluse behavior. The poems are not likely to be considered part of the transmission process Garfield talks about when referring to texts, even given the wide latitude afforded in what might be considered Buddhist texts. Nonetheless, Western practitioners clearly appreciate the aesthetic transmission of Buddhist ideas through a multitude of media—text, image, or music. This attraction for the aesthetic medium mirrors in some ways the initial acceptance of Buddhism in Japan more than 1500 years ago, when the art, design, and engineering of Buddhist statues, buildings, and holy artifacts preceded widespread understanding of the texts, which remained untranslated from the Chinese for hundreds of years. Unlike the Japanese back then, Western practitioners and scholars today absorb and usually understand canonical texts simultaneously with the appreciation of Buddhist artistic expression.

To conclude, Buddhism came to Japan tightly embedded in the material and intellectual culture of China, which was technologically far advanced over the indigenous systems of Japan. It was immediately attractive to the elites, who adopted it with minimal resistance. But in adopting Buddhism, the Japanese also sought to adapt it to things within their own culture they valued and did not wish to abandon. One of these was their love of nature and the favorite form for expressing that love, the thirty-one syllable *waka* poem. When the relatively peaceful era of the Heian period came to an end in the bloody warfare of the twelfth century, many courtiers looked to a different life, in the peaceful milieu of a mountain village, or *yamazato*.

In the mountain village, Saigyō and his companions were able to create a space in which they could live close to nature, where they could be alone yet still share the *yamazato* experience by means of their poetry. The mountain village exchange of Saigyō and Jakuzen is a way of encompassing within the boundaries of the words "mountain" and "village" all that the ideal of the mountain village meant to them. They compare and contrast their *yama/zato* life, and all of the natural phenomena of the mountain and village, the flora and fauna, bring to heart the loneliness of the mountain village. The mountain village is depicted as the ideal place from which to participate in the two most important endeavors of their age, the poetic tradition, representing the pursuit of aesthetics, and religious austerities, the practice that was to ensure true understanding and eventually salvation. Lonely the village might be, but it is a loneliness and a space in nature that can be shared with a person of the same heart, one who understands not only the religious significance of what they are doing but also its literary essence.

As an American translator of a poetic exchange deeply bound to a Buddhist tradition that itself had been transmitted and translated from India through China to Japan, I cannot help but feel the strangeness of being an outsider, but at the same time feeling an affinity as one who is also engaged in the process of transmission and translation. What is most remarkable is that in spite of the great barriers of language, culture, and time, it is genuinely possible to witness, interpret, and perhaps even participate in the exchange in our own day in our own idiom. The exploration of this exchange creates a transBuddhist moment of our own, and an understanding of what aesthetic sensibilities and religious devotion moved these poets some eight hundred years ago. Perhaps the twenty-first-century reader of these poems in English translation will recognize in them a common human longing that transcends time and culture.

Note

I would like to express my appreciation to the members of the TransBuddhism seminar of the Smith College Kahn Institute for their collegiality and contributions during the stimulating meetings we had together, and particularly to the editors of this collection, Abraham Zablocki, Nalini Bhushan, and Jay Garfield for their very helpful suggestions for revision that led to improvements on my original draft. I remain solely responsible for any errors or omissions that remain.

CHAPTER 7

Text, Tradition, Transformation, and Transmission in *Ghost Dog: The Way of the Samurai*

MARIO D'AMATO

O NE OF THE WAYS in which Buddhism enters the cultural imagination of the West is through film. This chapter addresses the imagination of Buddhism in the film *Ghost Dog: The Way of the Samurai* (Jarmusch 1999). I am interested both in how Buddhism has been imagined to play a role in the self-understanding of the film's protagonist and in how we—as scholars of religion interested in the transformation and transmission of Buddhism across cultures—might imagine Buddhism through reflecting on the film. I will not focus primarily on the Buddhist motifs in the film (although they are certainly present, even if Buddhism itself remains unnamed), nor will I argue that *Ghost Dog* is in some way a Buddhist film (although I think it is). Rather, I will use the film as the basis for a meditation on the concepts of text, tradition, transformation, and transmission in Buddhism.

First, a brief question: What does a violent film about an African American contract killer who imagines himself to be a samurai following the code of bushidō have to do with Buddhism? Quite a bit. "Bushidō" (lit., "the way of the warrior") is the name given to the imagined ethico-religious code followed by the samurai.[1] One influence on bushidō, and on samurai religion generally, was Buddhism, especially Zen.[2] So while the film employs Buddhist motifs, these are refracted through the lens of bushidō. One of bushidō's representative texts is *Hagakure* ("In the Shadow of Leaves"), composed by a Buddhist monk, Yamamoto Tsunetomo (1659–1719). *Hagakure* plays a central role in the film, with each chapter of the film beginning with Ghost Dog reading a passage from the text[3] and reflecting in some way the quotation from *Hagakure* that precedes it.[4] The text provides the vision for Ghost Dog's own understanding of himself as a samurai in a late twentieth-century urban American environment. According to a passage from *Hagakure* read in the film's opening scene, the way of the warrior is found in constant meditation on death—or in Buddhist terms, on the transient nature of things:

> The Way of the Samurai is found in death. Meditation on inevitable death should be performed daily. Every day when one's body and mind are at peace, one should meditate upon being ripped apart by arrows, rifles, spears and swords, being carried away by surging waves, being thrown into the midst of a great fire, being struck by lightning, being shaken to death by a great earthquake, falling from thousand-foot cliffs, dying of disease or committing seppuku at the death of one's master. And every day without fail one should consider himself as dead. (Jarmusch 1999; Yamamoto 2002, 17, 164)

In the film, Ghost Dog's life is indeed a meditation on death: as a contract killer, his profession revolves around the question of life and death. Hence from a thematic perspective, the film's violence highlights the bushidō—and by extension Buddhist—undercurrents of the film.[5] For those who are not familiar with the film, I have included a summary as an appendix.

Text

In Buddhism, as in various other religious traditions, the role of the text is fundamental. The dharma after all is only made manifest through specific collections of utterances—through scriptural texts such as sutras, or discourses of the Buddha, and treatises that further elucidate the meaning of Buddhist teachings. Without such fundamental texts, a religious tradition remains unarticulated and intransmissible; but with religious texts, followers of a tradition are offered a vision of life and the world. We might reflect on the centrality of the text for a religious tradition through considering the role of the text in *Ghost Dog: The Way of the Samurai*. In the film, Ghost Dog's very way of life, his entire mode of being in the world, is shaped by an ancient vision of the way of the samurai, a vision mediated for Ghost Dog by a specific text, *Hagakure*. As noted above, each chapter of the film is structured by a passage from the text, suggesting that Ghost Dog's life is a meditation on and embodiment of the text's vision of things. As Paul Griffiths points out, according to one early etymology "the [Latin] term *religio* derives from *relegere*, 'to reread'" (Griffiths 1999, 43), a point that emphasizes the general theme that being religious can be understood as undertaking a particular form of reading. Griffiths argues that a religious text is one which offers a vision of reality that is comprehensive, unsurpassable, and central. For a text to be understood as comprehensive, it must offer an "account of everything . . . nothing is left unaccounted for by it" (ibid., 7). For a text to be understood as unsurpassable, it must not "be capable of being replaced by or subsumed in a better account," which means that "the account's essential features [are] incapable of abandonment" (ibid., 9). And for a text to be understood as central, it must offer an account of things that is "directly relevant to what [one] take[s] to be the central questions of [one's] life, the questions around which [one's] life is oriented" (ibid., 10). Each of these three characteristics is exhibited in Ghost Dog's appropriation of *Hagakure*.

Comprehensiveness is certainly one aspect of the religious account around which Ghost Dog models his life. The initial passage from *Hagakure* quoted in the film—that one's life should be lived as a "meditation on inevitable death"—emphasizes the transitory nature of all things. Ghost Dog also quotes another passage from the text which highlights the ephemeral nature of reality:

> It is a good viewpoint to see the world as a dream. When you have some-
> thing like a nightmare, you will wake up and tell yourself that it was only a
> dream. It is said that the world we live in is not a bit different from this.
> (Jarmusch 1999; Yamamoto 2002, 82)

This passage resonates with the Buddhist theme that one should view one's life as an illusion constructed by one's own craving—an illusory dream to be dispelled through the attainment of awakening (*bodhi*). And another passage from *Hagakure* quoted by Ghost Dog contains a well-known citation from the Mahāyāna Buddhist *Heart Sūtra*:

> Our bodies are given life from the midst of nothingness. Existing where
> there is nothing is the meaning of the phrase, "Form is emptiness." That all
> things are provided for by nothingness is the meaning of the phrase,
> "Emptiness is form." One should not think that these are two separate
> things. (ibid.; ibid., 70)

Each of these passages exhibits the comprehensiveness that is characteristic of a religious account: each offers an account of the whole of existence. And each passage also exhibits a central motif of the Buddhist vision of things—transitoriness, ephemerality, and emptiness.

The aspects of unsurpassability and centrality can also be seen in other passages from *Hagakure* that are quoted by Ghost Dog. One passage states:

> It is bad when one thing becomes two. One should not look for anything
> else in the Way of the Samurai. It is the same for anything else that is called

a Way. If one understands things in this manner, he should be able to hear about all Ways and be more and more in accord with his own. (ibid.; ibid., 50)

Hence, learning alternate accounts of "the way things really are" should not lead one to consider abandoning one's own path in favor of another, but should lead one to a more profound realization of one's own "Way." Another passage states:

There is surely nothing other than the single purpose of the present moment. A man's whole life is a succession of moment after moment. If one fully understands the present moment, there will be nothing else to do, and nothing else to pursue. (ibid.; ibid., 68)

These quotes make it clear that Ghost Dog understands the religious account he follows to be unsurpassable and central: it is "incapable of abandonment" in Griffiths's terms, and it provides a pattern for his orientation to life and the world.

One reads religiously by directing one's entire existence toward embodying a religious account's very vision of things. In the film, Ghost Dog takes specific values recommended by *Hagakure* as central to his entire way of life, values such as non-attachment ("Every day without fail one should consider himself as dead"), spontaneity ("The Way of the Samurai is one of immediacy"), resolve ("It is a matter of being determined and having the spirit to break right through to the other side"), and, above all, loyalty ("If one were to say in a word what the condition of being a samurai is, its basis lies first in seriously devoting one's body and soul to his master") (Jarmusch 1999; Yamamoto 2002, 164, 60, 47, 66). We might say that Ghost Dog cultivates himself precisely in accordance with the vision laid out by the text.

While *Hagakure* is the centerpiece of Ghost Dog's religious vision, other texts also play a role in Ghost Dog's self-understanding. Especially significant in this regard is *Rashomon* by Akutagawa Ryūnosuke (1892–1927)[6]—the text given to Ghost Dog by Louise when he carries out the hit against Handsome Frank. Ghost Dog in turn reads it and lends it to Pearline, who later returns it to Ghost Dog (with the comment that "ancient Japan was a pretty weird place"), who then gives it to Louie. The loop is closed when Louise notices that Louie has her book, and she also recommends it to Louie. This text, iconic of the role of perspective in the construction of one's reality, is the most widely circulated text in the film. And indeed, the awareness of a multiplicity of conflicting perspectives—the diversity of competing "Ways" struggling to adapt to incongruous contexts—is an important dimension of this film.

As a counterpoint to Ghost Dog's religious mode of reading, we might consider the mafioso mode of reading. In the film, the mafiosi are often shown watching cartoons, with rather blank, mindless stares. These are the degenerate texts of a decadent subculture. They evoke no response from the "readers," serving as mere entertainment,[7] and do not contribute to any general sense of shared understanding among the members of the subculture. The texts consumed by the mafiosi do not offer a comprehensive vision of existence, nor of how one should relate oneself to the whole. The mafioso mode of reading clearly contrasts with Ghost Dog's own religious mode of reading, highlighting the strong connection between the practice of religious reading and the vibrancy of a tradition. It is only when a text is read as central to one's way of life that it may serve as the basis of a living tradition.

Tradition

There is no tradition without a text, at least in the abstract sense of an account of the way things really are, a vision of life and the world. But nor can there be a *text* in the religious sense without a *tradition* that takes the text as foundational: texts are not only read according to the modes of interpretation specified by a tradition but indeed are themselves only constituted *as texts* in the context of a tradition. A tradition involves a community and a history. As Griffiths states, "Religious readers do not read in isolation, either synchronically or diachronically. Their practices presuppose and engage with those who have already done what they are doing. Whence tradition" (Griffiths 1999, 69). Also illuminating here is Alasdair MacIntyre's concept of tradition as a "historically extended community in which practices relevant to the fulfillment of human nature can be carried out" (qtd. in Gutting 1999, 527). On this view, being a member of a tradition means participating in a community that shares the values presented in the tradition's texts. When one participates in a tradition—when one becomes a member of a historically extended community—one will endeavor to master the craft of self-cultivation recommended by the tradition's vision of things:

> To share in the rationality of a craft requires sharing in the contingencies of its history, understanding its story as one's own, and finding a place for oneself as a character in the enacted dramatic narrative which is that story so far. (MacIntyre 1990, 65)

Being a member of a tradition entails viewing oneself in the context of the tradition's history. And being a reader within a tradition means that one will endeavor to shape oneself in accordance with the tradition's texts.

> The reader was assigned the task of interpreting the text, but also had to discover, in and through his or her reading of those texts, that they in turn interpret the reader. What the reader, as thus interpreted by the texts, has to learn about him or herself is that it is only the self as transformed through and by the reading of the texts which will be capable of reading the texts aright. (ibid., 82)

So a central role is played by a tradition's texts: these texts provide the very vision of how one is to be in the world, how one is to properly cultivate oneself. These texts shape a religious reader since the "reader in his or her own life enacts and reenacts that of which he or she reads in Scripture" (ibid., 83).

In the context of the film's imaginary landscape we see two traditions, that of the Italian American mafiosi and that of the African American urban samurai. This is brought to our attention through Ghost Dog's reference to himself and Louie as belonging to two "ancient tribes." Each of these "ancient tribes" is marked by its specific ethnic and racial characteristics, but each also encompasses a set of shared values—a vision of how one should be in the world. Hence there is an important dimension of tradition in each way of life; each one occurs in the context of a community extended through time. It's clear that the mafiosi constitute a tradition: the Italian American mobsters often make reference to their way of life, drawing on the audience's cultural knowledge of the code of the mafia (especially as portrayed in popular culture)—a code which emphasizes loyalty, as does bushidō. Ghost Dog, too, lives his life in the context of a tradition. We see this in his interactions with other African Americans, including Pearline, who will eventually become his successor in his own peculiar hybrid tradition.

Ghost Dog also has brief but significant encounters with others who seem to belong to the African American urban samurai tradition. In one scene, Ghost Dog greets three African American gangsters in the street, one of whom hails Ghost Dog with the mantra-like refrain, "Knowledge to knowledge." In another scene, Ghost Dog sits listening to an extemporaneous rap by a group of African American hip-hop gangsters, whose lyrics evoke the experience of living with violence in the streets. And in a later scene there's a cameo appearance by the RZA—a founding member of the Wu-Tang Clan and the composer of the film's original music—who is credited as the "Samurai in Camouflage"; the Samurai in Camouflage greets Ghost Dog with the words, "Power and equality," to which Ghost Dog replies, "Always see everything, my brother." While these exchanges are brief, each is redolent with meaning, implying the sense that there are shared values among the somewhat hidden members of the African American urban samurai tradition.

But it is through his engagement with *Hagakure* that Ghost Dog participates most deeply, most reflectively, and most obviously in a tradition. While Ghost Dog understands himself to be a member of a rare and dying breed, it is significant that he does not take his approach to life to be entirely idiosyncratic: he views himself as a samurai, someone who is extending an ancient tradition into a modern environment. He is continuing to bring to life the "words of the ancients" (Jarmusch 1999; Yamamoto 2002, 47) through allowing those words to give form to his own life.

As noted above, a tradition provides the framework for properly interpreting—for properly reading—its texts. As MacIntyre points out, in its extended engagement with its foundational texts, a tradition must come to terms with "obscurities, discrepancies, and inconsistencies" found therein, which necessitates practices of interpretation, patterns of understanding by which such obscurities and inconsistencies might be respectively clarified and resolved (MacIntyre 1990, 84). The role of tradition in constituting a community of interpretation is represented in the film through Ghost Dog's interactions with his African American friends, Pearline and Raymond. Ghost Dog's initial conversation with Pearline, for example, is about books, ending with Ghost Dog lending her the copy of *Rashomon*, requesting that she share her own thoughts on the book after reading it. Furthermore, Ghost Dog's interactions with Raymond take place across the boundaries of language: the two are able to understand one another and develop a strong bond even while speaking different languages. These interactions convey the impression that meaning is more important than words—that the true meaning of expressions, utterances, and (by extension) texts is something beyond the specific words that convey it. This is reminiscent of the Buddhist principle of interpretation that true understanding relies on the meaning (*artha*) rather than the "letter" (Lamotte 1988), and also calls to mind the Zen idea of a special transmission outside the scriptures, apart from words and letters.

The interpersonal communication among the mafiosi, on the other hand, is stilted and disjointed. In fact, they often just sit together with blank looks, saying nothing. The mafiosi are unable to communicate effectively about anything, let alone their interpretations of texts (which are, after all, cartoons). All of this points to the decadence of the mafioso tradition: it's a tradition on the decline. When Ghost Dog carries out his attack against Vargo's gang, one of the fatally wounded mobsters remarks that at least "he's sending us out the old way," indicating nostalgia for a bygone era (albeit in rather unusual circumstances!).

Here it's also important to emphasize that the film's plotline concerns a hit that Vargo orders against one of his own men. Handsome Frank's affair with Boss Vargo's daughter, Louise, represents a breach of loyalty, a breach that demands reprisal; the reprisal in turn represents a second breach in loyalty, in that Vargo is forced to order the assassination of one of his own men; and that reprisal in turn leads to a further breach in loyalty, in that Louie is ordered to assassinate his own retainer, Ghost Dog. All of this indicates that the mafioso tradition is decaying from within—that the code of conduct which has been the basis of the tradition has begun to break down.[8] This breakdown in the mafioso tradition can be contrasted with Ghost Dog's unremitting commitment to the samurai tradition: Ghost Dog remains true to the value of loyalty even unto his own death. And Ghost Dog's loyalty highlights the point that the viability of a tradition depends on upholding the centrality of the tradition's texts—the "code" of the tradition. But as contexts change, maintaining the values of a tradition becomes more complex, which emphasizes the importance of a tradition's capacity to undergo transformations.

Transformation

Ghost Dog is not, of course, actually a samurai. The incongruity of an African American hit man for the mafia envisioning himself as a samurai, however, is part of the charm of the character and of the film as a whole. This is not the bushidō of medieval Japan. This is bushidō transformed. Indeed, the question of how to adapt traditional values to a new historical age even arises in a number of places in *Hagakure*. By the early eighteenth century, when *Hagakure* was composed, there was a period of relative peace and stability in Japan: the samurai were no longer the battle-hardened warriors they imagined their forebears to be.[9] *Hagakure* exhibits nostalgia for a martial age in which samurai were thought to live and die by the values of courage, duty, honor, and loyalty. However, it's no use lamenting what can no longer be:

> It is said that what is called "the spirit of an age" is something to which one cannot return. That this spirit gradually dissipates is due to the world's coming to an end. For this reason, although one would like to change today's world back to the spirit of one hundred years or more ago, it cannot be done. Thus it is important to make the best out of every generation. (Jarmusch 1999; Yamamoto 2002, 68)

For a tradition to continue it must adapt.

The vibrancy of a tradition is measured by its ability to transform and adapt to altered environments. Circumstances change, conditions change, contexts change. As Louie says in the film: "Everything seems to be changing around us. . . . Nothing makes any sense anymore." But which transformations represent genuine growth and adaptation, preserving authenticity in change? And which simply abandon tradition? These questions are by no means easily answered. And responses are never univocal: Does every Buddhist accept the Mahāyāna as a valid transformation of Buddhism? Does every Zen Buddhist consider Pure Land forms of Buddhism as genuine transformations of the Mahāyāna? What makes something "authentic," as opposed to a facile appropriation? Here, rather than approaching the issue in doctrinal terms, I will attempt to approach the question obliquely, in psychological terms.

In *Psychoanalysis and Religion*, Erich Fromm discusses two forms of psychoanalysis, one "which aims primarily at *social adjustment* and [one] which aims at the *'cure of the soul'*" (1978, 65). Fromm describes "social adjustment" in terms of helping the analysand to deal with unresolved conflicts and overcome specific symptoms, so that the analysand can achieve the "ability to act like the majority of people in his culture" (ibid., 73). The goal here is to "reduce the excessive suffering of the neurotic to the average level of suffering inherent in conformity to these [cultural] patterns" (ibid., 74). Fromm describes the "cure of the soul," however, as helping the analysand to achieve the "optimal development of a person's potentialities and the realization of his individuality" (ibid., 74), a role that places psychoanalysis in line with the highest aims of a religious attitude according to Fromm.

Fromm's account of psychoanalysis and (by extension) religion as "social adjustment" is consonant with Slavoj Žižek's criticism of the Western adoption of Buddhism. According to Žižek, Buddhism "enables you to fully participate in the frantic pace of the capitalist game while sustaining the perception that you are not really in it, that you are well aware how worthless this spectacle is" (2001, 15). Here Žižek understands Western Buddhism to simply be another technique for adjusting oneself to the conditions of late capitalism, so that one can ultimately become a better producer and a better consumer. Griffiths makes a similar point when he urges that the counterpart of religious reading is "consumerist reading."

Ghost Dog's appropriation of bushidō ideals is intended as a "cure of the soul." Through upholding these ideals, he directs himself toward realizing his potential and maintaining his integrity. Ghost Dog is not attempting to adjust himself to the circumstances of his late twentieth-century urban environment, but rather is striving to embody the values upheld by the tradition in which he participates—the "Way of the Samurai," or "the old-school ways." For Ghost Dog, the ideals of bushidō are paramount, and paramount among those ideals is loyalty: he upholds loyalty even to the point of his own death—which in itself might serve as the film's commentary on the incongruity of attempting to embody religious ideals in a time when the "spirit of the age" has been "gradually dissipated." At the same time, however, Ghost Dog's death also emphasizes what it would ultimately mean to uphold a tradition, that the tradition's values must become more important than one's own life.

William James argues that "when we think certain states of mind superior to others . . . it is because we believe them to bring us good consequential fruits for life" (James 1987, 22). On a Jamesian pragmatist account, the measure of authenticity and value is to be found in the results achieved: the true test of authenticity is in the attainment of a specified religious end—and any skillful means that can lead to such an end should be considered an authentic transformation. Buddhist traditions themselves have used this criterion to determine authenticity: Does the teaching lead to the cessation of the mental afflictions that bind one to cyclic existence?[10] Or, according to certain Mahāyāna traditions, to the attainment of nonconceptual awareness (*nirvikalpa-jñāna*) fundamental to buddhahood?[11] Relating the point to the concepts of "text" and "tradition," we might say that measuring a transformation's authenticity means measuring its capacity to achieve the embodiment of the ideals envisioned in a tradition's texts.

Transmission

What marks the successful transmission of the teaching? In Buddhism, transmission can be marked by full ordination into the monastic community, receiving the formal seal of mind-to-mind transmission (*inka*) in Japanese Zen traditions, being ritually initiated into a lineage of tantric practice in Vajrayāna traditions, or other means. But what might Jarmusch's film have to teach us about transmission? The key scene here is the final one—the only one that begins with a passage of *Hagakure* read by someone other than Ghost Dog. In this scene we hear Pearline reading the following lines:

> In the Kamigata area they have a sort of tiered lunchbox they use for a single day when flower viewing. Upon returning, they throw them away, trampling them underfoot. The end is important in all things. (Jarmusch 1999; Yamamoto 2002, 71)

What is the significance of this passage about something as seemingly mundane as lunchboxes? It is important to note here that in their first conversation, when Ghost Dog asks what she has in her lunchbox, Pearline replies "my books." This marks the beginning of their friendship, a bond based on discussing texts. In the film, Pearline's lunchbox functions (oddly enough) as a sign of her dedication to reading, a dedication that allows for her own transformation—a transformation marked by her reading the final passage quoted from *Hagakure*. Ghost Dog has successfully transmitted his tradition to Pearline: she will go on to cultivate herself in accordance with the text's vision of things, ensuring that the urban samurai tradition will continue. Although Ghost Dog himself has passed away, the vision that he endeavored to embody, the ancient tradition that he extended into a modern environment, will continue to live—to be concretely manifested in the world—through Pearline. And according to the way Ghost Dog lived his life, at the end of the day the continuation of the tradition is more important than Ghost Dog himself.

It is significant that Pearline—the successor of Ghost Dog's African American urban samurai tradition—is a young girl. This is in some sense incongruous: bushidō, after all, is a militaristic and paradigmatically masculine way of life. There is a point to this incongruity, however. For a tradition to be transmissible—in order for a tradition to be transmitted through history and across cultures—it must be able to adapt to different specific circumstances, personal as well as historical-cultural. Just as the meaning of a tradition's texts is something more than the "letter," so too must the values envisioned by a tradition (the *meaning* of a tradition) be something more than the specific modes through which those values are concretely embodied. A tradition must in some abstract sense encompass timeless and transcultural wisdom. For a tradition to become a "Way" (in Ghost Dog's terms) it must represent an ideal that can shape individuals in different eras and cultural contexts—whether that be "ancient Japan" or late twentieth-century Jersey City—and in different roles in life—whether as a hit man or a schoolgirl. The values upheld by Ghost Dog's urban samurai tradition—non-attachment, spontaneity, resolve, loyalty—can be embodied in different ways and in different specific circumstances, by a contract killer who carries out hits with precision, or a young girl who carries books in a lunchbox.

So when might we say that a successful transmission has occurred? When a specific form of life—a particular way of being in the world, a way of relating to the whole of existence through embodying the ideals envisioned by the texts of a tradition—emerges and continues in a different historical-cultural context. The transmission of Buddhism to the West is aided by scholars, translators, exegetes, filmmakers, and others. But it only actually occurs when the thoughts and practices envisioned by Buddhism enter into people's lives, and become embodied.

Appendix: Summary of *Ghost Dog: The Way of the Samurai* (Jarmusch 1999)

The film begins with an establishing shot of Jersey City, followed by a scene of Ghost Dog (Forest Whitaker) along with his pigeons on the rooftop shack that is his isolated dwelling, reminiscent of a late twentieth-century urban version of a Buddhist monk living at a mountain retreat. He is meditatively studying *Hagakure* and we hear his voice reading the first quote cited above, which sets up the entire first chapter of the film. Ghost Dog is a hit man who envisions himself as the samurai retainer of Louie (John Tormey), a small-time mafioso in a small-time, down-and-out mafia. Many years ago Louie had saved Ghost Dog's life, when as a young man Ghost Dog was being harassed and beaten by a gang of white men;[12] and in return, Ghost Dog had pledged his loyalty to Louie, as Louie's "retainer." Since then, Ghost Dog had performed a number of "perfect contracts" for Louie, communicating with Louie only through a passenger pigeon, and receiving his remuneration for the hits only once a year, on the first day of autumn.

The film's plot revolves around one particular hit, the last hit for which Louie employs Ghost Dog. Louie hires Ghost Dog to assassinate Handsome Frank (Richard Portnow), a mafioso who has been sleeping with Louise Vargo (Tricia Vessey), the daughter of the mob boss Ray Vargo (Henry Silva). The twist: like Louie, Handsome Frank works for Ray Vargo, so the mob is ordering a hit against one of its own "made men," a job which is considered appropriate only for an outsider like Ghost Dog. As usual, Ghost Dog carries out the hit efficiently but is surprised to see a girl at the scene (Louise). Louise remains calm and detached during the hit—perhaps too calm—and even gives Ghost Dog her book about "ancient Japan," *Rashomon*.

In the double-bind logic of the situation, Ray Vargo in turn orders Ghost Dog's assassination: he had, after all, killed one of Vargo's own men—although only through following instructions that had come down from Vargo himself. Louie meets with Vargo and two of Vargo's senior underlings, who form a rather odd pair: the underboss, Sonny Valerio (Cliff Gorman), who is curiously well-informed about hip-hop music; and an old consigliere (Gene Ruffini) who seems to be subject to dementia. During the meeting Vargo requires Louie to divulge everything he knows about Ghost Dog, ordering Louie to have Ghost Dog killed. As Sonny puts it, "Better him than you, right Louie?"

We see Ghost Dog in a park, listening to a group of African American hip-hop gangsters rapping about violence in the streets, and even invoking Ghost Dog's name in their lyrics. After they depart, Ghost Dog is approached by a young African American girl, Pearline (Camille Winbush), carrying a lunch-box filled with books. The two strike up a conversation and begin to develop a friendship, bonding through discussing books they've read. Ghost Dog lends Pearline the copy of *Rashomon*, on the condition that she later tells him what she thinks about it. The two of them also chat with Raymond (Isaach De Bankolé), an African American who has emigrated from a French-speaking country (De Bankolé is from Côte d'Ivoire) and whom Ghost Dog describes as his best friend. Oddly, while Raymond only speaks French and Ghost Dog only speaks English, the two of them have a meaningful rapport with one another. The film captures this through the use of subtitles: Ghost Dog's spoken words and Raymond's subtitled speech often paraphrase one another. At other points in the film, the two meet up and continue to develop their friendship.

Through the passenger pigeon, Louie sets up a meeting with Ghost Dog to let him know that Vargo has put a hit out on him. At the meeting, Ghost Dog saves Louie from being betrayed and killed by one of his fellow mafiosi. He shoots Louie in the shoulder to prevent any suspicion of his colluding with Ghost Dog: "Better me than you, Louie." Later returning to his rooftop dwelling, Ghost Dog sees that his pigeons have been killed. Knowing it to be the work of Ray Vargo's mafia, he determines that he must now attack Vargo and his mob.

Ghost Dog attacks the mafiosi while they're gathered at Vargo's residence, shooting everyone present except for Louise. He even shoots Louie—in exactly the same place he had shot him before—but the wound is of course not fatal. As Louie, Louise, and a fatally wounded mafioso drive away from the scene, the dying mobster points out, "You know, Louie, there's one good thing about this Ghost Dog . . . he's sending us out the old way."

This all leads up to the final showdown between Louie and Ghost Dog. Ghost Dog gives his few possessions to Raymond, except for his copy of *Hagakure*, which he passes along to Pearline. At the final showdown, Louie shoots Ghost Dog multiple times, but Ghost Dog does not return fire: his gun was not loaded.[13] It would be contrary to the samurai code for a retainer to kill his master. The film ends with Pearline reading a passage from *Hagakure*: "The end is important in all things" (Jarmusch 1999; Yamamoto 2002, 71).

Notes

1. The term *bushidō* first occurs in certain Japanese texts from the seventeenth century (G. Hurst 1990, 514; McFarlane 1990, 404). Hurst points out that "it would be a mistake to assume that there was one school called 'Bushidō'" (ibid., 515). Texts representative of what has been understood as bushido were composed during the peaceful Tokugawa period (1600–1868); such texts were "anachronistic in the extreme" (ibid., 520–21), exhibiting "an excessive attachment to the *ideals* of the late sixteenth century [during the Warring States period], focusing especially on loyalty, duty, and courage" (ibid., 515).

2. See Turnbull 2006, especially the chapters on "Buddha and the Bushi" and "Zen and the Samurai"; and Cleary's (2005) translation of "Notes on the Peerless Sword" by Zen Master Takuan Sōhō (1573–1645).

3. The only exception is the final chapter, which begins with Pearline—Ghost Dog's "successor"—reading from *Hagakure*.

4. Jarmusch states, "*Hagakure* even inspired the form of the film, because the book has these little aphorisms separated by a little symbol which gives you . . . a breathing space until the next thought. [In the movie] we present a section of our story and then break for a quote from *Hagakure*, to reflect or resonate with what's happening in the story" (qtd. in Spletzer 2000).

5. The film's violence also serves to place the film in relation to samurai movies, gangster films, and Westerns—although the genre boundaries become quite blurred in a Jarmusch-esque manner. As Jarmusch states, *Ghost Dog* "refers to action filmmaking, martial arts filmmaking, Westerns, yet I don't know if it is exactly any of those things" (qtd. in Spletzer 2000).

6. Two stories in this collection—"Rashomon" and "In a Grove"—provide the basis for Kurosawa's *Rashomon*, a film that centers on a purported murder recounted from conflicting perspectives.

7. Griffiths refers to such a mode of reading as "consumerist" as opposed to "religious" (1999, 40).

8. It is notable that two of the mafioso characters, the similarly named Louie and Louise, are in some sense exceptional: both are caught in the whirlwind of the breakdown of the mafioso tradition but attempt to maintain a degree of integrity. And both are connected to Ghost Dog and to the text, *Rashomon*: Louise gives the text to Ghost Dog, who then gives it to Louie.

9. "In fact, rather than think of the Tokugawa samurai as a warrior, it might be more appropriate to think of him as a government employee, a GS-12, for example" (G. Hurst 1990, 519).

10. For an overview of the standards of authenticity in Buddhist traditions, see Lamotte 1983/1984.

11. It is apropos that *Hagakure* also contains various passages emphasizing the importance of "no-mind" and the absence of discriminative thought: "What is called 'No Mind' is a mind that is pure and lacks complication" (Yamamoto 2002, 24–25); "Buddhism gets rid of the discriminating mind. . . . In the Way of the Samurai can a man be courageous when discrimination arises?" (ibid., 146).

12. We learn this later in the film through flashbacks. Interestingly, Ghost Dog's and Louie's flashbacks offer different versions of the episode: in Ghost Dog's flashback Louie shoots one of Ghost Dog's assailants to save Ghost Dog from being shot, but

in Louie's flashback Louie shoots the assailant when the assailant pulls a gun on Louie for interrupting their attack. This difference is reminiscent of Kurosawa's 1950 film, *Rashomon*, which is indirectly alluded to later in *Ghost Dog*.

13. The fact that Ghost Dog's gun is not loaded in the showdown scene is one of many allusions to Jean-Pierre Melville's 1967 film, *Le Samouraï*.

CHAPTER 8

Eastern Influences on Western Sport

Appropriating Buddhism in the G/Name of Golf

JANE M. STANGL

I N T H E C U L T golf film *Caddyshack* (dir. Harold Ramis 1980), Bill Murray, playing the well-seasoned groundskeeper of Bushwood Country Club, recounts to a wide-eyed young caddy a story of Tibet and his experience caddying for the Dalai Lama. He tells the strapping youngster, while holding a pitchfork under his throat, about "getting on as a 'looper'—a caddy . . ." on a course in the Himalayas. "So," Murray says, "I tell them I'm a pro-jock, and who do they 'gimme'? The Dalai Lama" (pronounced emphatically "lamb-a"). "The twelfth son of the lama—the flowing robes, grace, bald . . . striking!"

On the first tee the caddy hands the lama the driver. "He hauls off and whacks one," says Murray, "big hitter." He pauses and repeats. "He's a big hitter, the lama—long." Indeed, the lama proceeds to hit ". . . into a ten-thousand-foot crevasse right at the base of this glacier. You know what the lama says," Murray asks the youngster as he proceeds in an inane accent. "Gunga, ga-loonga . . . gunga-la, gunga-la." Seemingly, the lama had proceeded to swear in his native tongue. Murray's iteration then moves rapidly to a close at the 18th hole.

The monologue, which was apparently improvised on the spot by Murray, is amusing on several counts. First, there is the juxtaposition of the Dalai Lama's august personage with the supposedly prosaic game of golf. Second, the thought of the lama's ball disappearing into a ten-thousand-foot crevasse—a startling departure from the usual array of sand-traps and water-hazards—is both familiar and disconcerting: What golfer has not had a ball swallowed up by a course's unforgiving terrain? Third, the Dalai Lama's expression upon losing his ball reminds us of the curses that every golfer has uttered—while also suggesting that perhaps he is saying something profound and wise, using the vagaries of the golf experience that every golfer knows can be both a trial and a summit of wisdom to express his or her ideal, yet seemingly incomprehensible knowledge of the game. Beyond amusement, this bit is compelling because it evokes the experience that every golfer suspects, that within the game of golf there resides the potential to realize the ineffable, to attain a state of peace and clarity that, in other respects, seems more suited to the realm of religion than that of a sport.

Although the portrayal in *Caddyshack* is humorous, Buddhist ideas are in fact having a real and lasting impact on the game of golf as it is practiced and played through the greens of the United States today. Increasingly, golfers are drawing on Buddhist ideas and practices allegedly drawn from Zen to improve their handicaps, to make sense of their experiences, and even, in some cases, to seek spiritual fulfillment by finding the self, paradoxically, through losing the self altogether. Here, *Caddyshack's* other famous actor, Chevy Chase, in the character of Ty Webb, exhorts to such an approach stating, "there's a force in the universe that makes things happen. And all you have to do is get in touch with it, stop thinking, let things happen, and *be the ball*" (*Caddyshack* 1980). The idea of using golf as a microcosm of the self, as a venue to grapple with the challenges of ego-clinging and relaxation, and the prospect of acquiring greater wisdom about one's life (while, not coincidentally, believing that one can become a better golfer), have all led to a fascination with the applicability of Buddhist wisdom to contemporary sport and leisure practices.

The context for this work is my own life. I grew up as a middle child in a family of eight that included three talented and very athletic brothers. I was also blessed by the presence of an aunt who lived nearby and would relieve me from this boys-will-be-boys exuberance, and on dewy summer mornings, she would take me to the local golf course. On the course I found myself enraptured by the quiet calm and by my aunt's delight in the game, but more by her desire to teach me its rules and intricacies. My red Ball Jets would be sopping wet by the end of those early morning rounds, yet in her company I found stillness that no sandlot could provide.

Currently I have an academic career in sociocultural sport studies, and I provide golf instruction on the side. As I reflect on my own athletic history and intellectual growth in the world of sport, I see that it did not follow a traditional trajectory. Indeed, my engagement with sports led me in directions I could not have imagined. Particularly influential was my study abroad engagement as a student at the Universiti of Malaya in Kuala Lumpur where I played field hockey with men and trained in martial arts for the first time. In Malaysia, physicality melded with culture in a way I was unaccustomed to in the West, and I spent equally as much time attending festivals such as Thai Pusam and celebrating the incoming Chinese New Year, as I did on fields of play. Slowly, these experiences altered my roots, my athleticism, and my Catholicism. I woke daily to the Muslim call to prayer by the local Imam, gawked at Hindu temples, and marveled at pagodas. Of all these experiences, however, none made a greater impression on me than the experience of privately witnessing a Buddhist nun in meditative repose. The quietude of that moment captured me, and I vowed to incorporate the idea of serenity in more of my daily activities—physically and mentally. This current work emerges from these experiences of the juxtaposition of Western sensibilities about sport with Eastern spirituality. In this chapter, I examine the appropriation of Buddhism by Western culture, with special emphasis on the game of golf.

Golfing Bodies/Zen-like Minds

Millions of people across the world currently claim golf as their preferred form of recreation and leisure. In the United States, *Sports Illustrated* writer and critical commentator, Frank Deford, announced albeit facetiously in his piece "Hooked on Golf," that "golf has become an utter phenomenon, ubiquitous upon the earth, a dominant cultural force that has replaced most sensible, traditional American activities" (1998, 94). Guilty as charged, my own desktop swells with periodicals and literature about golf, but especially those pieces that engage the meeting of physicality and the transformed mind. Articles on such subjects abound, in newspapers such as the *New York Times*, and in weekly periodicals such as *Time* magazine (Hall 2003; *Time* 2003; Weld 2004). In addition, specialized publications in the domain of American-inflected Eastern spirituality, such as *Tricycle: The Buddhist Review, YOGA, Yoga Journal,* and *Shambala Sun,* as well as golf magazines, such as *Golf Digest,* and *Golf for Women,* all speak to the growing interest in incorporating some form of mindful practice into our everyday being and physical activity (Krucoff 2003, 120–24, 203; Lee and Nichtern 2007, 50–57; McCreddie 2003, 94; *Tricycle* 2006; Vickers 2004, 96–101; White 2003, 82, 85–89).

The catchy titles of these articles include: "Mind, Body, Books: A Healthful Balance," "Pre-round Poses," "Pumping Iron, Practicing Yoga," "Practicing with Loss" (a piece that asks us to compare the intensities of losing a tennis game to the loss of a child), "Insight from Injury," "It's Just Not Cricket," "The Quiet Eye," "Canyon Ranch Cure," and perhaps most telling of all, "Good Karma, Bad Golf," a tale of teeing it up with Losang Kunga Gyurme, known today as Lama Kunga Rinpoche, a Tibetan monk who "goes by George" (Das 2003, 82–84; Krucoff 2003, 120–24, 203; McCreddie 2003, 94; Roberts and Moss

2004, 46; Sens 2002, NE-1-NE-4; Vickers 2004, 96–101; Weld 2004; White 2003, 82).

In the most general sense, each of these pieces looks at some aspect of one's performance, whether in yoga, golf, or tennis. But each emphasizes that it is equally important to think about the task itself. For example, "The Quiet Eye" (Vickers 2004, 96–101), which focuses on the skill of putting the ball, engages meditative notions on the stillness of one's mind through a soft gaze—fixating one's head and eye movements to such a degree that conscious information is absent. Yoga, which offers golfers the important skill of "pre-round poses," is spa-like, miles away from the "Canyon Ranch Cure," but as in golf, its intersection between the physical and mental, and the incorporation of mindfulness encourages participants to build relaxed bodily awareness (Roberts and Moss 2004, 46; White 2003, 82).

In each piece, Buddhist techniques, meditative practices, and approaches allegedly drawn from Zen serve more as metaphoric guideposts than deep philosophical reflections that lead one into labyrinthine pathways where cacti and succulents become part and parcel of meditative acts. At "Canyon Ranch [Cure]" you can admittedly "stay as New Age or nuts-and-bolts as you like" (White 2003, 86). Here, most spiritual moments are marked by the [golf] seeker's improvement in length—that is, hitting the ball 50 yards farther!

Laden with understated attenuations toward Buddhist-like ideals, "Good Karma, Bad Golf" (Sens 2002, NE-1–NE-4) employs more believable strains of Buddhist sensibilities. Of course, like in *Caddyshack*, golfing with a lama may produce greater expectations of wisdom-laden narratives than distance in yards. Still, without engaging the eightfold path in the pithy way that another article entitled "Talk to Yourself . . . The Right Way" (Thompson 1997, 84–86) implores, Lama Kunga states more cogently, "suffering comes from anger, frustration [and] self-consciousness. If you play golf, you know what I mean" (Sens 2002, NE-2). Later, Lama Kunga—seemingly unaware of Ramis's Lampoon-like film *Caddyshack*, and the request from Murray's looping stint with the Dalai Lama to pay him "a little something for his effort"— delights in the film's expectation and the lama's response. "Oh there won't be any payment," the Dalai Lama supposedly declared. "But when you die . . . on your deathbed . . . you will receive total consciousness" (*Caddyshack* 1980). Hereafter, author Josh Sens takes the liberty of linking the four noble truths to religion—golf and Buddhism of course, and though this lama offers him tutelage on the thirteen stages of enlightenment, none grace the *Golf Digest* pages. Lama Kunga's best advice on golf: "let go of your expectations," that is, relinquish your [golfing] desires (Sens 2002, NE-1).

Playing Conscious Golf

In 2004, *Golf Digest*, a magazine with more than a million and a half subscribers, published a special report on the future of golf's relationship to the mind–body business. Spurred on by Ernie Els's and Phil Mickelson's respective successes in major championships, the author tells us what we now know, namely that "the mind can help us play better golf (if we'd just quit fighting it)." The article is entitled "Finding the Zone" (Diaz 2004, 134–45, 178). Following Mickelson's 2006 Master's championship play, *ESPN* re-affirmed again that "Lefty" (Mickelson) was at peace and clearly "playing within himself"—sport parlance for equanimity (Maisel 2006). Two months later, in June of 2006, Mickelson graced the cover of *Sports Illustrated*, crouched in a near-fetal portrayal of defeat after blowing a one-shot lead on the final hole of the U.S. Open. The venerated hero quickly became the "Crack-up" (*Sports Illustrated* 2006).

Time, in its August 4, 2003, feature piece, "The Science of Meditation," suggested more consumeristic takes on uniting the mind and body with articles such as; "Just Say Om" and "A Shopper's Guide to Meditation" (Bjerklie 2003; Stein 2003). More recently, a January 2007 follow-up issue on the mind and body encouraged similar sentiments. In both pieces, references to work at the University of Wisconsin–Madison labs on meditation and monks helped support the mind–body connection (*Time* 2003). Like the professional athlete who generally claims no less than 10,000 hours to hone his or her skill, the "Lama in the Lab" engages in no less than 10,000 hours of meditation—sitting in quiet repose, thus furthering evidence that keen mind–body skills take repetition and practice (Ericsson and Charness 1994, 725–47; *Time* 2003). In a relatively recent piece entitled "The Emergence of Sport and Spirituality," Ian Lawrence argues that sport in modern society embodies a new spirituality; it fulfills the spiritual void left by the dispersion of traditional religious forms. Here Lawrence suggests that if we must choose among religions per se, we may do well to adopt Buddhism, which acknowledges that life is a journey (Lawrence 2005).

Ironically, the notion that life is a journey is not particularly Buddhist, and what emerges from these mainstream renderings about our newly acquired state of consciousness is a cursory connection of sport to seemingly deeper spiritual and mindful values—physicality cum spirituality that often yields trite aphorisms. Consider Lawrence's point as it transfers to the sport lover's T-shirt—"baseball is life," "soccer is life," "golf is life." Evident in this perspective is a value-laden philosophical bent toward pithiness that may arguably suit the supposedly less-evolved Western mind.

It is precisely such succinct dicta that offer us a Buddhist-inflected approach to sport yet deprive us of the richness of Buddhist doctrine and teachings. This discourse forces us to reconsider the stake that cultural appropriation has in changing minds. Cultural appropriation—literally, *taking* from one culture something that is not its own—may appear to be a stretch given the global scope of the game of golf and globalization in general (see Cole 2002) yet it is the assumptions behind such taking that warrants a more critical appraisal (Ziff and Rao 1997). Appropriating Buddhism from this trajectory is not without its own history; indeed, today's (American) Buddhism is described as a tapestry of American religious life, not a set of beliefs to be taken on faith but a set of observations about life, the sources of suffering, and the end of suffering—based on one's own set of experiences (Eck 2001).

From Classics to Contemplatives

Golf, a game credited as rich in terms of sport literature, is arguably under-investigated in terms of scholarship. As such, golfing literature appears widely in mass consumer bookstores, though the texts are largely experiential and laden with numerous "lessons" (Stoddard 1994, 21–34). The lessons these writings impart often stand in as metaphors for life per se, and as such they remain ideas, ideas that are acquired from some place at some point in time yet conform to dominant social arrangements to such a degree that they shape our organization of experiences more broadly. The lessons in this context appear as almost inevitable—much like my own dewy fable that frames this chapter. Deford articulated this point similarly, "golf has risen above criticism. Even for those pledged to document it, golf isn't a sport so much as it is a sacred way of life" (1998, 96). Regarding golf as sport: books, novels, and throngs of metaphoric tales are spun around the game's charm, and as will be made clear in a number of titles, precedents for these yarns often connect notions of Zen and the mind in the broadest sense.

Two classic texts that meld physicality, the mind, spirituality, and specific sports when taken together arguably offer a gateway to this more recent trend. *Zen in the Art of Archery* (1953) by Eugen Herrigel and *Golf in the Kingdom* (1972) by Esalen Institute founder Michael Murphy are spiritual sport classics, the former on Eastern philosophy and archery, and the latter on golf and mysticism. These pieces are filled with anecdotes that offer as many lessons on life as they do knowledge on their respective sport. In Herrigel's volume, D. T. Suzuki's introduction describes the "everyday" mind, and the importance of the unconscious to the success of practitioners—from art, to fencing, to swordplay and archery, where full presence of the mind necessitates detachment. Suzuki's presence in this context is instructive. Although Herrigel's goal is to have the skill become spiritual—for the performer to become purposeless and egoless, to not only detach oneself from the skill but to free the self from the self—the text became appropriated in sport quite differently. For example, the discipline of sport psychology picked up Herrigel's thesis and took it as the archetype for a genre of how-to texts with titles that incorporate terms such as *zen*, *consciousness*, and *inner-workings*, in order to draw in the mystery and lure of games in which consciousness impedes the progress of the practitioner.

Buddhologists may argue that Buddhism has been corrupted and complicated by various academic and religious traditions, and one might argue that sport traditions join in this enterprise of corruption as well (Lopez 2005). Suzuki, credited to some extent with "liberating" Zen, is simply part of this long narrative that incorporates individual experiences and present-day events, ahistorical as they seem. Murphy's decidedly more metaphorical reflection, *Golf in the Kingdom*, plays on the Buddhist principle of veneration for one's teacher. Shivas Irons is the renowned character who unearths the "religion o' the game" (Murphy 1972). The tale is replete with reference to prayers, higher laws, grace, holy men, mystery, and mystical allure, all set in golf's birthplace—Scotland, at the fictitious links of Burningbush.

Golf, tennis, or yoga may make the "taking" of Buddhism easier because of these sports' individual focus, but applying Buddhist sensibilities to team sports generates even broader cultural appeal. Here it is instructive to look to another sport in which the Buddhist link has been articulated and supported. In the 1990s the rise of basketball superstar Michael Jordan led many to notice one of his teachers—the former Chicago Bulls coach Phil Jackson. In *Sacred Hoops: Spiritual Lessons of a Hardwood Warrior* (1995), Jackson, a self-described Zen Christian, sprinkles his text with quotes from Lao-Tzu and Thich Nhat Hanh to Carlos Castaneda and Eugen Herrigel. More striking than Jackson's eclectic approach to the dance of basketball in which he engages principles of meditation, selflessness, and compassion is his cafeteria-style way of adapting principles and concepts that are deeply meaningful to Taoism, Zen, and Native American spirituality. Playing the role of the venerated teacher himself, Jackson offered applied experience as the real teacher as he carved his career through earlier stints as a coach in the Continental Basketball Association (CBA) and Superior Basketball League of Puerto Rico. His path to Chicago was littered with obstacles; in other words, he too suffers. Describing life in the CBA, Jackson offered examples on the challenges of what he called "enlightenment management." Jackson suggests that in engaging Buddhism, particularly its ideals about right action as a principle of the eightfold path, he nearly ended his coaching career. Fundamentally, he believes that love of the game is what motivates players, not winning, nor salaries: "They live for those moments when they can lose themselves completely in the action and experience the pure joy" (1995, 79).[1]

Lessons through Books: "Be the Ball"

During the 1990s and well into 2000, many treatises reflecting approaches such as Jackson's appeared—each promising to bring more of the "wisdom of the East" to the Westerner. This genre of enlightenment seeking was notably stretched to golfers. Tim Gallwey's 1998 revision of *The Inner Game of Golf: The Art and Zen of Learning Golf* (Hebron 1990); *Beyond the Fairway: Zen Lessons, Insights, and Inner Attitudes* (Wallach 1995); *Extraordinary Golf* (Shoemaker 1996); *Golf and the Spirit* (Peck 1999); *Be the Ball* (Jones and Doren 2000); *Conscious Golf* (Hendricks 2003); Deepak Chopra's *Golf for Enlightenment* (2003); and Roland Merullo's *Golfing with God* (2005), all offer glimpses of this ideal. While these books vary in style as fables, instructional pieces, professional advice compendiums, spiritual guides, and how-to psychologies, they all address the game by engaging the value of a more mindful approach to golf as a particular practice, hence using the game as a meditative or more contemplative form of exercise.

Golfing with God offers a wonderful example of how appropriated ideas about spirituality and religion's place in golf take on Westernized forms. In Merullo's novel, Hank Fins-Winston, the protagonist, meets God in multiple forms as he golfs his way through heaven. In chapter eight, a "fellow on the plump side" emerges as his next golfing companion. He carried an air of calmness, moved with elegant stillness, and "had a way of smiling" (2005). He never used a tee, never took a practice swing, and eliminated the usual practice of lining up a putt. No swagger, no ego, no aggravation. Fins-Winston's playing companion on that day was, of course, the Buddha, and the Buddha's calm precision was designed to infect Fins-Winston to such a degree that the protagonist would find himself playing with an unconscious reflexivity of his best self.

Indeed, it is the Zen Buddhist tradition that provides the basis for many of the central concepts articulated in this subgenre of work as applied to sport. This tradition is most openly referenced in the works of Wallach and of Hebron. In *Beyond the Fairway*, Zen sayings preface chapters and the protagonist begins with the confession that, "for much of his life, he felt intuitively that golf could connect him to pure, clear streams of consciousness" (Wallach 1995, 2). This particular tale is spun between spiritual hazards, Himalayan foothills, and exploration of the game's most sacred sites, as well as sanctified rituals. Written to appeal to the mystical and visionary golfer, Wallach's book is a metaphorical journey toward enjoying each stroke on the way to the hole. The opening Zen golf koan best exemplifies the spirit of his tale:

> A new member of the golf club was anxious to learn about the course and said: "I have only recently become a member. Will you be gracious enough to show me the way to the first tee?" The Head Pro said: "Do you hear the murmuring of the stream?" The new member said: "Yes, I do." The Head Pro said: "Here is the entrance." (3)

By employing the very idea of a koan, the reader is treated to the notion that with deeper reflection and awareness one can enter an elusive domain wherein wisdom presides, and better yet, the entrance to golf is found. The koan as parable sets the stage by suggesting that the new student, who is anxious to learn, asks the venerated teacher, the pro, how to join the community of golf. In Buddhist vernacular this can be alternately read as the student's desire for instruction in the game (the dharma), to be found behind the open door to the community's entrance (the sangha). Hence, the way to golf is through the self.

In addition to more conscious and mindful practices there is the notion of "flow"—widely credited to psychologist Mihaly Csikszentmihalyi (1990). This concept is central to *The Art and Zen of Learning Golf* (Hebron 1990). Indeed, "go with the flow," serves as a mantra in many sports—avoid resistance, be open to immediate experience. Contrary to other texts in this genre though, Hebron is more generous and forthcoming with lessons from Zen. Paraphrasing "the Zen idea," Hebron suggests that the practitioner tap into an inner ability that will allow maximizing his or her potential without trying, but doing so "in the tradition of trying" (Hebron 1990). Not quite Chevy Chase's *Caddyshack* quip to "be the ball," but close. Hebron applies these ideas to golf by addressing the benefits of awareness and visual learning, citing an example of the average golfer being aware of the differences between a high handicapper and a professional's swing. Hebron urges that one must work with absence, for example, excluding from the mind all extraneous thoughts. Unlike other texts in the subgenre, Hebron moves beyond the pithy explanations of applied spirituality. He expands on Zen's history, its benefits, its principles, and its ideas, though in modestly abbreviated and sometimes cursory ways.

The Inner Game of Golf (Gallwey 1999) is built around three main aspects of the golfing experience: enjoyment, learning, and performance. Although Gallwey advocates a greater desire for the former two, most golfers interrupt this balancing act with a tendency toward outcome, that is, performance, perhaps underestimating the former aspects, which can offer joy, satisfaction, and fulfillment. How well we perform, or *do* golf, becomes more allied with *being* a particular type of golfer—scratch or 14-handicapper, for example—than with being at peace with the challenges of the game itself. As golf teacher Harvey Penick noted, thinking too much about how you are doing, when you are doing, is disastrous (Penick and Shrake 1992).

Penick, widely revered as the consummate teaching professional, was known for his teaching through parable. Through a different lens, *Golf and the Spirit* (Peck 1999) and *Golf for Enlightenment* (Chopra 2003) take the everyman's story of golf approach, enriched by these authors' public reputations as spiritual beings with broad social capital. It is the beauty of the game, compounded by the human's unrelenting ability to master it, that speaks to one's soul. Peck, a self-identified Zen Buddhist turned Christian mystic, constructs an imaginary course of 18 holes through allegorical titles and twists. The notion of paradox itself rests at the center of each approach. His text is rich and reflexive, engaged with proclamations about the place of freedom, perspective, time, and God in the golfer's life. These portrayals reflect Peck's roles as psychotherapist, author, lecturer, and advocate devoted to extolling the virtues of consciousness.

Deepak Chopra uses fable rather than explicit instruction. His protagonist, Adam, encounters seven profound lessons on spiritual strategies that move beyond the game's essence to the essence of life. Each text takes us through life's journeys, led by chapters that pull together rhetorical chants of mindfulness, accounts of being and presence, recommendations to cultivate detached passion, admonitions toward transcendent knowledge, and the acceptance of uncertainty. Both Peck and Chopra suggest that for each of us the repetitive rituals of golf are guides to our own individual, yet basically human path.

In *Conscious Golf* (2003), Hendricks engages Zen explicitly, arguing that one must empty oneself in order to learn. Nonetheless, Hendricks links golf to business, taking each to be a way to address life. Breathing, emptiness, awareness, and truth all travel in and out of tales of flat tires, children, policemen, and popular management guides. *Zen Golf* (2002), a hot seller by Dr. Joseph Parent, also offers "a lot more than golf." Parent appeals to golfers' psyche and to our fears about what others think, arguing that this internalized judgment clouds our performance. Parent introduces the pun of PAR—preparation, action, and reaction. His path to mastering the mental game encourages mindfulness meditation techniques that he claims to have acquired through disciplined training with the Tibetan Buddhist master Chögyam Trungpa Rinpoche. Awareness, breath, posture, and body scans are all recommended in the context of the wisdom and rhetoric of the lessons Parent learned in his Buddhist training.

Golfers are wont to rationalize their performance failures. The first tee in particular serves as the ground on which all excuses for the future inept flight of the ball are based. Ösel Tendzin, Chögyam Trungpa's American dharma heir, and Parent's teacher as well, offered this advice on complaining, as shared by Parent: "don't complain, about anything, not even to yourself" (2002, 14). Snippets of advice from the Shambhala tradition founded by Trungpa, and allegories that reference the eleventh-century Tibetan Buddhist meditation master Milarepa, serve as mini-introductions to the subsections of the book. Parent's work, lauded as "a roadmap to inner confidence [and] self-awareness," is endorsed by PGA professional Vijay Singh as "powerful—easy to comprehend and apply," the consummate text engaging the place where spirituality meets the swing (Parent 2002, back cover).

These books purport to show the golfer how to obtain a clear, calm, and focused mind in the service of the game of golf—and, in so doing, to become a competitive player. Ironically, it is Fred and Pete Shoemaker in *Extraordinary Golf* (1996) who address Zen the least, yet arguably deliver its principles the most. By stressing the idea of "extrospection," the Shoemakers suggest focusing attention on reality in order to develop awareness. On balance, the most important accomplishment is the mastery of time between shots—an estimated 95 percent of playing a round. They argue that golf requires one to rid oneself of presence. For example, the grip—the golfer's essential connection to the skill itself—which demands awareness of hand tension, should be absent from self-consciousness. It is the absence of self-consciousness regarding one's grip that makes it possible for one to cultivate one's awareness most completely. To play extraordinary golf by the Shoemakers's standards is to be purposeful *about* the game, rather than *at* the game. Purposefulness necessitates an absence of formulas and a presence of mind, asking *why* we play the game, not *how*.

Definitions: Lost Ball

My own thinking about the transmission and appropriation of Buddhism to sport is most influenced by Newman Robert Glass in *A Third Reading of Emptiness* (1995) and Brian Pronger in *Body Fascism* (2002), to which I now turn. Glass explores the workings of emptiness or nothingness; of affirmation, presence, or positive (co)dependent arising; and the workings of negation, difference, or negative (co)dependent arising. He argues for a third working of emptiness called "essence." He suggests that emptiness be approached through affect, emotion, force, or *desire*, not simply cognitively. Pronger's work, subtitled *Salvation in the Technology of Physical Fitness*, builds on Glass's notion of desire, and applies it more directly to fitness, health, and sport-related pursuits, urging that we pay attention to our own bodies:

This means heightening our awareness of how the body perceives the scripting discourses that we are using to understand and produce the [bodies' effects.] That is, it is a matter of trying to see the effects that our language—our scripting conventions in the technoculture of physical fitness—have on the body, from the perspective of *the body*. (Pronger 2002, 152)

The Nike phrase "just do it," or Chase's famous expression, "be the ball," hardly bring us closer to an enriched sense of sport as spiritual or religious practice. Pronger's and Glass's works take us to greater philosophical depths by drawing on the writings of Dōgen Kigen, the great Japanese Zen Master of the thirteenth century. In their view, *zazen*, drawing on the dichotomy of attachment/ non-attachment, offers a profound awareness of interdependence. Glass relays the Buddhist concept of "emptiness" as an awareness that arises from the movement of thinking to "pure non-thinking," which ultimately allows us to become attuned to and more accepting of impermanence, while Pronger strings together the project with a "drawing-penetrating-absence-presence of movement" (2002, 152). Glass describes this as "a shift from attachment to non-attachment through a specific practice of thinking understood here as the 'presencing' of all that is" (1995, 2).

Connecting all of this to golf, however, is difficult. Still, there is one consistent desire in golf that literally handicaps many recreational players. That is the desire to hit the ball—far! Being preoccupied with this desire leaves many golfers without a ball at all; at least once it takes leave on its flight path. I often tell beginning golf students, "do not become attached to your golf ball—ever." Why? Because eventually you will lose it, and a lost ball creates a very different opportunity, especially for others who eventually find it—in the water, behind a tree or a rock, under a leaf or organic debris—later on. Hence, your ball is no longer yours. This perceptual approach can be met by the more skilled and mindful golfers as they advance through the game and the stroke becomes more finely tuned. The ball itself then become an object of the flight path generated by a presence of movement absent attachment. That is, by being wholly present the golfer meets the ball at a state of rest. By virtue of the swing the golf ball will be moved into its flight path and again come to another state of rest, where the golfer re-presences himself or herself—in golfing parlance this is known as addressing the ball. It is this very act of repetition that challenges the golfer's sense of attachment and impermanence. Still, in the rules of golf one of the typical conundrums is the question of when is a ball deemed as lost.

While much popular psychology takes as its goal the strengthening of a sense of self, Buddhism has always advocated awakening *from* a sense of self, also in the service of mental health and optimum performance. In Pronger's view, this self-emptying allows desire to issue in physical movement in the context of that absence. Pronger describes this "openness without limits" where emptiness means *being* in "full alterity." He explains: "This compassionate desire is pure, unfettered love. In such love there is no abyss, no abjection, no fear, no loathing. Instead . . . a profound acceptance." Accordingly, this bodily practice, this movement, is "enlightened movement—the body of enlightenment, the body of ultimate reality—the practice of movement that is produced in compassionate, non-aggressive desire" (2002, 92).

Golfer as Universal Subject

Although the golf-enlightenment genre may offer a new *discourse* about golf, and may even produce better *golf*, what the genre does not do is explore its own roots. These texts use Zen, on the one hand, to make sense of the game of golf, but on the other hand, are silent about Zen's place in Western consciousness at large, with the consequence that the lessons expressed about golf are presented as decontextualized universal truths. That is, Zen attributions are often presented as if they emerged from within the newly refined awareness of the golfer as universal human subject. In Buddhist philosophy, for instance, the absence–presence (doing–being) dichotomy has been the subject of both ancient and current academic debate. At the most basic level, Zen's influence within and connection to Japan and to China is also hidden, occluding the cultural matrix in the context of which these ideas were formulated.

Any discussion of golf and Buddhist sensibilities is incomplete without some mention of Tiger Woods. Woods, the golfing phenomenon, has arguably "blitzed" the intense psychologizing of the game. In *The Chosen One* (2001), David Owen draws attention to Kultilda, Tiger's Thai mother, who allegedly "steeped him in the Buddhist tradition" in which she was raised. According to his father, Tiger's mother's spiritual teachings are what provide the athlete with the sense of mental peace and calm that steel him during competition. Tiger himself was quoted in a 1996 *Sports Illustrated* piece that he "liked Buddhism because it's a whole way of being and living. It's based on discipline and respect and personal responsibility" (Owen 1988). Golf culture listens to Tiger, and connects his greatness with his supposed Buddhism.

It remains to be seen whether the cultural hook of golf will yield a new Western variant of Buddhism's ancient enlightenment project. The texts of "Buddhist" golf show little engagement with the complexities of the many variations that arose as Buddhism traveled outward from India. Nor is there any mention of sutras or bodhisattvas, and only rarely of nirvāṇa. Nevertheless, golf has come to constitute a surprising bridge—facilitating, if problematically, the transmission of Buddhism to the West as well as its transformation in the West. While this interjection is not wholly bereft of Buddhist sensibilities, we must not be seduced into the view that golf constitutes the new vehicle to enlightenment. Tennis anyone?

Note

1. It is interesting that Michael Jordan's post-basketball career finds him an avid golfer playing to a 1.2 USGA handicap (see Bestrom et al. 2007). It is, however, impossible to know whether Jordan's natural athletic prowess, his training in Phil Jackson's philosophy, or a more intuitive love for the game led him to this level of play.

PART III

Transformation

CULTURAL ENCOUNTERS at their most productive spawn new interpretations, re-weightings, and novel alignments between ideas new and old. The transmission and translation of historically Buddhist ideas and practices into the North American and more broadly global context has produced just such a transformation of Buddhism in our time. As part of this transformative process, ideas previously nonexistent or at the periphery move to center stage; voices previously silent come to be heard, and the juxtaposition of different models of ways to live results in a rich hybridity of thought and practice.

A reassessment of the role of women in Buddhist communities is one instance of this transformation. Karma Lekshe Tsomo documents a fascinating tale of just such a transformation in the lives of Buddhist nuns accomplished through a circulation of ideas about what is possible for women from across the globe, integrating insights from traditional Buddhism and Western feminism. Transformations also occur when insights, texts, and practices from different cultures are joined and when each is revitalized in the process. Nalini Bhushan and Susan Darlington both explore the ways in which modern European ideas inflect and transform Buddhist theory and practice. Bhushan examines the contributions that psychoanalytic thought can make to Buddhist psychology. Darlington demonstrates that contemporary Thai Buddhism has incorporated important ideas from Western environmentalism. Mark Blum raises important questions about whether transformations of these kinds and of this magnitude deliver a Buddhism that is still recognizably Buddhist.

Transformation inevitably raises a fascinating complex of questions for the future of Buddhism. In a fundamental sense, Buddhism has always been about transformation: the transformation of an individual agent from ignorance to a state of enlightenment. These chapters demonstrate that Buddhism is not just an *agent* of transformation; as it is disseminated among diverse peoples and cultures, Buddhism itself is transformed as well.

CHAPTER 9

Global Exchange

Women in the Transmission and Transformation of Buddhism

KARMA LEKSHE TSOMO

D ESPITE ITS ASPIRATIONS to facilitate liberation and enlightenment for all, and despite the fact that enlightenment has no gender, gender inequalities have existed in Buddhist institutions throughout their history and remain prevalent in Buddhist societies today. In all Buddhist cultures, women have historically devoted themselves to preserving and transmitting Buddhist teachings and values, and they continue to do so. Only recently, however, have their contributions begun drawing the broader attention they deserve. Many argue that this attention is closely linked with the transmission of Buddhism to the West and the reciprocal impact of Western cultures and ideas on Buddhism.

As interest in Buddhism has grown rapidly in countries around the world, Asian and Western Buddhist feminists, practitioners, and scholars have increasingly become aware of the textual, historical, and institutional biases that have helped perpetuate these inequalities (Gross 1993; Paul 1985). As observers focus on gender issues across the Buddhist traditions, their gazes sometimes coincide and sometimes are refracted at different angles. To examine all the complex currents of feminist thought and their intersections with Asian Buddhist traditions is clearly too much to cover in a few pages. In this chapter, I simply trace a few of the major vectors of convergence, congruence, and divergence in women's perceptions of the global transmission and transformation of Buddhism.

In the last few decades, a global initiative to recognize and to encourage the contributions of Buddhist women has emerged and gathered remarkable momentum. The diverse, international nature of this movement has allowed for an unprecedented exchange of information about Buddhist women's experiences that transcends traditional boundaries and limitations. Buddhist women in dialogue are integrating theory and practice, art and activism. Students and teachers, lay practitioners and ordained, Theravāda and Mahāyāna, are learning to appreciate diverse traditions, perspectives, and reference points. Differences of language, culture, and Buddhist affiliation that have kept women isolated in their own environments until now are being transcended in a dynamic worldwide movement.[1] Parochial attitudes that have kept women in the shadows of Buddhist history are now being brought to light, examined, and reconsidered. Buddhist women's diversity, which once seemed like a colorful but nearly insurmountable barrier to interethnic communication and understanding, is being reworked into a vibrant tapestry of unifying strength. Buddhists of all descriptions are increasingly being challenged to expand their thinking and to reevaluate the traditional subordination of women. Patriarchal preconceptions and structures are giving way to new, inclusive ideals and ways of working that are changing the way Buddhism is understood and practiced, both locally and globally. A new revaluing of women, incorporating and drawing strength from both Buddhist and feminist values, is one of the most visible and significant features of the current global transformation of Buddhism.

Since becoming a Buddhist nun in 1977, I have traveled to many monasteries and dharma centers throughout the world. On these travels, I have been fortunate to observe the lives of Buddhist women and to learn more about their experiences, the choices they have made, their sources of inspiration, and the difficulties they encountered along the way. The experiences and concerns of Buddhist women in Asia are often quite different from those of Buddhist women in North America. There are also significant differences among the experiences and concerns of Asian, Asian American, and non-Asian Buddhist women living in North America. Most generally, Asian Buddhist women are concerned with subsistence, education, healthcare, and preserving their Buddhist heritage; Asian American Buddhist women are concerned with juggling their careers, families, and cultural values; and non-Asian Buddhist women are concerned with meditation, gender issues, and social justice.

Women Transmitting and Transforming Buddhism in the West

Since the earliest transmission of Buddhism to North America, women have made indispensable contributions. Applying their skills in organizing, teaching, translating, communicating, fund-raising, cooking, cleaning, and all the essential tasks needed to establish and maintain Buddhist centers, they have worked tirelessly to create opportunities for others to learn and practice the Buddhadharma. Since the 1960s in particular, their discipline and dedication have established a solid foundation for the future growth of Buddhism in North America. As in Asia, Buddhist women have worked ceaselessly for the dharma and the welfare of others, often behind the scenes. Nuns, laywomen, and women who self-identify as neither lay nor ordained[2] have founded and supported countless Buddhist centers. Even though women often work in supportive roles within patriarchal frameworks and some centers continue to favor male teachers from Asia, where men are privileged in education and training, Buddhist women's leadership and contributions are becoming increasingly prominent, in both North America and Asia.[3] Gradually, women have begun to take on teaching and leadership roles that are transforming traditional attitudes toward women's spiritual capabilities and status within Buddhist institutions. Buddhist women's voices are reaching beyond their communities and becoming part of a new global discourse. The American *bhikṣuṇī* Pema Chödrön has appeared on television with Oprah Winfrey and Bill Moyers, and her book *When Things Fall Apart* is a staple among Oprah's Book Club fans.

During the past twenty years in all these Buddhist communities, a trend toward greater visibility, independence, recognition, and equity for women has begun to emerge. One example is that, in their struggle for economic survival and adjustment to American life, Asian immigrant women have been assuming new roles that reflect changes in traditional assumptions about gender. With higher standards of education and greater economic sufficiency, some have begun to question the supportive roles that women traditionally play and to take leadership positions in Buddhist temples. Internationally, as women become better educated, financially independent, and socially mobile, many begin to reevaluate gender stereotypes, pollution taboos, educational inequalities, and discriminatory passages in Buddhist texts. They especially begin to question their subservience and to address the legacy of neglect and subordination of Buddhist nuns.

The transmission and transformation of Buddhism to the West is integrally related to developments in Asian Buddhism in recent history. Although Buddhist traditions interacted and co-mingled during the early centuries of Buddhist development in India, in subsequent centuries the Buddhist traditions developed distinct identities, with relatively little interaction among them. All that began to change in the 1960s when Buddhism attracted the notice of a new countercultural generation of Americans seeking alternatives to war, consumerism, and organized religion. Unencumbered by inherited loyalties to specific Buddhist traditions, those whose interest was piqued by Buddhist thought were free to explore a wide variety of philosophical approaches and spiritual practices. In a process that transcended specific traditions, they explored Zen, *vipassanā*, Tibetan, and other Buddhist practice styles, consciously selecting compatible elements and rejecting others. This pan-Buddhist approach is visible in the teaching styles of prominent Western Buddhist teachers who draw from many Buddhist traditions (Gross 1999).[4] Many Buddhist centers open their doors to teachers from different traditions and seem eager to learn from them. Theravadin practitioners learn Tibetan *tong-len* ("taking and sending" meditation) and Tibetans learn *vipassanā* ("insight" meditation), through the mediation of Western practitioners.

Among the ideas circulating back to Asia from the West is a reassessment of traditional attitudes toward women. The idea that women have bad karma and can redeem themselves primarily through generosity is starting to be seriously questioned. The customary practice of grown women bowing at the feet of young novice monks is beginning to appear a bit odd. Just as Buddhism has enriched the lives of countless women in the westward Buddhist diaspora, women's voices are beginning to influence traditional Buddhist attitudes and assumptions. These reciprocal influences, both subtle and overt, are widespread and very influential in the rethinking, repackaging, and reformulation of Buddhism in the global community.

Transmission and Transformation of Asian Buddhism

The dismal situation of Buddhist nuns was the catalyst for the creation and growth of Sakyadhita, the first active international organization of Buddhist women. At the time of the Buddha, thousands of women reportedly left household life, became *bhikṣuṇīs* (fully ordained nuns), and achieved liberation (*nirvāṇa*). In the ensuing centuries, however, patriarchal domination reasserted itself, leaving nuns on the margins of most Buddhist societies, largely undernourished and uneducated (Roth 1970).[5] By 1987, the dire circumstances of nuns became the theme of the first international conference on Buddhist women, held in Bodhgaya, India.[6] Gathering strength, Buddhist nuns, laywomen, and their allies formed a worldwide alliance called Sakyadhita International Association of Buddhist Women. This alliance of women dedicated to peace and justice has helped expand women's vision of themselves as full participants in a global revival of interest in ancient Buddhist teachings.

Inspired by this global consortium, many women have begun to teach, translate, build monasteries and retreat centers, initiate community service projects, seek ordination, go into intensive retreats, and pursue higher education. The multicultural exchanges at bi-annual international conferences have given women an appreciation for all Buddhist traditions and other religious perspectives. At the first Sakyadhita conference in 1987, a group of sixteen Sri Lankan laywomen and nuns gathered the determination to revive their country's own legacy of full ordination for nuns after a lapse of nearly a thousand years; within twenty years, their aspiration had virtually been accomplished (De Silva 2004; Goonatilake 2006; Wijayasundara 1999). After discussing the importance of education for Buddhist women at the same conference, Tibetan women began intensive studies of philosophy and debate, a scholastic tradition previously dominated by men. After twenty years of study, some will soon be eligible to receive the *geshe* degree, an historical breakthrough for women.

The networks of friendship and scholarship that have developed out of the Buddhist women's movement are models of transnational collaboration, Buddhist ecumenism, and interreligious understanding. Many of the conceptual boundaries that previously existed between Buddhist women have dissolved. Buddhist women's cooperation has expanded far beyond the conferences and also beyond Buddhism, to global interfaith and development initiatives.[7] By creating a global forum for Buddhist women, Sakyadhita has not only given women a forum for expressing their concerns but also has drawn international attention to the history, development, and needs of Buddhist women, heretofore frequently missing (and dismissed) in feminist discourse, Buddhist institutions, and global development forums. The emergence of Buddhist women as a dynamic global force—active both in the transmission and transformation of Buddhism and in the transformation of attitudes toward women and attitudes of Buddhist women toward themselves—exemplifies the complex and multidimensional flow of influences between Asia and the West.

One of the most important ways that women are influencing Buddhism is their persistent questioning and critique of gender discrimination. Buddhism is attractive to many Western converts because it promotes universal values such as compassion and wisdom above identity loyalties and dogmatism. After closer contact with Buddhist traditions, however, many discover the inconvenient fact that, although women in Buddhist societies enjoy considerable social freedom, they are not fully included in Buddhist institutions, and many Buddhist women lack even basic religious freedoms. Not only are most archetypes of enlightenment and most Buddhist teachers male, but decision-making power within most monasteries and Buddhist organizations is also generally concentrated in male hands.

The late twentieth-century phase in the internationalization of Buddhism brought many women to a new awareness of their own identity. Meditation helped women to transform destructive habits, such as self-deprecation, and to cope more effectively with stress, anger, disappointment, and loss. As women from Asia and the West became linked through Buddhist practice, they shared their feminist insights, becoming more aware of the gender discrimination that still subverts an ideologically egalitarian tradition. As the realization of gender discrimination in Buddhist institutions dawned, and after working through their disillusionment and discomfort, many women began to discover a new sense of their own identity as Buddhist women. In formal and informal circles, they began to forge new alliances that unite women across boundaries of class, education, and experience, and to work toward correcting gender disparities in Buddhism. Gradually, with Buddhist and feminist insights flowing in both directions, a dynamic international Buddhist women's movement emerged and continues to thrive.

Although Buddhist perspectives and feminist perspectives spring from different sources and employ different methodologies, they share much common ground. Both recognize the importance of self-understanding and the fallacies inherent in essentializing identities. The Buddhist ideal of liberation from cyclic existence and the feminist ideal of liberation from gender injustice differ in scope, but they do share a common concern to alleviate the sufferings of the world, especially those of the disadvantaged and oppressed. Like the feminist movement, the Buddhist women's movement encourages women's leadership, scholarship, spiritual growth, and creativity. Buddhist feminist awareness is expanding and maturing naturally, taking its own unique form, and gradually influencing Buddhist institutions.

Buddhist Monastic Life for Women

When I was a young woman, I wanted to be a monk. It took years of reflection before I began to question why the terms "monk" and "nun" elicit such different responses in me, and why the image of a monk conjured up such a different, more attractive image in my mind. The life of a nun is not easy and the low status of nuns in many Buddhist societies makes ordination a difficult choice for women. In contrast to monks, who are quite universally respected, supported, and even revered, nuns often experience hardships and humiliation. Before 1987, nuns in Sri Lanka were often viewed as little more than beggars; in Thailand they were viewed as laity in the garb of nuns. Even in Taiwan, where the status of nuns is relatively high, nuns routinely address one another by highly esteemed male relationship terms (Chang 2008; Winklemann 2008).[8] In the Tibetan tradition, even after decades of dialogue, the monastic hierarchy still has not agreed to establish a *bhikṣuṇī* sangha. Although the idea of a man wanting to be called a nun is unimaginable, some American women happily call themselves monks. When questioned, they say that "monk" is a generic term for a monastic, rather like saying that "mankind" describes all of humanity. In time, after years of discovering and questioning my sexist conditioning, I became reconciled to my identity as a woman and a nun and wholeheartedly embraced it.

Today, women are influencing Buddhism in part through their interest in monastic practice. It is said that Buddhism is only really established in a land when the monastic sangha is firmly established, and there is still much work to be done to establish Buddhist monasticism in North America. The City of Ten Thousand Buddhas, Shasta Abbey, and Tassajara Monastery, three monasteries in California, typify the diversity of approaches to monastic practice found in small, widely dispersed monastic communities across the continent.

In Buddhist societies, monasteries are the principal sites for the study and practice of the Buddha's teachings. Monasteries are considered zones of safety, because observing the Vinaya (monastic discipline) helps one develop mindfulness and guard against moral transgressions. Historically, Buddhist monasteries have provided a safe environment for women to receive an education and engage in spiritual practice without worries about personal appearance, family responsibilities, romantic entanglements, and sexual exploitation.

Here I use the English terms "ordination" and "nun" for the sake of convenience, but such use requires explanation as the terms they translate have different connotations in a Buddhist context than they do in a Christian context. A Buddhist nun or monk does not preside over sacraments and does not necessarily perform ritual functions. The first step in becoming a Buddhist nun is the "going forth" (*pravrajya*) or "leaving the household life." According to tradition, she subsequently receives three levels of ordination: the ten precepts of a novice nun (*śrāmanerikā*),[9] the precepts of a probationary nun (*śiksamānā*), and eventually the more than three hundred precepts of a fully ordained nun (*bhiksunī*). A monk receives the same ten precepts of a novice and is known as a *śrāmanera*, then receives the two hundred–plus precepts of a fully ordained monk (*bhiksu*). The English term "nun" can also be used to denote a celibate female Buddhist who observes eight, nine, or ten precepts without belonging to any of these traditional categories.

The rules and procedures that govern the sangha are contained in the Vinaya, the texts of monastic discipline. The three rites of the sangha that are essential for Buddhist monastic life: (1) full ordination (*upasampadā*); (2) the bi-monthly recitation of the *Prātimoksa Sūtra,* which contains the monastic precepts (*uposadha*); and (3) the assembly held at the end of the three-month rainy season retreat (*pravāranā*). The rite of full ordination for monks requires the presence of ten *bhiksu* precept masters (five in a remote area), whereas the rite of full ordination for nuns requires the presence of both ten *bhiksu* and ten *bhiksunī* precept masters.[10]

The advantages of monastic ordination can be understood by citing some of the reasons for observing the precepts: (1) the precepts support the practice of mindfulness and alertness in everyday actions; (2) the precepts support the development of renunciation by limiting the number of possessions monastics may keep; (3) the precepts prevent monastics from becoming overly involved in worldly affairs, to limit distractions and allow more time for mental development; (4) the precepts help foster respect for others; (5) the precepts provide a standard of deportment that inspires the respect and support of the lay community; and (6) the precepts encourage the restraint of the senses, which is necessary for achieving liberation. Additional advantages to monastic ordination include: (1) by living in a supportive community of like-minded practitioners, monastics are protected from certain worldly temptations; (2) because the laity provides them with material requisites, monastics are free from having to make a living and therefore have more time for mental cultivation; (3) because monastics are celibate, they are free from the responsibilities and distractions of family life; and (4) because monastics have opted out of worldly life, they are free from ordinary societal obligations.

The ordination of Buddhist nuns began during the Buddha's lifetime, over 2,500 years ago. When his aunt and stepmother Mahāprajāpatī requested permission to join the monastic order, the Buddha is said to have hesitated at first, given the patriarchal social climate of the time. But when questioned about women's ability to achieve the fruits of Buddhist practice, he agreed that women had equal potential to purify their minds and achieve liberation (nirvāṇa). This affirmation marked the beginning of the order of Buddhist nuns (bhikṣuṇī sangha) that flourished under Mahāprajāpatī's leadership and continued to exist in India for some fifteen hundred years.

From India, King Ashoka's daughter Sanghamitra took the lineage to Sri Lanka in the fourth century B.C.E. In the fifth century C.E., the Sri Lankan nun Devasara took the lineage to China and from there it spread to Korea, Vietnam, and Taiwan. Tens of thousands of fully ordained bhikṣuṇīs continue to practice in these countries. In the early years, monastics lived a wandering lifestyle. Even today, the ordination rite begins with the formula of the four reliances: relying on alms for food, rags for clothing, trees for shelter, and cow dung and urine for medicine. Gradually, the Buddha agreed that the nuns and monks could accept invitations to meals, donations of robes, more permanent shelter, and additional medicines. Because of instances of sexual assault against nuns, the Buddha observed that it was not safe for them to take shelter in the forest and instead allowed them to stay in vihāras (monastic dwellings) or temporarily with families. Over time, Buddhist nuns and monks began to settle into monastic communities, usually located near a town or village where they could go for their daily alms round. Today, most Buddhist nuns in the world live in monasteries. Some live alone, however, in solitary retreat, or in small retreat communities.

As Buddhism spread throughout Asia, communities of fully ordained monks were established and thrived, but communities of nuns were not always established alongside them. There is no conclusive evidence that the lineage of full ordination for women was ever established in Cambodia, Laos, Mongolia, Thailand, or Tibet, for example, though there is inscriptional evidence of a *bhikṣuṇī* sangha in Burma. The *bhikṣuṇī* sangha died out in India, Nepal, and Sri Lanka around the eleventh century C.E., but it has been reintroduced in the last twenty years with the help of *bhikṣuṇī*s from Korea and Taiwan. A vibrant international movement to institute full ordination for women in all Buddhist societies is now underway (Tsomo 2004).

Women's Ordination Rites and Rights

Age-old patriarchal patterns have been replicated in the sangha, despite the fact that there is no philosophical justification for male dominance in the Buddhist monastic community. Given a new global ethic of respect for human rights and the fundamental Buddhist principle that the dharma and its fruits are accessible to all, regardless of gender, the legislation of subordinate status for any group must be seriously questioned. Feminist textual analysis of the Vinaya, similar to feminist theologians' textual analysis of the Bible, may be the next frontier in Buddhist studies.

The dual ordination procedure for nuns is enshrined in the eight special rules (*gurudharmas*) that Mahāprajāpatī purportedly accepted in exchange for her admission to the sangha. These eight special rules vary among different schools of Vinaya, and their historicity is anything but clear (Kusuma 2000).[11] They stipulate the nuns' dependence on the order of monks in such important matters as ordination, instruction, and reinstatement, despite the fact that nuns' communities generally function independently of monks' communities. The first *gurudharma*, which requires even the most senior *bhikṣuṇī* to bow to a brand-new *bhikṣu,* is particularly grating to the sensibilities of women raised with ideals of gender equity. Although it is likely that the *gurudharmas* were instituted considerably after the lifetime of the Buddha, they remain as socially sanctioned protocols in Buddhist traditions. Even if it could be established that Mahāprajāpatī agreed to abide by these rules, it is still far from clear that all *bhikṣuṇī*s up to the present day should be obligated to follow them. This is relevant today, because if renunciant women are obligated to follow a set of ancient protocols that clearly discriminate against women,

Westerners are likely to reject Buddhist monasticism as archaic, sexist, and hypocritical.

Today Buddhist nuns living in numerous countries throughout the world attempt to abide by codes of monastic discipline formulated in ancient India, while simultaneously adapting to local etiquette and contemporary cultural mores. Even in the most traditional Buddhist settings, it is difficult for nuns today to live on alms alone and to adhere strictly to all the precepts. At present, especially from the standpoint of Western women, the most obvious discrepancy between orthodox Vinaya practice and the needs of modernity is the lack of full ordination for women in certain Buddhist traditions. It is therefore clear that Vinaya and modernity require mutual accommodation. Although women have access to full ordination in the Chinese, Korean, Taiwanese, and Vietnamese traditions, they currently have access to only novice ordination in the Tibetan tradition. In the Burmese, Cambodian, Lao, and Thai traditions, although tens of thousands of women shave their heads, don monastic robes, and receive eight or nine precepts, they do not have access even to novice (*sramanerika*) ordination; in fact, they are ordinarily regarded as Buddhist laywomen (*upāsikās*) living like nuns.

Since 1987, Sakyadhita International Association of Buddhist Women has campaigned continuously for gender equity, especially with respect to education and ordination. Inspired by Sakyadhita's biennial international conferences and grassroots social activism, Buddhist women have begun to work toward making full ordination available in all Buddhist traditions. It is possible, however, for nuns to receive ordination from *bhikṣuṇī*s of another tradition.

The first breakthrough came in 1988 when the Nepalese nun Dhammavati and two of her disciples received full *bhikṣuṇī* ordination in a ceremony conducted at Hsi Lai Temple in Los Angeles (LeVine and Gellner 2005). The second breakthrough came in 1996 when Kusuma Devendra and nine other nuns from Sri Lanka became *bhikṣuṇī*s at a ceremony conducted in Sarnath, India (De Silva 2004; Li 2000). Another twenty Sri Lankan nuns received full ordination in 1996 at a ceremony conducted in Bodhgaya, India. Since then, Sri Lankan *bhikṣu*s have presided over numerous full ordination ceremonies for hundreds of Sri Lankan nuns. Nuns from Burma, Indonesia, Thailand, and other countries have also been ordained in these ceremonies.

Progress toward achieving full ordination for women in the Tibetan tradition has been slow. A few nuns of the Tibetan tradition have received full ordination from other traditions, but their ordination is not officially recognized and these nuns have not been able to institute a *bhikṣuṇī* lineage within the

Tibetan tradition as a whole. His Holiness the 14th Dalai Lama has repeatedly expressed his support for the full ordination for women, but states that such a decision must be made by a council of senior *bhikṣus* and cannot be taken by him alone. Senior Western *bhikṣunī*s practicing in the Tibetan tradition have formed a Committee of Western Bhiksunis to research ways to institute the *bhikṣunī* lineage and to answer the objections of those who oppose it. These nuns have traveled to Hong Kong, Korea, and Taiwan to receive full ordination and are concerned with opening up opportunities for nuns who may find it difficult to travel to foreign countries and prefer to receive ordination within the Tibetan tradition.

The reluctance to institute *bhikṣunī* ordination in the Tibetan tradition is based on two premises. The first is a doubt about the origin of the *bhikṣunī* lineage practiced in China, Korea, Taiwan, and Vietnam, and whether the lineage has been transmitted uninterruptedly since the time of Mahāprajāpatī. This objection has now been resolved by the discovery of texts that document the unbroken continuity of the *bhikṣunī* lineage in China.[12] The second issue concerns the method of conducting the full ordination in traditions that have no living *bhikṣunī* lineage. The Theravāda[13] and Tibetan Buddhist traditions have preserved the *bhikṣunī* Vinaya texts but do not have living *bhikṣunī*s in their own traditions to conduct ordinations. Therefore, the question is which method of conducting the *bhikṣunī* ordination is preferable and most likely to be considered valid: (1) by *bhikṣus* alone; (2) by *bhikṣus* and *bhikṣunī*s who all belong to the Chinese, Korean, or Vietnamese traditions; or (3) by *bhikṣus* and *bhikṣunī*s who belong to different Vinaya traditions (e.g., Tibetan *bhikṣus* together with *bhikṣunī*s ordained in the Chinese, Korean, or Vietnamese traditions). The third procedure was used to restore the *bhikṣunī* sangha in Sri Lanka, with subsequent ordinations conducted by Sri Lanka *bhikṣus* and *bhikṣunī*s.

Buddhist feminists around the world have worked to find a mutually acceptable solution to this dilemma. The lack of equal opportunities for women to receive full ordination contradicts Buddhism's claim that men and women have equal capacity and equal opportunity for spiritual practice and progress. As long as women in some Buddhist traditions lack access to full ordination, they lack the optimal conditions for fulfilling their ultimate potential. As long as Buddhist women anywhere remain deprived of opportunities for personal and spiritual development, then Buddhist women overall can be said to be deprived.

Directions of Transmission and Transformation

It is often taken for granted that all the impetus for improving the status of Buddhist women is coming from the West, as if women elsewhere were incapable of recognizing inequalities and oppression. The assumption that feminist awareness is a Western invention to be gifted or imposed on women in other parts of the world is patronizing, inaccurate, and evidence of a Eurocentric bias that has no place in feminist discourse. The daring initiative of the Buddha and Mahāprajāpatī in founding an order in which women participated fully with men is a liberating narrative in Buddhist societies. Women across time and cultures have had their own, often very sophisticated, ways of expressing resistance to gender injustice. At the same time, it would be naïve to ignore the fact that liberative ideologies have accelerated feminist awareness throughout the world in recent decades and given rise to many streams of feminist thought. The picture is hence more complex than is often assumed.

Westerners are importing a Buddhist tradition that was very liberating for women in the fifth century BCE South Asian context, but nevertheless does contain patriarchal, sometimes sexist, elements that were taken for granted in that context but are at odds with twentieth-century North American liberal sensibilities. When American Buddhists speak out against gender discrimination in Buddhist liturgy and social praxis, Asian teachers who may at first be incredulous often come to recognize the sheer hypocrisy of these internal contradictions. With those insights, many gradually become forces for changing attitudes toward women and other gender minorities, at least in the West.

On the one hand, whether female or male, it requires concerted discipline to live a dedicated celibate life in a society that places great value on seeking pleasure. On the other hand, Buddhist monastic life provides a refuge from stereotypical gender expectations and an alternate to the distractions, temptations, and anxieties of a consumer society. Being outside the mainstream of contemporary life provides many opportunities to develop patience, humility, wisdom, and compassion. Even if only a small percentage of Buddhists are inclined toward ordination, the monastic ideal is a powerful symbol of wholehearted commitment to the Buddhist path and one that should not be limited by gender.

Buddhist women in North America run the gamut, from mothers, corporate executives, self-styled visionary Vajrayāna *yoginī*s, to celibate nuns. For some, the Buddhist teachings are a source of wisdom for skillful parenting (Conover 2001; Desmond 2004; Miller 2006; Napthali 2008); for others, the teachings are practical methods for coping with everyday challenges and relationship distress. For some, an interest in Buddhism solves riddles about the mysteries of life; for others, interest developed tangentially from an interest in political issues, such as the campaign for a free Tibet. In some ways, the symbiotic relationship between Tibetan refugees and their Western donors and fund-raisers can be used to illustrate the reciprocal flow of Buddhist influences from Asia westward and back. As the plight of Tibetan political exiles in India and Nepal captured the world's attention after the Chinese communist takeover of Tibet in 1959, many Western sympathizers, especially women, began to sponsor Tibetan refugee children and monastics. An interest in the Tibetan cause led to admiration for H. H. Dalai Lama and often to an appreciation of spirituality and to Tibetan Buddhist culture especially. The Western fascination with Buddhism has awakened some Asian youth to a renewed appreciation for their own cultural heritages. Mutually beneficial reciprocal influences between Asia and the West extend to politics, food choices, music, and gender issues.

Women in North America who are interested in Buddhism have been influenced by a new global ethic of gender equality, and many recognize a resonance between the Buddhist teachings and their own values. Having grown up with roughly equal educational opportunities, they apply themselves to the study and practice of Buddhism as ably as men. In fact, Asian Buddhist teachers who live and teach in the West are often supported in their endeavors by the skills and dedication of women. Gradually, many of these teachers are able to cut through their own sexist conditioning and develop a more appreciative attitude toward women. They develop a more egalitarian style of teaching, consciously or unconsciously, and begin to realize the resonance between gender equity and the Buddhist teachings. In these ways and many others, Buddhist and feminist ideas and influences flow back and forth between Asia and the West, with benefits both for women and for Buddhist societies.

Buddhist women have become the topic of numerous university courses, research projects, and conferences. Through their research on Asian Buddhist women's history and practice, North American scholars have begun to document, affirm, and spark a transformation in both their subjects' self-perception and their own. These research projects not only contribute to scholarship on Buddhist women but also to intercultural awareness and solidarity among women. Buddhist women have been active participants in interreligious dialogue among Hindu, Christian, Jewish, and Muslim women. Women are increasingly being included in international interreligious gatherings that were hitherto almost exclusively male.[14] Both formally and informally, Buddhist women are taking their places alongside their Catholic sisters at such gatherings as the Interfaith Alliance, Monastic Interreligious Dialogue,[15] and the Women, Faith, and Development Alliance. Meetings between women scholars, and practitioners of the world's religions have sparked dialogue on such quintessential topics as suffering, monasticism, and family. The movement for full ordination has sparked dialogue among women of diverse Buddhist traditions and is a prime example of global transmission and reciprocity.

There is still much work to be done to understand and document the intersections between Buddhism and feminism in the current global transmission of Buddhism. One of the most striking features of the global exchange is changing attitudes toward women. Certainly, women will continue to be visible, active, and vital in its transformation.

Notes

1. Nuns such as Bhiksuni Cheng Yen from Taiwan, Bhikkhuni Dhammananda from Thailand, Bhikkhuni Kusuma from Sri Lanka, Bhikkhuni Molini from Burma, and Dhammavijaya from Nepal inspire and activate others around the world through their Buddhist practice and community development work.

2. The term "neither lay nor ordained" is used variously to describe married clerics in Japan, *ngakpa*s in Tibet, *anagārikā*s and *yogi*s in Theravāda countries, and holders of *bodhisattva* precepts in American Zen centers. In any sense, the term challenges the traditional assumption that serious Buddhist practitioners are celibate monastics.

3. Among the numerous prominent Buddhist women teaching in North America today are Tsultrim Allione, Jan Chosen Bays, Charlotte Joko Beck, Sylvia Boorstein, Pema Chödrön, Thubten Chodron, Ruth Denison, Karuna Dharma, Christina Feldman, Joan Jiko Halifax, Zenkei Blanche Hartman, Seong Hyang (Barbara Rhodes), Chan Khong, Anne Carolyn Klein, Chimey Luding, Wendy Egyoku Nakao, Enkyo Pat O'Hara, Tenzin Palmo, Susan Ji-on Postal, Yvonne Rand, Khandro Rinpoche, Marcia Rose, Sharon Salzberg, and Yeshe Wangmo. Among the pioneering women teachers who have already passed away are Gesshin Prabhasa Dharma, Ayya Khema, Khechog Palmo, and Jiyu-Kenneth Roshi. The names of prominent Buddhist women teaching in Asia today would fill a book.

4. For example, Joseph Goldstein, an American who teaches *vipassanā* meditation from the Burmese tradition, also explored *Dzokchen* and understands both systems as skillful means rather than as statements of absolute truth.

5. The neglect and derision of nuns has a long history. At the time of the Buddha, in addition to "harlot," a frequent term of abuse was "daughter of a witch" (*iti-kitikaya dhitam*).

6. Sakyadhita International Conferences have been held in Bodhgaya (1987), Bangkok (1991), Colombo (1993), Ladakh (1995), Phnom Penh (1998), Lumbini (2000), Taipei (2002), Seoul (2004), Kuala Lumpur (2006), and Ulaanbaatar (2008). These conferences have been the starting point for a series of anthologies on Buddhist women.

7. Sakyadhita was represented at the UNIFEM conference in Helsinki in 2007 and at Breakthrough: The Women, Faith and Development Summit to End Global Poverty held at the National Cathedral in Washington, DC, in 2008.

8. Carole Winklemann explores the linguistic strategies Himalayan nuns use to negotiate their increasing feminist awareness in the context of cultural survival.

9. The ten precepts of a novice Buddhist nun or monk are to abstain from: (1) taking life; (2) taking what is not given; (3) sexual intercourse; (4) lying; (5) taking intoxicants; (6) wearing ornaments or cosmetics; (7) singing or dancing; (8) sitting on high or luxurious seats or beds; (9) accepting gold or silver; and (10) taking untimely food.

10. Twelve precepts masters are required in the Mūlasarvāstivādin tradition practiced by Tibetans.

11. See Bhikkhun Kusuma (2000), in which she discusses the inconsistencies inherent in these rules. Her research demonstrates that the eight *gurudharma*s are almost certainly later interpolations.

12. The Chinese *bhikṣuṇī* lineage from 357–511 C.E. is documented in the *Pi-chiu-ni chuan* (*Biographies of Bhikṣuṇīs*). The lineage from 512–1930 C.E. is documented in the *Hsu Pi-chiu-ni chuan* (*Sequel Biographies of Bhikṣuṇīs*). These two texts are included together in the *Pi-chiu-ni chuan-shu* (*Complete Biographies of Bhikṣuṇīs*) (Taipei: Fo-chiao Publications, 1988). Because this is the lineage of full ordination for women that was subsequently transmitted to Korea, Taiwan, and Vietnam, and because it is the only *bhikṣuṇī* lineage available to Buddhist nuns today, the matter of establishing its unbroken continuity in China is critically significant.

13. The Theravāda tradition relies on the Pāli canon. Theravāda Buddhist countries include Burma, Cambodia, Laos, Thailand, and Sri Lanka. Theravāda communities are also found in Bangladesh, China, India, Indonesia, Malaysia, Nepal, and Vietnam.

14. The World Day of Prayer (October 27, 1986) and the Day of Prayer for Peace (January 24, 2002), both convened by Pope John Paul II in Assisi Assisi, Italy, were laudable efforts to unite followers of the world's faiths. As usual, however, women filled the pews rather than the stage. Considering the backlash that resulted from the pope's efforts to foster interreligious understanding, the muted presence of women is not surprising. As an extreme example, Archbishop Lefebvre, Emeritus Bishop-Archbishop of Tulle, regarded the 1986 gathering as "a public sin," accusing the pope of ruining the church and of making a mockery of the creed. *Si Si No No*, Society of St. Pius X, District of Asia, February 2002, No. 45. In response to charges of blasphemy and the claim (by Cardinal Kasper, among others) that "Christians cannot pray with members of other religions" (*Osservatore Romano*, January 5, 2002), religious representatives prayed in separate rooms at the 2002 gathering, rather than together.

15. I vividly remember the Monastic Interreligious Dialogue, an ongoing exchange program between Benedictine Catholics and Tibetan Buddhists that occurred in Dharamsala in 1988. The Benedictine team consisted of three nuns and three monks, whereas the Tibetan side was represented by eighty monks at the Institute of Buddhist Dialectics. When I was summoned to provide hospitality to the nuns, we immediately recognized our solidarity and conspiratorially set about comparing the prospects for the ordination of women in our respective traditions. After expressing both despair and faint rays of hope, the Benedictine nuns asked why no Tibetan nuns had been included in the dialogue, and I recommended they take up the question in their audience with H. H. Dalai Lama. Thereafter, nuns and nunneries became full participants in the exchange.

CHAPTER 10

Toward an Anatomy of Mourning

Discipline, Devotion, and Liberation in a Freudian-Buddhist Framework

Nalini Bhushan

Freud's "Mourning and Melancholia" (1917) articulates an influential and persuasive psychoanalytic model of mourning that renders comprehensible, rational, and indeed, gives shape, to one form of human suffering, that borne of tragic loss, the death of one's beloved. Freud invites us to conceive, in interestingly novel ways, of the mental and physical process of profound mourning as *disciplined*. His introduction of the concept of discipline into the raw existential experience of profound mourning is fascinating in itself. This discipline, which gives shape to the mourning process, and makes possible a rare species of devotion, is indispensable for the sufferer's eventual liberation.

This eventual freedom from suffering is itself secured by an initial, and more circumscribed freedom in a different domain—one that makes possible attachment to the dead beloved. But this secured freedom to love one's dead beloved, in turn, and almost paradoxically, frees the mourner from the grip of the love object and facilitates her return to the realm of reality. This realm, according to Freud, is the realm of the living. The ways in which the model articulates and justifies these connections between discipline, devotion, and the different domains of freedom will occupy my attention throughout the chapter.

I juxtapose Freud's analytical model of mourning with a Buddhist folk tale that centers on the suffering of a young woman named Kisagotami as she experiences and comes to terms with the death of her only child. Traditional interpretations of this tale use it to elucidate elements of Buddhist psychology and morality. In particular, the story of Kisagotami showcases the familiar Buddhist accounts of the road from ignorance to enlightenment, the universality of suffering, the possibility of liberation from suffering, and ends, also in a familiar way, with a moral lesson from the Buddha concerning the need to shed an egocentric perspective on one's own suffering.

As I attend to this narrative, I'm interested in part in extracting for discussion just these ideas regarding the path from bondage to liberation, and from ignorance to enlightenment. These ideas are at the heart of Buddhist theory and practice. But I'm also interested in taking a closer look at the nature of Kisagotami's existential crisis and at the procedural character of her mourning, and to examine these both from first- and third-person perspectives. This will underscore mourning's inextricably public and social dimensions. I argue that keeping the focus on *what it is like* for Kisagotami in turn allows a reader to take in the tale in a qualitatively different way. For it forces us to take a second, more critical look at the assumptions about the kinds of epistemic ignorance and moral deficiency that Kisagotami is often taken to embody that both cause and constitute her suffering in many standard accounts of the story.

Simultaneously critical of and fortified by both the Freudian and traditionally Buddhist accounts of the place and significance of mourning, I select from each of them ingredients for a composite mental model that appropriates vocabulary from each in order to explain the phenomenological and procedural character of the psycho-physical-social state of mourning and its place in the life of the grieving individual. Along the way I raise questions for both traditions: What assumptions ground Freud's account of a non-pathological response to this kind of suffering and of the state of mind that represents the cessation of such suffering? *Is* preoccupation with the dead beloved a way of escaping the fact that the person is *dead*? Or could it be a distinctly non-escapist acknowledgment of the continued presence of the dead beloved? Are the Buddhists quite right to characterize this preoccupation as a form of moral deficiency, based on ignorance? Instead, and depending on the uses that they serve, might it be appropriate to interpret some manifestations of "ignorance" as manifestations of "knowing"? Or, to judge some sources of ignorance as more knowledge-conducive than others? Might certain forms and contexts of ignorance in effect put one on a path to enlightenment?

Freud's Account of Mourning and Health

"Profound mourning," says Freud, is characterized by

    (a) an excruciatingly painful feeling;
    (b) a relinquishing of any interest in the outside world except as it serves to recall the dead person;

(c) an inability to care for a new love object;

(d) a relinquishing of any activity that does not connect with the dead beloved in some way. ("Mourning and Melancholia," 162)

We have here the kernel of the idea of welding rational and emotional processes in the context of excruciating psychological pain caused by the death of the beloved. This welding results in a striking instance of psychological and physical discipline, as the mourner, both physically and emotionally, gives up all connections to people, places, and activities unrelated to the beloved. Given that healthy people are naturally drawn to seek such connection, a coherent, sustained, and multi-pronged disciplinary process is necessary to allow the mourner her singular focus on the physically absent beloved. In Freud's terms, here we have an "inhibition and circumscription in the ego [which] is [in effect] the expression of an exclusive *devotion* to its mourning" (165, emphasis added). In other words, the discipline that she undergoes, as she denies herself typical connections, makes possible in her case a singular kind of devotion not typically experienced by those who are not in crisis.

Freud's assessment of the mental status of the mourner in question is crucial to his overall account. What she experiences, and the way in which she responds to what she experiences, he argues, is normal, emotionally healthy, and rational given the particularity of her context. In this context, the felt excruciating pain is justified; the suffering is real—that is—not an excessive or ignorant response of a temporarily crazed person. Loss is real, for Freud, and the sudden loss of a loved one due to physical death is perhaps the clearest and most uncontroversial instance of a loss that is real and to which an emotional response that might be inappropriate or unhealthy in other circumstances is both appropriate and healthy.

But while the *person* is in fact stable in this context, the *situation* inside and outside of her is inherently unstable. For the grieving *person*, the mental and physical labor of the mourning process serves to recreate the physically dead beloved as an internal object, psychically real to her and experienced as an existence palpably distinct from her. In this way, love escapes annihilation.

The *situation* of the person is, however, inherently complicated and ultimately unstable. For the mourning self, in effect, refuses to accept what Freud calls "the test of reality"—the reality that the beloved is now dead and absent forever from her world. This objective instability eventually makes its way into the mourner's temporarily stable world. For ultimately, the very mourning process with its mental and physical discipline, its laboring in the service of ensuring the presence of the dead beloved, will, quite naturally, lead to her turning away from her dead beloved, "returning" the mourning individual back to objective reality, the material world of actual physical objects, other living selves, and rendering her as a person accessible to her senses. But how does this work?

Let us imagine a situation involving a husband and wife who work at the same institution and have a practice of going home together at the end of the day. They meet each day outside the science building at five. The woman arrives earlier. She waits, and watches her beloved walk down the long corridor toward her. His features gain definition with each step. At last, he is by her side, fully present, entirely determinate.

Imagine this woman as a widow. After the sudden death of her husband, she maintains their tradition and her ritual. Day after day, she waits outside the door. She watches lovingly as her husband walks down the corridor toward her. How could this happen? There are many possibilities.

Perhaps she "morphs" a living individual who happens to be walking down that very corridor. She re-creates him as her late husband. As his features gain definition, they become her husband's, perhaps even re-creating the final moment of his presence, perhaps dissolving at some critical moment.

Perhaps she accomplishes this without the help of a living prop, replaying, and, in this way, reliving the event entirely in her imagination, "while all the time the existence of the lost object is continued in the mind" (166).[1] Freud proposes instructively that the deployment of a prima facie bizarre strategy by the mourner is not only within the realm of normal but that it is disciplined and necessary to her ultimate health.

This return and repetition in the wife's process of mourning is played out with "every single one of the memories and hopes which bound the libido to the object" (166). This is necessary to the "emptying out" of every memory and hope. Freud argues that in the end, every *successful* instance of a re-living will, by that very token, simultaneously *fail* the test of reality and so lead one gently back to reality. The widow successfully completes the rendezvous with her husband every day at five, despite her husband's physical death. The labor of her mourning, the discipline and devotion to her lost husband is precisely what allows her this glorious freedom to remain in his presence and to preserve his presence in her life.

Nonetheless, each time she successfully re-establishes and affirms this peculiarly intimate connection, she also sees, in the very act of bringing him to presence, that he is in another, equally important sense, not present. That he is *not* alive. And so the repetition of this ritual of bringing to presence allows her to integrate his absence into the narrative of her own life, not as a brute, empty space, but as the absence in the external world of something at the same time forever present to her. She sees this, and accomplishes this self-transformation, precisely because she is a woman who *is* "normal," and she remains normal, and even healthy, as she endures and undertakes the painful process of grief.

According to Freud, mourning is constituted by a gradual shift in perspective. This shift is accomplished through reliving one relived event at a time. In this repetition, reality intrudes, gradually and imperceptibly, but inexorably. This leads the mourner to the second stage of detachment, as she comes to experience fully the unreality of the imagined beloved, the reality of the late beloved as physically gone, however imaginatively present, and this allows her to detach from the love object and to reestablish connections with the real, that is, the living world.[2]

Thus, step by step, the self detaches itself from this object and regains its freedom and spontaneity. The end of mourning, in this model, is a return from the world of the dead to unambiguous dwelling in the world of the living. On this account, the mourning process would be pathological at either extreme—of pathological denial of attachment as well as that of pathological attachment. In the first case, in such denial, were the labor to be foregone, what appears as immediate freedom from the dead beloved is more productively read as a psychologically unstable response to the reality of relationship (that is, that while physical people die immediately, relationships do not). It is pathological not to see suffering where it does exist. In the second case, if the mourner were to perseverate in her attachment to, and exclusive desire for, the dead beloved, to continue to experience the dead beloved as fully present, the emotional process would shift from mourning to what Freud calls "melancholia" (typically manifested in excessive self-reproach and guilt). It is pathological to see suffering where it no longer (justifiably) exists.

Freud's account emphasizes two aspects of mourning. First, and primarily, Freud underscores the psychological reality of felt, unbearable pain experienced by the self in mourning. Second, he emphasizes the empirical fact that the self responds to such suffering by a process of detachment, and this in two stages: first, the self must detach from the actual world; second, the self must ultimately detach from the non-actual world it constructs in the first moment of detachment. The first, apparently pathological, but in fact normal, process, he argues, is the precondition of the second.

Both stages are understood as internal psychological dynamics, driven by actual circumstances, and are understood as processes that are non-self-conscious and not deliberately chosen, though they are clearly deliberate and motivated from within. The situation is better seen in terms of two different descriptions under which processes may be viewed as conscious and deliberate. To go back to the earlier example of the widow, her rendezvous is conscious and deliberate; the bringing to presence of the beloved is conscious and deliberate, under one description. But these processes are not conscious and deliberate under another description. What is automatic, and dynamically driven, is the unconscious process of detachment; but that is always achieved through a conscious and deliberate process represented, undertaken, and experienced at a very different level, and under very different descriptions. Both forms of detachment, that is, detachment from the actual world, and, ultimately, detachment from the non-actual (unreal) world, make certain kinds of attachment possible. It is the first that is of particular interest to Freud because of the kind of cognitive and affective labor that is involved in forging an attachment that is sustained and sustainable only by a radical detachment from objects, individuals, and communities toward which one would normally gravitate.

The second stage of detachment is the natural, and more obviously healthy, culmination of the first (even though its goal is the opposite of stage one of detachment, involving as it does the move away from the non-actual dead beloved). Moreover, as we have seen, these two stages are not entirely sequential. The second detachment, which appears to be an opposing process, is actually the mirror image of the first detachment. This aspect merely comes to predominate later in the mourning process.

The first detachment is psychologically peculiar although normal in the context of one suffering from profound grief. It is a withdrawal from everything that has no relation to the dead beloved. Note that when Freud characterizes the first detachment as that which gives the mourning individual freedom for absorption into the dead beloved, he uses the term "devotion" to underscore the exclusivity—indeed, the singularity—of the fixation on the dead person. Detachment in one domain thus provides an opportunity for connection in another. One might call this the *economy* of mourning.

Economy in one domain allows for surplus in another, and thus for the freedom and leisure to solidify this devoted absorption. Moreover, according to Freud, there is the activity of return, of repetition, as the dead person is brought back vividly and freely for the grievant, as every event is brought up and relived, time after time. While this may be seen as an aspect of devotion, with continual return as a way to solidify memories of the dead beloved, it has an additional and seemingly paradoxical function, which is that of weaning the beloved away from her devoted absorption, and bringing her back to the real world.

Kisagotami: The Mother Who Mourns the Loss of Her Dead Child

There are many versions of the Kisagotami legend. I will narrate a version that captures the core of the tale,[3] underscoring the parts I find most illuminating.

There once lived a poor, young woman named Gotami from the village of Savatthi, who was so thin (*kisa*) that she was known as Kisa-gotami.[4] Although poor, she was of intellectual and moral depth, and, emanating a light of inner beauty, had the good fortune to marry into a wealthy family. She soon conceived and gave birth to a son. Gotami's well-deserved domestic happiness, with a good husband and a male firstborn admired by all, was short-lived: in a little over a year, her son died unexpectedly of an illness. This was her first intimate experience with the death of a loved one, and her only child at that.

It was customary for male relatives and community members to take possession of the dead body, but Gotami rejected this custom. Not only did she refuse to relinquish possession of the body of her child but she was determined to cure her son by finding the right medicine for him. So, carrying her child on her hip, she went from house to house, inquiring of its inhabitants whether they might help supply her with medicine that would bring her son back to life. She received a range of reactions from her community, including many who scorned or mocked her for her obvious mental derangement, and some who pitied her for her naïveté and for her unhealthy obsession with an obviously dead child. Finally she came to the door of a wise man who, recognizing that the source of Gotami's bizarre behavior was profound grief, sent her to the physician for all manners of suffering, the Lord Buddha himself.

Gotami presented her dead child to the Buddha and asked him, as she had asked many others before, for medicine for her son. The Buddha replied that he did in fact know of such a medicine but that Gotami would have to acquire it herself. When pressed further he revealed this medicine: white mustard seeds. Gotami's task was to return to the village, and to the houses she had recently visited, and to obtain a small quantity of mustard seeds. But these seeds, he emphasized, could come only from a household that had never experienced the death of a daughter or son.

Gotami was overjoyed at the prospect of securing such readily available medicine and returned to the village and repeated her visits to each house, this time with the concrete request for mustard seeds. Every house she visited had mustard seeds, as they are a staple in cooking for all households, but she began to realize that there was no household that had not lost a daughter or a son. As she received the mustard seeds with one hand, she returned them with the other. By the end of the day she came to the realization that there was no medicine to cure her child. She then came to accept two things: that her child was in fact dead, and that she was not the only person to experience profound grief—that death and grief are universal conditions of human life. The legend ends with Gotami burying her son and returning to the feet of the Buddha as his disciple, becoming a nun, reading the scriptures, and eventually finding joy and liberation from all forms of suffering.

What is significant about this story, in the standard Buddhist interpretation? This is a story about profound loss, about a profound mourning as a response to that loss, and about the process Gotami undergoes in ultimately coming to accept it *as* a loss. But the story is at its core a story about morality, and about the nature of our epistemic access to moral truths. Given the kinds of moral blindness to which we are subject, one needs a spiritual teacher to guide one along the moral path from deficiency to perfection.

In the story, the Buddha teaches Gotami two powerful lessons: that all human beings are similarly situated in this universe, no matter what their particular differences might be, as death is every human's inevitability; and that one's individual interests, projects, and passions are not inherently more valuable than those of others. One is a lesson about the universality of suffering and is an epistemic lesson that allows her to arrive at the right moral conclusion regarding respect for all humans as fellow sufferers. The second is a distinctively moral lesson about the defect of narcissism and about bringing Kisagotami to recognize her form of suffering as due to an extreme form of narcissism.

The Buddha imparts this lesson in a very specific way: not by giving her directly a universal experiential truth (e.g., "All humans experience the grief that comes with death"), or a direct moral truth (e.g., "Narcissism is bad"). He instead teaches her indirectly, by having Gotami travel a path of her own to final acceptance, one that was deeply personal. From a Buddhist perspective, then, one reads the story of Kisagotami as one that involves a shift from ignorance to enlightenment, and perhaps even from the pathological and morally deficient to the enlightened normal.

This is certainly a compelling reading in its own right. While the teacher provides the epistemic and moral parameters for the path on which she travels, without which she would surely falter, the story emphasizes that a person has to find her own way to the truth. At a meta-level, it underscores the Buddhist emphasis on narrative rather than theory as the focus in the ethical domain (Garfield 2006; Hallisey 1996; Hallisey and Hansen 1996).

It is the method of the Buddha that is most striking in the story. He is compassionate above all else, and his compassion is evident in the way that he provides the opportunity for epistemic and moral improvement in a context and on terms that make sense to the grieving subject.

This is the traditional reading, and it is certainly a reasonable one. I now propose an alternative reading of the story, based in part on some of those very concrete Freudian insights I have underscored earlier in this chapter. Those Freudian insights allowed this ancient story, one told in a very different place and at a very different time, to come alive for me, turning Gotami into a character with whom I could empathize. When I read the story in this way, I recognized Kisagotami as quite a different person than the one she is portrayed to be in the more traditional reading.

The standard interpretation makes Kisagotami out to be, at best, a pitiable woman, temporarily mentally deranged in her grief, suffering from a massive delusion as to the status of her own child. She is naïve and simplistic rather than sophisticated in her sorrow, certainly narcissistic in her obliviousness of the manner of her imposition on others, and in need of the hand of an outside teacher, or a therapist, or, in this case, the Buddha, to bring her to certain moral realizations.

Indeed, it is difficult to put one's self in Gotami's shoes from a contemporary perspective. Her crisis feels ineluctably third person—I can see *that* she suffers, but her bizarre behavior prevents me from feeling it *with* her. The register of her suffering is alien in the degree of its seeming ignorance ("who will give me medicine for my child?" in the context of his death). In contrast, the actions and words of the Buddha come as a relief to the reader—clarifying, compassionate, and instructive. The difference between the states of knowledge and ignorance could not be clearer.

With Freud's psychoanalytic mourning narrative close at hand, however, a different image of Kisagotami emerges. Kisagotami is far from pitiable. On the contrary, she now strikes one as a strong woman suffering the worst kind of existential crisis that life could possibly present. What could be more excruciating than suffering the sudden death of one's only child?[5] In the context of such a crisis, one might argue that the *pathological* response might well be to quietly acquiesce to the situation, for instance, to having one's child taken away (by male relatives, for the last rites), something Kisagotami refuses to do. The denial of the magnitude of this loss, is, from a Freudian perspective, just as pathological as the obsessive attachment to the dead beloved in the long term.

This insight—about a radical redistricting of what is normal and what is pathological in the context of a crisis—we find in Freud in its most fundamental form, who points out that: (a) profound mourning is in fact characterized by excessive absorption into the beloved, to the exclusion of all else; and (b) that this is rational and a sign of health rather than delusional and a sign of derangement.

Kisagotami's carrying around of her dead child from house to house, and her repeated identical request of each household, now emerges as a *literal,* that is, *physical* manifestation of the psychological process of return and repetition described by Freud. He argues, as we have seen, that precisely this kind of process is *healthy* in the context of mourning, precisely because it is a necessary condition of an individual coming to face reality and to return to a healthy *nongrieving* psychological state.

On this interpretation, Kisagotami's problem isn't simple ignorance or a stubborn refusal to accept the fact of death. Rather, Kisagotami's incomprehension of death simply reflects the mystery of death (the emotionally transgressive quality of the finality of life), which is an inextricable part of the mystery of life—a mystery that cannot be solved directly by the intellect (as the Buddha realizes, when he refrains from advising her to "just get over it") but can only be effectively and *efficiently* approached emotionally and experientially, solved by what turns out to be a disciplined process that involves absorption, repetition and, finally, release. And so it is that she returns her dead beloved child to her hip again and again, as it seems she must, confronting individuals in her community again and again with the physicality of her grief. Part of the genius of the Buddha's prescription is that he prescribes a process that will be repetitive, that will be volitional, that will begin in detachment from reality, and will thereby issue in attachment to reality, and will accomplish all of this over sufficient *time* for the process to be genuinely healing.

But this is not simply Freudian theory anticipated. In a twist to the Freudian interpretation, it is this community that will, individually and jointly, constitute "the test of reality" that eventually brings her to acceptance. According to Freud, as we have seen, the psychodynamics of mourning are interior, are individual. Freud never mentions the role of community per se in the mourning process. This is a defect that the tale remedies. For the folk narrative (in all of its versions) makes central and indispensable the role of the community, and in particular the structure of social relations, in bringing about Kisagotami's realization and ultimate liberation from suffering.

I will end this section with two final observations. First, although it is clear that Kisagotami's practice isn't one that is recognizably "yogic"—in the sense that yogic practice typically involves a course of mental and physical training that an individual has *chosen* to undertake in order to achieve enlightenment—the death of her child nonetheless casts her, without her desire or consent, onto the yogic path; and that what appears as a desire for attachment, and thus as a symptom of her ignorance, is really part of the process toward detachment, an unconscious and instinctive knowing that puts her on the path to enlightenment. What is it that makes her a candidate for enlightenment? An instinct to discipline in response to one of life's greatest challenges, one that life's greatest teacher, experience, has thrust upon her.

Kisagotami's sensibility, then, is yogic. We can see her on at least part of the eightfold path toward liberation from suffering. Thus, as part of the mother's mourning process, we witness the following stages:

> withdrawal (*pratyahara*)—of senses from the outside world;
> one-pointed-ness or concentration (*dharana*)—what Freud describes as the internalized or introjected object—the individual who has died being recreated in the mind, in Kisagotami's case revealed in her concentration on her lifeless child who she refuses to accept as dead; and
> absorption (*dhyana*)—when this concentration becomes spontaneous (the child willed into part of her actual world).

On this alternative interpretation, the significance of the role of the Buddha is his recognition in Kisagotami of this particular potential for enlightenment, which he goes on to facilitate in the way depicted in the story. The emphasis is not so much on the negative—the ignorance qua unknowing that is responsible for Kisagotami's suffering, but rather on the positive—on an aspect of life that she is able to experience firsthand, in the raw and most powerfully. If this is at all characterizable as an "ignorance," it is simultaneously a form of "knowing," which in turn makes it possible for her to move to enlightenment.

Second, what is so striking in the tale for being so crucial to Kisagotami's progression, and for being so conspicuously absent in Freud's analysis of the process more generally, is the role that society plays in the mourning process. The possibility that a self can successfully both undergo and overcome grief at the individual level is simply not entertained in any of the Buddhist tales that are about loss. There is a deep insight here, it seems to me, that a Freudian might productively take from the tale of Kisagotami: the activity of mourning is most successfully undertaken and completed when it is not confined to the inner space of individual emotion, allowing for the physical and social aspects of loss as integral parts of an expanded psychological anatomy of mourning.

Toward a Hybrid Theory of Mourning

In this section I provide the beginnings of a more satisfactory conceptual framework for understanding mourning. The Freudian and Buddhist accounts each supply some of the conceptual resources necessary for an account of the phenomenology, cause, and trajectory of mourning that is more intellectually and emotionally satisfying than either provides on its own.

Whatever the details, any satisfactory account of mourning must take seriously the first person, phenomenological, and incontrovertibly existential character of mourning. This is an irreducibly subjective dimension. It is not apt for moral evaluation. It is singular, and individual, and below the threshold of the moral domain.

Mourning is far more than the qualitative experience of the individual. Freudians and Buddhists alike share the insight that mourning is voluntary and procedural in nature. But they differ regarding how these properties are to be understood. Freud's account allows us to see what we might call "willed ignorance" as a healthy and legitimate blocking off of reality that provides the space for the grieving individual to comprehend, both intellectually and emotionally, what she otherwise finds incomprehensible (Safran 2003). This suggests the possibility that ignoring an event is constitutive of a form of knowing.

This is at odds with the Buddhist approach. On the one hand, Kisagotami's exercise of will is seen in the Buddhist context as an exercise of extreme narcissism and cannot therefore be similarly justified. I take the Freudian point on this matter. On the other hand, the Buddhist account gets right the procedural character of mourning, the social dimension, and the necessarily public aspect of the mourning process. An account of the mourning process that attends only to the inner, private space of the mourner (as Freud's does) fails to capture adequately all aspects of mourning. The anatomy of mourning has a psychological, physical, and social dimension. It also has a personal and public dimension.

What the Buddhist account provides is the broadest theoretical framework for understanding the basic human condition. It is that human beings suffer, and that the suffering, of whatever kind, is due either to: (a) attachment, (b) aversion, or (c) confusion regarding the nature of reality. I think that situating loss in general, and the mourning process in particular, within this broader context, with suffering in general caused by these three basic factors, allows us to understand better the fact that suffering due to death is not fundamentally different in kind from suffering due to greed, or due to anxiety attacks, or due to pressure from having papers due the next day. This is to "normalize" in its public and social aspect (in sharp contrast to its qualitative aspect) the status of the mourner.

Finally, the Buddhist view of reality is broad as well, and provides us with a way of understanding the relationship between living and dead selves in a different way than Freud does in his sharp separation of the objective worlds of the living and the dead. For Freud the realm of the real is, quite literally, the realm of the living. In Tibetan Buddhism (the Bardo teachings), life and death are not sharply distinguished polar opposites. Bardo (Intermediate State) theory emphasizes instead phases of a life–death spectrum, with death itself not viewed as an end to one's reality but rather as a transformative moment, offering a chance for enlightenment. Even if we bracket the theory of rebirth in the context of which this theory emerges, Bardo is an instructive way to think about the life process and its relation to death. All states are intermediate. We who are living are corpses in the making; the dead are in transition from one form of presence to another (Sogyal Rinpoche 1992).

This idea of a spectrum in turn can provide us with the conceptual resources to resist drawing the line between what is pathological and what is normal in ways that outstrip both traditionally Freudian and traditionally Buddhist understanding. Specifically, the presence of the dead beloved might well continue to persist in an individual's life well beyond what Freud would claim to be normal; and by the same token, this presence might be interpreted in ways other than as an embodiment of an extreme form of narcissism, as understood by the Buddhists. But developing this outline in more explicit detail—of the subjective, social, public, and metaphysical dimensions to the anatomy of mourning—and making the case for a persisting presence of the dead beloved as a sign of health specifically lacking excessive obsession or narcissism, is a potential subject for another chapter.

I have argued that the story of Kisagotami achieves a level of truth and authenticity, a felt truth that renders the story timeless and cross-culturally powerful, exposing in the raw the human condition. But this reading requires that it *not* be read as primarily imparting a moral lesson from the Buddha, nor one that describes a particularly poignant form of ignorance that takes shape in the person of the hapless Kisagotami. Indeed, I have argued that both of these moral and epistemological points, while they may certainly be extractable from the story, take us away from what is psychologically, physically, and socially real.

In reading the Kisagotami story, instead, as a tale from the first-person perspective of a woman suffering the loss of her only child, one sees in its details the very heart of the tragedy understood existentially—a personal world of justifiable suffering to which we, as outsiders, have access, if we could only recognize it for what it is from that first-person perspective. In so doing, it is not simply the descriptive details but the qualitative dimension of her suffering that get activated in the heart and mind of the reader: an activation that allows an imaginative identification with the core of her suffering, cutting through the cultural, historical, and religious specificity of the narrative, replacing one's sense of the strange and removed with a painful sense of the familiar. In contrast, when one foregrounds the moral lesson, as it happens with the more standard reading, one in effect thrusts, willy-nilly, both Kisagotami and us as readers, into the more public, more universal world of a shared recognition of what is a nonexistential though perhaps moral truth of the universality of suffering. In the end, the difference in these two interpretations may be one of emphasis, but where one places the emphasis is not a trivial matter.

My goal has been to show that in using both Freudian and Buddhist insights in interpreting the tale, we benefit in several ways. In appropriating Freud, we have a richer account that makes possible a more empathetic understanding of Kisagotami as she moves toward enlightenment in the Buddhist sense. In appropriating Buddhist insights, we have an enriched account of mourning that underscores the crucial role played by a *society* as it participates in and bears witness to physical acts of repetition in an individual's mourning process, and its contribution to her dawning recognition of a moral truth, a dimension that is neglected in Freud in his emphasis on the inner, psychological, and individual, aspect of the mourning process.

Notes

A much earlier version of this chapter was read as a paper at the Vedanta conference at Miami University, Oxford, Ohio, in September 2002. A sketch of the current version, which includes the analysis of the tale of Kisagotami, was presented at the TransBuddhism seminar at Smith College in April 2004. Thanks to Peter Gregory and Richard Millington for useful comments on that sketch. Finally, thanks to Jennifer Nery, Cynthia Townley, Jay Garfield, and Abraham Zablocki for their thoughtful comments on a more detailed recent version.

1. In Freud's words, the object is "clung to through the medium of a hallucinatory wish-psychosis" ("Mourning and Melancholia," 166).
2. If a person does not reach this stage in the mourning process, continuing to be connected to the beloved in the manner described without succumbing to the test of reality, then what is normal has turned pathological. There is no specification of

a time frame in Freud for the mourning process, after which it would be deemed pathological.

3. *Dhammapada* 114, Book 8, Story 13 (Burlingame 1969).

4. Hereafter I will use these two names—Gotami and Kisagotami—interchangeably.

5. It is crucial to point out that Kisagotami's verses of liberation in the *Therigatha* embody the very palpable sufferings that were particular to women at that time, such as the death of children and being co-wives.

CHAPTER 11

Translating Modernity

Buddhist Response to the Thai Environmental Crisis

SUSAN M. DARLINGTON

I T I S H A R D to breathe in Bangkok. The capital of Thailand is a sprawl-ing and congested city with major air and water pollution. Energy demand is high, forcing a dependency on oil and natural gas and the develop-ment of resources such as hydroelectric power. Large-scale dams bring addi-tional problems of alternating flooding and drought, loss of agricultural and forest land, and relocation of large numbers of people. Since the 1960s, Thai-land has faced an environmental crisis that has steadily worsened. Rapid eco-nomic development based on a Western model of growth, industrialization, and consumerism has led to depleted forests, soil erosion, polluted air and water, and massive problems of hazardous and industrial waste.

Thais have responded to the crisis and the broader social changes brought on through modernization in both conventional and creative ways. Ironically, many use a Western concept of environmentalism to deal with the problems they see as brought on by a Western model of development. Others take what they see as distinctly Thai or Buddhist approaches, rejecting or changing West-ern concepts. Some of these latter approaches have now found their way back to the West as Buddhist activists and environmentalists in the United States are adopting and adapting them to build environmental awareness and practice.

One of the most creative responses to Thailand's environmental problems draws on Buddhism, local culture, and Western environmental and scientific concepts. This approach is exemplified by a small number of Buddhist monks, called environmental monks (Thai, *phra nak anurak*), who have begun envi-ronmental conservation projects on the local level. The innovative ways in which they use the religion reflect the growing international movement known as *engaged Buddhism*. As with engaged Buddhists in other parts of the world (in both Asia and the West), the Thai environmental monks are rethinking and reinterpreting aspects of Buddhist practice in response to ideas, concepts, and pressures introduced through the processes of economic globalization and modernization. Thus, the ancient philosophy of Buddhism, through their reinterpretations, is proving responsive to modern issues.

The goals of environmental Buddhism, based on both the ecological concept of interconnectedness found in deep ecology (Devall 2000; Halifax 1990; Macy 2000) and the Buddhist concept of interdependent co-arising (*paticca samuppada*), emphasize modern, scientific methods and ancient religious principles.[1] In this way, the environmental monks are neither "modern" nor "traditional." The monks' interpretations of religion and science, and tradition and modernity, do not fall into clear-cut categories, but rather represent a creative blend of approaches appropriate for a changing world. Their example complicates and highlights the tensions inherent in the environmental crisis itself, and the questions facing Thai society as it attempts to deal with the crisis. The presence of these monks challenges Thais at all levels of society to confront what it means to be modern or traditional, local or global, Thai, and even what it means to be Buddhist.

Thai environmental monks did not invent the idea of using Buddhism to deal with environmental issues. Buddhists across Asia and America point to scriptures that document reverence for nature and ground ecological activism in Buddhist teachings. His Holiness the Dalai Lama includes environmental issues in his call to make Tibet a zone of peace; the Korean nun Jiyul Sunim has fought the destruction of a sacred mountain to build a railway tunnel; and American Buddhists draw from different forms of Buddhism to express concerns about, and responsibility for, nuclear waste, deforestation, water usage, to name only a few cases (for more examples, see Kaza and Kraft 2000; Tucker and Williams 1997). The Thai activist monks receive support from the International Network of Engaged Buddhists (INEB), a nonprofit organization that brings together Buddhists from around the world concerned about social justice. Beyond the Buddhist world, a movement linking religions of all kinds with ecology has been growing worldwide over the past several decades. The actions of the Thai environmental monks are, however, the products of their own reflections on the practice of Buddhism in contemporary society. If influenced by the philosophy of American Transcendentalism, as argued by Mark Blum (chapter 12), these monks are unaware of this process and the debates about authenticity that surround it.

In this chapter, I examine the activities of Thai environmental monks through three examples: tree ordinations, long-life ceremonies for rivers, and natural, integrated agriculture. All three activities are innovations within Buddhist practice. Trees do not really become monks; the lives of rivers are only extended if people change their behaviors and stop polluting them; and natural farming is a response to chemical-based, intensive agriculture worldwide. Yet, despite the debates over the scriptural basis of these actions, their symbolic value and practical effectiveness cannot be denied. In a nation that faces severe environmental problems and rapid growth of consumerism and development, the use of innovative Buddhist practices to address these concerns has begun to affect people's behavior. Indeed, albeit slowly, over the past two decades, these practices have seen some success in transforming the environmental milieu of Thailand.

Environmental Monks

Environmental monks perform rituals that symbolically mark the relationship between Buddhism and nature, such as ordaining trees and performing long-life ceremonies for rivers. They also establish integrated, sustainable agricultural farms, protected community forests, and wildlife sanctuaries. As a central tenet of their interpretation of Buddhism, they teach the responsibility of humans for the natural world.

The environmental crisis to which these monks are responding is the result of Thai society buying into global capitalism and rapid economic and industrial growth. The monks' response takes an ideological stance that critiques this form of modernization, arguing that capitalism and consumerism are pulling people away from spiritual practice. Capitalism, they argue, emphasizes greed, ignorance, and anger, the three root evils in Buddhism. The monks call for a return to religion and religious values as a guide for living simply and purely, with an emphasis on community-level society in which people care for each other and are sensitive to the impacts of their actions on others.

While this interpretation can be seen as emphasizing tradition over modernity, and even idealizing the past, the monks' methods and interpretations of Buddhism are themselves modern. They are influenced by and draw from the international environmental movement, as well as the transnational socially engaged Buddhist movement.

The term *engaged Buddhism* is attributed to the Vietnamese monk, Thich Nhat Hahn. In his opposition to the Vietnam War in the 1960s, he argued for the importance of using Buddhist principles to work for social justice and peace. The concept of engaged Buddhism as a means of responding to modern social problems emerged concurrently in many Buddhist societies in the mid-twentieth century. Initially, activists who took a Buddhist approach focused on local issues and communities. Globalization, however, not only brought capitalism and multinational business but also introduced alternative ideas intended to help people oppose dominant concepts of large-scale economic development and rapid growth. Buddhists concerned with social issues in different nations began to support each other as part of this process. In 1989, the Thai social activist Sulak Sivaraksa founded the INEB, an organization that brings together socially active Buddhists. Information and ideas exchanged at INEB conferences and through the journal *Seeds of Peace* have sparked new actions on the local level. The actions of engaged Buddhists, whose work is grounded in Buddhist philosophy, are contributing to a rethinking of the application of Buddhism in the modern world.

Environmentalist monks in Thailand emerged from a small group of monks who were engaged in rural development work that aimed to counter the capitalist-heavy development policies of the government and big business. These monks work closely with environmental nongovernmental organizations (NGOs), which have the knowledge of ecological technology and environmental science that the monks lack. The methods the monks use—especially rituals—bridge science and culture, bringing and translating new ideas and approaches to rural villagers. The rituals, while based on traditional ceremonies, have only been performed in this manner since the late 1970s. Integrated agriculture, for example, has no scriptural basis in Buddhism. Yet both rituals and Buddhist-based natural farms mediate the tension between what is seen as "traditional" and "modern," and reinforce the value of spirituality in dealing with environmental problems.

Thailand's Environmental Crisis

One of the results of the policies of intense economic development that the Thai central government has promoted since the 1960s has been a dramatic increase in environmental problems. The national government recognizes the seriousness of the environmental crisis, and in the 1990s enacted legislation to deal with environmental issues. The Enhancement and Conservation of National Environment Quality Act of B.E. 2535 (1992 C.E.) aimed to strengthen environmental policymaking, encourage decentralization of environmental quality management, and create legal rights and responsibilities for individuals, environmental NGOs, businesses and government agencies (Laird 2000, 318–19). Thailand's 1997 constitution also incorporated environmental protection provisions.[2]

Despite such governmental support, the nation's environmental problems continue to grow at an alarming speed. Economic development leads to increased energy and resource use—electricity, oil, natural gas, water—and greater pollution levels and environmental degradation. Excessive pesticide and chemical fertilizer use contributes to river, water, and land pollution and poor soil fertility. This vicious cycle leads to further chemical use, pollution, and environmental damage.

In addition to the depletion of its fertility, agricultural land is disappearing. Urban growth consumes farmland. Golf courses, industrial sites, and housing developments replace rice paddies. Urbanization and industrialization create the very modern problems of hazardous and electronic waste, in the form of spent chemicals, oil, old computers, and cell phones, to name just a few. Natural marine environments (mangrove forests, coral reefs, coastal beaches) are vanishing in favor of commercial shrimp farms (resulting in the salinization of both mangrove and coastal rice paddy land) and tourism.

The most visible—and debated—environmental impact of economic development is the loss of Thailand's forests. Statistics on deforestation between 1961 and 1998 vary, depending on the source. According to the Royal Forest Department (RFD), forestland decreased from 53.3 percent of the nation's total land in 1961 to 25.6 percent in 1998.[3] Various environmental NGOs place the figure much lower, claiming only 15 percent of forest cover remained by the early 1990s (Hirsch 1993, 26–27; Pinkaew and Rajesh 1992, 22–23; Trébuil 1995, 68). Definitions of what can be counted as forest cover differ as well. Some groups, including sectors of the government, incorporate monoculture plantations, such as eucalyptus and tangerine groves, as forested land. Forest loss results in the degradation of watersheds, decrease in biodiversity, floods, and severe water shortages. In 2002, the RFD claimed that forests had recovered to 33.4 percent of the nation's land, due primarily to reforestation efforts and better control of forest fires (RFD 2002, 29). Problems of environmental degradation overall, however, continue to grow at a serious rate. In addition to the direct impact on the natural environment, the problems also affect people's quality of life, ranging from health problems, increased stress, struggles to find basic resources such as water, conflict over land and natural resources, and the effects of growing consumerism underlying much environmental destruction (Fahn 2003; Laird 2000).

Buddhist monks became aware of environmental problems in a number of ways, but primarily through experience and observation. Witnessing environmental change and its negative impacts on people motivated many monks to engage the issues actively. For example, Phrakhru Pitak Nanthakhun of Nan Province long had concerns about the declining state of the forest surrounding his home village. As a child, he walked through the forest to school in the 1960s and early 1970s. As the economy shifted to a monetary base, farmers began to plant crops for sale rather than for subsistence. They were attracted to the visions of financial success offered by seed company representatives who came into the area. On his walks, Pitak noticed the forest gradually disappearing as it was cleared for cash-crop fields.

Planting cash crops such as string beans and feed corn had two kinds of negative effects. First, most of the farmers fell into ever-deepening debt as they borrowed from the companies to purchase the seeds, fertilizers, and pesticides to grow the crops. The companies bought the harvest but often not at the price initially offered. They also upheld strict standards of quality and crop size, which the farmers could not always meet. Second, cash cropping entails monoculture— growing a single crop repeatedly in the same fields. In addition, the corn rows tended to be planted vertically on hillsides, promoting soil erosion and water runoff. The chemical fertilizers and pesticides pushed by the companies polluted the soil and water. The experiences of the villagers in Nan Province paralleled those of farmers across Thailand. By the late 1970s, awareness of the problems arising from cash cropping and industrialization led many Thais to join the growing worldwide environmental movement.

Environmental Movement

The environmental crisis in Thailand serves as a pivot point for an ongoing debate about the nation's involvement in globalization and economic development. It also highlights issues concerning the introduction and adoption of ideas and concepts from the West into Thai culture. The government has adopted a Western model of development and pressed ahead as rapidly as possible with little to no regard for environmental and social consequences. The rapid development has generated opposition: many oppose its environmental consequences, while others object to the resulting increase in poverty and the growing gap between rich and poor. The extent of the environmental crisis has spurred these groups to unite in their opposition to the government's policies. Approaches and tactics have varied, from student and farmer protests, to the formation of new political parties and people's organizations, to a dramatic increase in environmental NGOs, to community environmental projects. The irony is that this coalition itself borrows heavily from the West, especially from the environmental movement.

Environmentalism is a relatively new concept worldwide, emerging in its popular form in the mid-twentieth century in the United States with the publication of Rachel Carson's *Silent Spring* in 1962. The concept appeared in Thailand in the early 1970s. One of the key factors that sparked the student-led protests in 1973 that brought down the ruling military triumvirate was the discovery of poaching of endangered wildlife in a national park by high-ranking military personnel. The new, democratic government gave some attention to environmental concerns, even while dealing with many other social issues and competing political forces. The first National Environmental Quality Act was enacted in 1975, establishing the National Environment Board (Hirsch 1996, 23). The political factors of the era quickly overshadowed the environmental ones, however, as Thailand entered a tumultuous period of political action, protests, and campaigns to empower rural people. This period culminated with the violent attack on Thammasaat University students by right-wing paramilitary troops on October 6, 1976 (Bowie 1997). As politics shifted back to the right, environmental issues fell to the side for the next decade.

In 1985, a proposed cable car up Doi Suthep in Chiang Mai, the sacred mountain site of a revered temple, Wat Phra That, helped to reignite environmental concerns in conjunction with other social issues and worries. Ironically, the Tourism Authority of Thailand (TAT) proposed the cable car to reduce the environmental impact of increasing numbers of tourists visiting Wat Phra That. The only way to get to the temple was by way of a narrow roadway that was congested and saw frequent accidents (Chayant 1998, 266). TAT viewed the project as a form of cultural or ecotourism that would attract more people to Chiang Mai and contribute to its economic growth (Chayant 1998). The people of Chiang Mai, including many Buddhist monks, did not agree.

Local monks joined with students, environmentalists, NGOs, academics, journalists, and local residents in an effort to prevent the construction of the cable car. Some protesters argued the cable car would damage the biodiversity of the forest that it would cross on the way up the mountain. Others pointed out the lack of public involvement in planning the project, seeing it as an example of harmful economic development that ignored cultural and public concerns. The monks who joined the effort raised concerns about the potential disruption of the peace surrounding the temple and the resulting commercialization of one of the most sacred sites of northern Thai Buddhism.[4] Making the links between Buddhism and the environment strengthened all the arguments against the cable car—ecological, economic, and cultural. While the arguments varied, the effect was a unified opposition that at least postponed the construction of the cable car in 1986 (Chayant 1998). (Chayant noted that the project is periodically revived, but as of early 2007, it had not gone further than occasional discussion [1998, 267].) The case also marked the first entry of Thai Buddhist monks into a public discourse of opposing development that would affect both the natural environment and the religion.

Goals of Activist Monks

Socially engaged Buddhism in Thailand did not begin with the cable-car struggle; well-known monks such as Buddhadasa Bhikkhu and Phra Prayudh Payutto had taught social responsibility as a critical component of practicing

Buddhism for decades, although from different perspectives (Swearer 1997). Other monks worked on the local level, undertaking rural development work to help counter the impact of economic development on villagers' lives. The monks who became involved in the cable-car protests represent a segment of the Buddhist sangha concerned with social justice and its relationship to religious teachings. Their interpretations of Buddhist teachings, methods, and social issues often differ, both from each other and from the mainstream Buddhist hierarchy within which they must work. Regardless of their interpretations of the religion's philosophical traditions and history, Thai activist monks believe it is part of their responsibility as monks to work to end suffering and to help people move along the path toward enlightenment.

One high-ranking monk who undertakes rural development work in Chiang Mai is Phra Buddhapochana Varabhorn (Chan Kusalo). Observing the growing struggles of northern Thai farmers through the 1960s as economic change influenced village life, he first opened a school in Chiang Mai City for boys from the surrounding countryside. His aim was to provide them with the educational tools to return to their villages and help people modernize based on Buddhist principles of compassion and self-sufficiency. Buddhapochana was concerned about the spread of greed and consumerism that accompanied rapid

Phrakhru Manas Natheephitak, abbot of Wat Photharam, Mae Chai, Phayao Province, credited with performing the first tree ordination in 1988.

economic growth. In 1972, he established the Foundation for Education and Development of Rural Areas (FEDRA) in the nearby town of Mae Rim. Through FEDRA, Buddhapochana expanded his work into several villages, assisting rural communities to develop according to Buddhist principles. He set up local rice banks, from which villagers could borrow rice at low interest rates (repayable in rice) during the months before they could harvest their crops. He provided water buffaloes so farmers could plow their fields without paying excessive fees to outsiders who owned buffaloes or gas-powered plows. And he hired recent college graduates to teach villagers environmentally friendly agricultural methods and to help them organize their communities to promote sustainable development. FEDRA now works in more than thirty villages on agricultural development, has a handicrafts school for women who reside in rural areas, and markets handmade products directly in Thai cities and overseas to help women supplement their agricultural incomes (Darlington 1990).

Phra Buddhapochana frequently states that spiritual and material development must go together. He believes that people cannot truly work toward spiritual development if they are starving or worried about where their children's next meal will be found. Through helping them learn to support themselves without going into debt, he aims to increase their understanding of Buddhist teachings and practice.

Environmentalist monks have a similar philosophy. They see their work serving multiple goals: helping to relieve the suffering caused by economic growth and environmental degradation; helping people learn to help themselves and therefore be able to help others; and maintaining—or even re-creating—a place for religious practice in a rapidly changing world.

It is this issue of having a place for religion that underlies much of the work of activist Buddhists. Their efforts to relieve suffering serve as a bridge between village life and global concepts of environmentalism and sustainable development. The centerpiece of their approach is religious practice; in particular, adapting well-known rituals as a means of translating new ideas into culturally recognizable forms.

Tree Ordinations

The best-known activity of environmentalist monks is the tree ordination (Darlington 1998). Marking trees as sacred with orange robes is not unknown in Buddhism (for example, bodhi trees wrapped with orange monks' robes are all over Thailand, as well as in other Buddhist countries). However, using *ordination* to protect the forest is anything but traditional. Phrakhru Manas Natheephitak of Phayao Province in northern Thailand was the first monk to perform tree ordinations to promote environmentalism, beginning in the late 1980s. He emphasizes the symbolic value of the ritual, noting, however, that only humans can *actually* be ordained. Phrakhru Manas adapted the text of a Buddha image consecration ceremony to sanctify the tree and forest rather than *bhikkhu* ordination texts. Saplings were placed around the image during the rite, conferring sanctity on them as well. Villagers who participated referred to the blessed saplings as *ordained*, thus coining the phrase for the new environmental ritual (Pipob Udomittipong, personal communication, January 15, 2007).

Monks choose a variety of texts for these rituals, emphasizing the consecration of the tree and the forest and using the opportunity to teach Buddhists' responsibilities and connections with nature. Villagers view the rituals more literally, as they often consider the trees to be ordained. Their behavior toward trees wrapped in orange robes is similar to the respect they show monks: they *wai*, or bow with palms together, to such trees when they pass. The popularity of tree ordinations as well as the criticisms they receive from the Buddhist monastic establishment and media are grounded in the villagers' version of the rite. Environmental monks play upon the tension between what they see as the scriptural meaning of the rituals, which teaches religious and environmental principles, and the popular meaning among villagers to get people's attention and promote their message.

After visiting Phrakhru Manas and other monks engaged in conservation work during early 1990, Phrakhru Pitak Nanthakhun of Nan Province realized the value of action and example for gaining villagers' commitment to environmental work. Prior to this visit, Pitak had preached about the importance of caring for the forest and the natural environment, but villagers continued to clear the forest for cash crops. He sponsored his first tree ordination in his home village in 1990, using it to mark the establishment of a protected community forest surrounding the village. The community forest was a shared area that the villagers agreed to conserve and protect, limiting the cutting of trees and forbidding hunting. The tree on which he focused was the largest in the forest, and was considered the "king of the forest" in northern Thai tradition. Its ordination symbolized the consecration of the entire forest.

Phrakhru Pitak chose the texts for the ceremony carefully. The ordination ritual, while following the basic structure of a *bhikkhu* ordination, used texts from various parts of the scriptures that he felt taught lessons of responsibility for nature and the importance of self-sufficiency (on which he builds sustainable agricultural projects). However, the tree was wrapped in the used orange robes of a *bhikkhu* to mark symbolically its sanctity and to remind the villagers *visually* of the mutual dependence between them and the forest. A few days before the ritual, a Buddha statue had also been placed at the base of the tree as a focus for reverence and a further reminder of the Buddhist basis of the act.

The day before the ritual, the villagers conducted a ceremony to ask permission of the village tutelary spirit to ordain the tree and consecrate the community forest. Through this non-Buddhist ceremony, the villagers incorporated their spirit beliefs into the larger process of protecting the forest. Pitak did not participate in this rite, but by agreeing to its performance, recognized the importance of the complex syncretic religious and cultural practices of the villagers (Kirsch 1977). In the process, he acknowledged the existing reverence villagers had for the forest, as well as their respect for and fear of the spirits living within it. While some environmental monks criticized Phrakhru Pitak for using spirit beliefs in conjunction with tree ordinations, it is difficult to compartmentalize villagers' beliefs. Pitak carefully balanced the expectations of his own behavior as a Buddhist monk and the broader belief system in which he was raised (Darlington 2003).

Rituals draw on the respect lay people have for the religion and the monks. Tree ordination rituals symbolically recreate the relationship between monks and the laity. Through ordination, men (and even young boys) give up their lay social status and take on the highest status in society. Novices go from being boys subordinate to their parents, teachers, and all adults, to having even their parents bow to them after ordination. While not fully ordaining trees, the tree rituals symbolically raise the status of the forest, highlighting the respect that humans should show. These ceremonies draw on the power of ritual, creating an emotional commitment to the preservation of the forest among the participants. Evidence of this commitment was visible when I visited Phrakhru Pitak's home village in October 2006. The state of the forest that was consecrated and protected through a tree ordination sixteen years earlier was remarkable. The forest was still lush, green, and cooler than the surrounding area. I witnessed villagers genuflecting at the Buddha image at the base of the ordained tree as they passed on their way to collect renewable forest resources such as mushrooms, broom grasses, and fruits. The former headman, who was in office when the tree was ordained but stepped down in 2001, commented that villagers will selectively cut trees in the forest but only with the permission of the entire village. In contrast, the land surrounding the consecrated forest was denuded of trees and mostly covered in corn fields. It is still unknown whether the consecrated forests can survive the continuing pressures of economic growth, but so far the rituals have had a positive effect.

The tree ordination is a creative use of traditional rituals to promote the modern concept of conservation (see Blum, chapter 12, for a discussion of the authenticity of this use). While many Buddhist environmentalists worldwide point to aspects of the Buddha's teachings that they see as supporting conservation work (such as the fact that the Buddha was born, enlightened, gave his first sermon, established several residences and meditation sites, and passed away in forests), there was no environmental crisis like the one we face today during the time of the Buddha. Scholars debate the degree to which the Buddha was concerned with people's lives and conditions in this world as compared with aiding them in their spiritual goal of releasing themselves from worldly suffering, and whether environmental concerns have any scriptural basis (Harris 1991, 1995, 1997; Swearer 1997; Tucker and Williams 1997). Yet Buddhism has evolved dramatically since the time of the Buddha, developing into many new forms as it spread. Tree ordinations and other environmental rituals are perhaps evidence of another way in which Buddhists have adapted their religious beliefs and practices to a new situation, one informed by global pressures and influences.

Long-Life Ceremonies

While tree ordinations have particularly captured the imagination of Thais and foreigners alike, they are only one kind of ritual used by environmental monks to gain the commitment of lay people and to encourage them to undertake conservation projects. Individual Thai monks perform various rituals, drawn from the rich diversity of Buddhist practices, which they feel are appropriate to the particular environmental problems faced by the villagers they serve. For example, Phrakhru Pitak adapted a traditional northern Thai ritual to the cause of healthy rivers. This ritual is usually performed at the behest of someone who is ill or old in an effort to promote a long and healthy life. Here, Phrakhru Pitak, again following a precedent set by Phrakhru Manas in Phayao Province, conducted the *suep chata*, or long-life, ceremony in a different context to raise concern and stimulate action for polluted waterways and to protect the fish that live within them.

In 1993 he invited more than twenty monks from across northern Thailand to join him in performing the ritual for the first time, calling for long life for the Nan River, which flows from the province's highlands to connect with the Chao Praya River in the heart of Thailand's agricultural basin and on through Bangkok. They conducted the ritual, chanted Buddhist *suttas* for the river and the participants, and celebrated Pitak's recent ecclesiastical promotion. The audience included monks from across Thailand, provincial and city dignitaries, and villagers from all along the river's path within Nan and neighboring Phrae provinces.

The ceremony culminated two months of data collection by NGO workers and local volunteers on pollution of the river. Groups of two to four people had walked sections of the river's edge documenting things such as fertilizer run-off, trash dumping, and laundry sites. An educational fair ran for two days surrounding the *suep chata* ritual. Posters showed the pollution data accompanied by photographs of piles of trash and soap suds along the river. Other displays illustrated the fauna and flora of the region, and threats against them due to deforestation and rapid economic growth.

Beyond performing the ritual and holding an educational and cultural fair, Pitak used the event to establish a fish sanctuary in a section of the river. A fish sanctuary had been created the year before at a village upriver from the city. It served two purposes. First, it highlighted that water pollution kills fish, thereby linking the problem of river pollution to people's economic livelihood. And second, it offered a way to foster the renewal of the fish population. Within the protected section of the river, no one was allowed to catch fish. Monks and local people fed the fish in this area, luring them into the sanctuary where they could breed and grow in safety. As the fish population grew, fish moved out of the protected area, where people could catch them. The village that originated the idea received a national environmental award in 1999 for its innovation and success in rejuvenating the fish population.

Phrakhru Pitak invited the provincial governor to open the long-life ceremony for the river and purposefully located the fair on property belonging to a military instillation along the river just outside Nan City. By including both military and governmental officials as key participants in the event, Pitak avoided the kinds of conflicts that some environmental monks elsewhere in the country had faced when they were perceived as being critical of government policy (on some of these conflicts, see Reynolds 1994; Taylor 1993b).

As with the tree ordinations, the long-life ceremony for the river intended to bring attention to the environmental and social problems arising from rapid economic development. Phrakhru Pitak combined religious and environmental teachings, embedding them in a celebration of local culture. Incorporating provincial and military officials in the event placed the ritual within a larger political and social sphere, symbolizing the work of Phrakhru Pitak and his supporters, as well as local environmental NGOs, as part of a *national* endeavor. Rather than marking local issues as falling under the hegemony of a national agenda, Pitak pulled national agents into his project, making concerns for the local situation the center of attention. In particular, Pitak's use of Buddhism and local culture shifted the usual balance of power from the center (Bangkok) to the periphery (the rural provinces), and garnered the cooperation of national players with his agenda. This cooperation has not always been the case for environmental monks, however, as they often struggle against the goals, policies, and practices of the national government and big business.

Conflicting Agendas

Phrakhru Pitak uses tree ordinations and long-life ceremonies as a way of raising awareness among villagers about environmental issues, such as the relationship between deforestation and drought. In the weeks leading up to the performance of a ceremony, he and a group of NGO workers run discussions and slide shows about deforestation, ways in which people can prevent it, ecologically sound agricultural methods, and—most important for Pitak—the interconnections between the environment and Buddhist teachings. I noticed through watching several of his slide shows that Pitak does not include much scientific detail. He begins with cartoon morality stories drawn from the Jataka tales of the Buddha's former lives. Pitak uses names of local people in the tales, pulling in and amusing the audience. The tone then shifts, as he incorporates photographs of lush forests and the wildlife that lives within them. Gradually he introduces pictures of deforestation and environmental problems. For a shocking end, Pitak shows several slides of the impact of a dramatic flood in southern Thailand in 1988 that killed more than three hundred people. Photographs of bloated human bodies floating downstream shake up the audience.

Environmentalists and the government blamed the 1988 flood on excessive deforestation in the hills, which resulted in erosion and the inability of the forest to hold the heavy rains during the monsoon season. The following year the government instituted a ban on commercial logging (Pinkaew and Rajesh 1992). Unfortunately, the ban did not solve the problems of deforestation. Illegal logging done for monetary gain by businessmen and others continues even today. The government also sponsors "development" of forestland, which allows the establishment of monoculture plantations such as eucalyptus and tangerines (Lohmann 1991). Large dams are constructed to provide electricity and water for urban areas, flooding rural farms and forests, damaging the natural environment, and resulting in the dislocation of thousands of people. And in areas unaffected by these government-sponsored projects, villagers themselves continue to clear the forest for cash cropping, or to sell their land to developers for plantations, housing developments, resorts, or golf courses. The fact that these problems have persisted, and even grown, despite the logging ban, underscores the ongoing importance of the environmental monks' work.

Beyond local projects and rituals, these monks have periodically come together since the early 1990s to discuss the challenges they face, and their methods and approaches in dealing with them. These seminars are organized by various NGOs, such as the Thai Interreligious Commission for Development (TICD) or the Wildlife Fund Thailand (WFT, an affiliate of the World Wildlife Fund), or Sekhiyadhamma, an organization that supports socially active monks, originally established by TICD but now run by monks themselves. Participation ranges from as few as twenty to as many as two hundred monks. Underlying the seminars I have attended is the recognition among the monks of their shared aim of relieving suffering and their opposition to the hegemony of the central government and big business, directly or indirectly. Their main goal is to find ways that Buddhism—through its ethical principles, teachings, and practices—can counter what the monks see as the dangers of capitalism and consumerism.

The case of the Pak Mun Dam illustrates several key issues these monks address and engage, as well as the way in which larger concerns can envelop the monks. On the one hand, this example shows the sensitivity of both government and business forces to the power of alternative ideas of development and modernity, and on the other, it highlights the spirituality that the environmental monks represent. The Mun River runs through the northeastern provinces, providing water and a livelihood for many people. In addition to facilitating the irrigation of farmland, the river contains fish on which many of the poor in the northeast depend. In 1991, the Electrical Generating Authority of Thailand (EGAT) began construction of a dam along the river. Hydroelectric power offers relief to the high energy demands of Thailand's urban centers, especially Bangkok, and promotes the nation's growing industry. Opposition to the dam erupted immediately, coming from both national NGOs and local organizations and people. Opponents emphasized environmental damage and the loss of livelihood for local people resulting from the impact of the dam. The dam would threaten the main fish species in the river and would flood large areas of farmland.

In 1991, TICD and the Project for Ecological Recovery (PER) sponsored a seminar at a temple in Ubon Ratchatani Province. The seminar brought together more than fifty monks interested in conservation to share their experiences of different local attempts to apply Buddhist environmental practices and principles. On the third day of the seminar, the organizers arranged a study tour of the dam construction site for the monks. They also visited some of the villages that would be affected. As they arrived at the dam, the monks were met by more than two hundred armed police and special military units who followed them as they toured the site. Although no direct confrontations occurred, the police continued to follow the monks as they returned to the temple, even carrying their weapons into the temple compound.[5] Given

Buddhism's emphasis on nonviolence, bringing guns into a temple compound was highly disrespectful.

The temple abbot demanded an apology from the governor of the province, Saisit Phornkaew, who had ordered the police to follow the monks. A month after the incident, the governor arranged a meeting at the temple. I attended that meeting with several NGO workers from TICD and PER and two environmentalist monks who had been at the earlier seminar. We reached the temple just before the governor arrived. The monks and NGO workers expected an apology and an explanation.

After making a religious donation, the governor explained the government's concerns surrounding the monks' attention to the Pak Mun Dam. He claimed that he did not see the monks themselves as a problem, and he had not ordered the police to carry weapons. He had been worried that the seminar was a vehicle for negative influences from leftist NGOs and university students from Bangkok, which would have been damaging to the reputation of the monkhood (sangha). He also stated that he feared influence from Burmese and Sri Lankan monks, who were known to be political activists. These disruptive influences, he argued, could threaten the stability of Thai society and needed to be monitored. Although he admitted that the police and military had acted improperly, he felt that their observation of the seminar was justified to protect both society and Buddhism.

The meeting, covered modestly by national media, defused the uproar over the armed police entering the temple compound. The governor left seeming pleased with himself; however, the monks involved were not pleased. They felt he had further insulted them by trying to placate them, and by equating their interest in the dam and concerns for the impact it would have on both people and environment with "disruptive" elements in society. Additionally, there was clearly no connection between the seminar and Burmese monks, who have too many life-threatening issues of their own to attend to, leaving them no time or reason to interfere in environmental debates in Thailand. Finally, as for involvement by NGOs and students, representatives of both had indeed participated in planning and running the seminar out of the desire to promote social and environmental justice. Yet, while considering themselves opposed to many government policies, these students and NGOs were not like those who, after the 1976 protests and crackdown, had joined communist insurgents in the jungle after fleeing violence in the capital. In the 1990s, the NGOs and students took the approach of working within the system to bring about social change, rather than literally fighting it.

The governor's response and explanation seemed to push the monks into a firmer position of opposition to the dam and the larger policies it represented.

Some of the monks were adamantly opposed to the dam and critical of the government even before the incident during the seminar. Others had tried to temper the monks' positions, arguing that the sangha stood for the middle ground and should model efforts to mediate conflicting opinions. The monks with whom I spoke after the governor's brief visit indicated that the incident had clarified for them the importance of their position against unbridled economic growth.

At the same time, the monks from the region surrounding the dam remained concerned about extreme positions. Most of the villagers had no problem denouncing the dam and calling for its cancellation. Some of the monks argued for moderation; they recognized the negative effects of the dam and equated it with the root evils in Buddhism, particularly greed. They agreed with environmentalists who argued for changes in the lifestyles in Bangkok so that less electricity would be required, rather than damaging rural areas to support urban demand. But they were also troubled by the anger displayed in some of the lay protests against the dam. Drawing from Buddhist teachings, they took the middle ground, balancing between conservative and radical positions, representing the local people and their culture against the demands of modernity represented by the dam and Bangkok. They did not, however, stand for tradition or a static society—it was clear that they recognized that society is changing. They came to realize that trying to stop change was unrealistic and would only result in alienating the people who look to them for guidance in dealing with the broader world.

Ultimately, the Pak Mun Dam was built. Evidence demonstrates that the environmentalists and villagers were correct; there are fewer fish in the river, and many villagers were relocated from the flooded lands. Livelihoods have been damaged, and many people still seek restitution for what they have lost. In response to local demands, four months a year the dam is opened, allowing water to flow and villagers to fish. Nevertheless, tensions surrounding this dam, and others, remain high, and the debates over their impact remain unresolved (Fahn 2003, 89–96). As with the logging ban, the case of the Pak Mun Dam served to strengthen the commitment of environmental monks to find moral and cultural solutions to Thailand's environmental problems. Their approach continues to be one of seeking alternatives to large-scale development and integrating concepts that originated in the West, such as sustainable agriculture and ecological science, into their religious teachings.

Integrated Agriculture

In addition to creating protected community forests through tree ordinations and challenging people to change their behavior to protect rivers and water

life, Phrakhru Pitak and other environmental monks introduce integrated agricultural methods by encouraging villagers not to plant cash crops, but instead
to mix native crops and livestock that mutually support each other, negating
the need for chemical fertilizers and pesticides.[6] For example, many farmers
plant native rice with fish in the flooded paddy fields. Fruit trees surround the
paddies, drawing from the water as well. Chickens and pigs root among the
fruit trees, eating the fallen fruit and discarded rinds, thereby fertilizing the
fields naturally. Peas and other nitrogen-producing crops are interspersed
among the other plants. Crops are chosen based on the nutrients they produce
as well as those they require, creating symbiotic relationships among the plants
and animals. The monks recognize that merely protecting nature is not sufficient if people do not have alternative sources of livelihood to replace cash
cropping and clear-cutting the forest.

Phrakhru Pitak mentored one farmer, Dang, to convert his feed-corn fields
into an integrated and natural agricultural farm. Using funds raised through
donations to his environmental work, Pitak helped Dang purchase some fruit
tree seedlings, native rice, and other seeds.[7] He contributed money toward the
payments Dang owed to the company that sponsored his cash cropping, which
began to bring down his debt. Dang attended seminars run by NGOs on integrated agricultural methods, where he received additional support to get the farm
established. When I visited his farm four years after he switched to integrated
agriculture, Dang was managing several acres of land that were covered with
fruit trees, natural rice paddies, and herb gardens, and were swarming with chickens and pigs. He claimed he had paid off his debt and even had a small surplus
of funds. He had been able to do this by: (1) not having to buy food (a perennial
problem when all of a farmer's fields are devoted to a single crop), and (2) selling
the surplus organic crops and livestock. Dang now receives many visitors every
year hoping to learn methods of integrated agriculture.

Another environmentalist monk in Nan Province, Phra Somkit, also promotes integrated agriculture. Rather than financially supporting individual
farmers, Somkit established a model integrated agricultural farm on temple land.
On several acres directly behind the village temple, his farm at first appeared
chaotic and overgrown to me. Walking through it with him and his brother, who
manages the farm work, I quickly realized the complexity and beauty of the
plan. A fishpond provided water for native dry rice, banana, papaya and mango
trees, and other perennial crops. Pigs and chickens roamed the farm, rooting out
weeds and insects and fertilizing the land with their excrement.

At the top of a hill, Phra Somkit proudly pointed out the diversity of plants
growing freely. This place, he told me, had been cleared years ago by his father to
make way for growing feed corn. The land supported the corn for only a few years

before erosion and decreased soil fertility inhibited production. At that point, his father donated the land to the temple to make religious merit from the gift.

His father's donation of land adjacent to temple grounds motivated Phra Somkit to learn about sustainable or renewable forms of agriculture. He also adapted the Buddhist tradition of *bindabat*, the monks' daily alms rounds for food. In addition to allowing villagers to make merit through giving him food, he encouraged them to donate land to be placed under his care and used for the integrated agricultural farm.

Phra Somkit's farm demonstrates the benefits of integrated agriculture to the local farmers. The high yields, in addition to the regeneration of degraded land, appeal to the farmers. They volunteer to work on the farm as a new form of merit making and to gain the knowledge and skills necessary for this agricultural approach. Phra Somkit receives visitors from across Thailand and around the world. He claims that more than a thousand people every year come to see and learn from his farm, including university students from the United States, Europe, and Japan.

The farm, its visitors, and the new ideas it introduces into the village illustrate the ways in which activist monks serve as intermediaries between village life and the larger world. Through his fastidious Buddhist practice and teaching, Phra Somkit receives the respect of the villagers. At the same time, he uses his position to filter ideas, concepts, and values entering the village, hoping to steer villagers away from models of consumerism and development that he believes will incur debt and suffering. Instead, he selects methods and concepts he hopes will help villagers adapt to, and be engaged in, the world in ways consistent with Buddhist values, avoiding the dangers of uncontrolled economic growth.

Monks as Agents of Change

Monks hold the highest social position in Thailand. Even when monks come from outside their local area, villagers tend to trust them. They represent the Buddha, and villagers respect their spiritual goals and practices, seeing them as teachers and leaders. Until the kingdom's education system was modernized and centralized in the late nineteenth and early twentieth centuries, most formal education occurred at the temple. Even with that function largely replaced by government schools, the monks play an influential role in village life. They are in a position to introduce and mediate new ideas to local people, and they have the potential to act as agents of change. This potential was recognized by the national government, which used monks throughout the twentieth century to promote its agendas of economic development and nationalism.

In the early twentieth century, wandering forest monks[8] helped the Thai government establish control over remote areas that, historically, had few political or cultural links to Bangkok. Although the use of the forest monks to serve such political motives was controversial, their presence in peripheral areas and the respect villagers had for them enabled the central government to pull these regions under its control (Kamala 1997; Taylor 1993a).

Beginning in the 1960s, the government again used monks to extend its influence and agendas into peripheral, rural areas. The central government established two Buddhist development programs, *Thammacharik* and *Thammathud*, through which monks worked with minority peoples in mountainous northern regions and rural Thai people in remote, poor areas on the borders with Laos and Cambodia. The goals of these programs were multifold: (1) to introduce economic development to relieve poverty; (2) to promote Buddhist practice (and

Environmental monks (including Phrakhru Manas Natheepitak) at tree ordination site on river near Mae Chai, Phayao Province.

even conversion, in the case of the primarily animist mountain peoples) according to central Thai tradition; and (3) to integrate remote areas into the nation. The first two goals served the third, as the government believed that through economic development and Buddhist practice people would feel a stronger connection with Thai culture and the nation. Community development programs run out of the two Buddhist universities in Bangkok fulfilled similar goals (Ishii 1986, 140–42; Keyes 1971; Somboon 1977, 1982; Tambiah 1976, 434–71).

The monks involved in these programs introduced new concepts of economic development and material culture into remote regions. Although many, if not most, of the monks believed in the religious motivations of their work, the consequence was to pull people from what had been relatively isolated areas[9] into a national and global economy and a national concept of citizenship (which included being Buddhist as a central component of national identity).

In the same way, the monks today who oppose the government's development goals and the consumerist trends in the country act as a conduit for alternative ideas—of modernity and globalization, as well as interpretations of religion and social justice—to rural people. Mostly the monks work quietly and garner little attention beyond the local area. Several, however, have become famous for their work. Phrakhru Pitak Nanthakhun and Phra Somkit, for example, both attract numerous visitors from across Thailand and beyond, who come to see how the monks use the methods and philosophies of Buddhism to support their environmental work, and how these lessons might be applied elsewhere. They are frequently invited as speakers at seminars across Thailand, and both have won environmental awards.

Environmental monks also work to gain the support of the sangha administration. Early in the movement, members of the sangha hierarchy criticized environmental monks for undertaking activities they considered inappropriate for monks, such as the condemnation of state economic development policies. For example, Phra Phothirangsri of Chiang Mai believed he was passed over for ecclesiastical promotion because of his vocal opposition to the Doi Suthep cable car in 1986 (personal communication, September 9, 1992). When Phrakhru Pitak sought more information in the late 1980s about the negative ecological impact of eucalyptus trees in response to Nan Province's plan to reforest with eucalyptus plantations, the provincial sangha administration asked him to explain his involvement in this secular issue. His argument demonstrated that his primary concern focused on the suffering of rural people as a result of environmental degradation and convinced the sangha administration of the Buddhist motivations behind his work.

The sangha hierarchy also questioned the use of rituals for social change, particularly tree ordinations, which some saw as violating the Vinaya. To counter such critiques, Phrakhru Pitak carefully consulted his superiors during the planning process for environmental rituals such as tree ordinations and long-life ceremonies for rivers. The long-life ceremony in 1993 incorporated a celebration of his ecclesiastical promotion along with raising concerns about the environmental condition of the Nan River. These cases illustrate the struggles environmental monks have faced from the monastic institution and overcome through careful consideration of the Buddhist bases of their activities. While their work is not publicly condoned by the sangha leaders, they rarely face the questioning that occurred early in the movement. Gradually, environmental monks have won over their superiors through the same mediation process used to gain the support of the laity—by introducing and translating new ideas through careful Buddhist interpretations.

Buddhism and Alternative Modernity

Environmental monks continue to work against forces they feel are potentially destructive to both society and the natural environment. They do not try to turn back time to some idealized past in which villagers supposedly provided for themselves and one another. Instead, they embrace alternative forms of development and modernity, borrowing concepts of ecology and sustainable agriculture from the international environmental movement that can be adapted to fit Thai cultural settings.

These ideas are brought into Thailand through a range of means. Academics, government officials, multinational businesses, and Thai and foreign NGOs all act as conduits for transporting and transmitting ideas from the West into Thailand. These agents bring knowledge—NGOs in particular introduce alternative approaches to the mainstream emphases of the government. Activist monks translate this knowledge into forms the Thai people, especially villagers, can use. As a result, they also translate and transform Buddhist practice, tying Buddhist principles with social justice and the natural environment in ways that did not exist in the past. Given Thailand's cultural identification with Buddhism, such public changes in how Buddhism is understood and practiced also modify what it means to be Thai.

At the same time, the creative actions of this handful of Thai monks are echoing back across the Pacific to influence Buddhists in the United States. Just as the Thai environmental movement followed the rise of the movement in the United States, American Buddhists are beginning to look at the actions of Thai monks as models for strategies to promote environmental awareness in the United States.

In late 2006, I encountered a complex example of the ways in which Thai activist monks are impacting the environmental thinking and actions of the American sangha. I was contacted by a documentary filmmaker working on a film about emerging faith-based environmental movements in North America.[10] She had questions about the Thai environmental monks and, specifically, the tree ordination ritual. She wanted to know the details of the ritual as they were considering asking one of the groups they were documenting whether they would perform one to be included in the film. An American group, Green Sangha, is a nondenominational spiritual community dedicated to environmental action. Although not specifically Buddhist—despite its name—the group cites several engaged Buddhist leaders among its sources of inspiration, including the Dalai Lama and the American Buddhist environmentalist Joanna Macy.

The possibility of their conducting a tree ordination raises the issue of appropriation. For example, would the spirit of the ritual remain the same if it was done at the filmmakers' behest rather than through "authentic" religious and environmental motives? Or, given Green Sangha's emphasis on protecting the environment, would it really be wrong if they decide to conduct a tree ordination? Their activities focus on changing people's behavior to minimize the destruction of forests, particularly through paper usage. A tree ordination could, as it does in Thailand, get people's attention, especially in the United States where such rituals are unusual.

The idea of integrating a tree ordination ritual, the practice of which originated in Thailand, into a documentary on an American spiritual environmental movement illustrates the global nature of Buddhism today. It also highlights the eclectic nature of Buddhist practice in the United States, crossing denominational, ethnic, and national boundaries. The case cannot be easily categorized as "local" or "global," as the cyclical nature of change and its mutual pressures and influences are complex and multidirectional.

These examples of the environmental monks illustrate the ongoing adaptability of Buddhist principles and practice. The Thai people, as active players in the modern world, look to their religion for guidance regarding how they should live in a rapidly evolving world. Buddhism, when interpreted through the lenses of social justice and social welfare, has become a positive, active force in Thai society for dealing with modernity on its own terms. Simultaneously, Thai Buddhist environmentalist activism is reverberating in the United States, inspiring Americans of various persuasions—religious and ethnic—to think and act creatively to incorporate spirituality in the efforts to preserve the earth. This small, grassroots movement that arose in response to the pressures of the modern world in rural Thailand epitomizes the unexpected directions that globalization can take and the high degree of cultural exchange it produces between disparate activists who previously knew little about their respective efforts to protect the environment in their own local contexts. Far from being an isolated, local movement, Thai Buddhist environmentalism has become a factor in the evolution of contemporary Buddhism, and perhaps even in the development of an American socially engaged practice.

Notes

1. Buddhist environmentalism, as with all forms of environmentalism, is not a single, unified, cohesive movement. Different approaches and groups within Buddhist environmentalism draw on various interpretations of ecology, and have differing degrees of scientific knowledge. Western Buddhists in particular most often draw from deep ecology.

2. A coup d'état in 2006 abrogated the 1997 constitution. I do not know whether the new constitution raises similar environmental concerns.

3. The 1961 statistic is from the website of the Thai Royal Forest Department (RFD) (http://www.forest.go.th [accessed August 15, 2005]), as well as England 1996, 60, and P. Hurst 1990, 46. The 1998 figure was estimated by the Food and Agriculture Organization of the United Nations Forestry Department in 2000 from RFD reports from 1999 (http://www.fao.org/forestry/site/22030/en/tha [accessed August 15, 2005]).

4. For a discussion of the significance of sacred mountains in Northern Thailand, see Swearer et al. 2004, especially 33–35 on reactions to the cable car.

5. A month after the seminar I saw a video of it, including the tour of the dam site and affected villages. The video was shown at another seminar for environmental monks of Northeastern Thailand sponsored by TICD to demonstrate solidarity with the monks involved. It also showed armed police and military personnel entering the temple during the first two days of the seminar, before the monks toured the dam site. Police and military were monitoring the conference before the monks showed any public interest in the dam, implying the government was concerned about all the activities of environmental monks, not just those that touched on controversial issues.

6. *Integrated agriculture*, as used by Thais, would be considered an aspect of the concept of *permaculture* in the United States.

7. Funds donated to Buddhist monks during rituals such as tree ordinations are considered a form of religious merit making for the donors. Usually donated funds are used by the monks for their needs and for temple maintenance. In this case, the funds are used to promote the environmental work of the monks.

8. Forest monks, or *phra pa*, are monks who remove themselves from society to isolated forest locations (sometimes temples or meditation centers, sometimes caves or groves) to practice meditation. They are also referred to as *phra thudong*, or ascetic wandering monks.

9. Rural villages were not completely isolated, as long-established trade routes with regional centers connected them with both the dominant political kingdoms to

which they belonged and neighboring kingdoms. Many villages in the north, for example, traded with places in Laos and Burma as well as the various minor kingdoms of Lanna (a major Northern Thai polity).

10. The film, *Renewal*, came out in 2007 and was produced and directed by Marty Ostrow and Terry Kay Rockefeller.

CHAPTER 12

The Transcendentalist Ghost in EcoBuddhism

MARK L. BLUM

W ITHIN the worldwide ecology movement, the cause of environ-mentalism among countries with Buddhist populations, both East and West, is of high interest. In particular, the participation of the sangha in such activities, while certainly not traditional, nonetheless reflects a healthy activist stance toward societal problems. This kind of involvement is absolutely essential for Buddhism, and indeed all religions, to grow and prosper in the rapidly changing world today, for Buddhism is not only surrounded by that world, it is part of it. Nonetheless, I was taken aback when I read Sue Darling-ton's description (revisited in chapter 11) of a ceremony that took place in 1991 at which trees were *ordained* in a ritual conducted by twenty Buddhist monks in Northern Thailand and attended by approximately two hundred villagers. Darlington describes the phenomenon of "environmental monks" in Thailand in detail and shows how they represent a healthy example of how some Bud-dhists in traditional cultural settings are absorbing useful ideas into their practice from Western scientific and environmental knowledge for the express purpose of protecting their physical environment. But my concern is with what the idea of ordaining trees or "performing long-life ceremonies" for rivers means both to us in the West and to Buddhism as a religion. At the very least these actions imply agency in the receiving body, which in a Buddhist context is defined as karmic accountability. Ordination specifically is a ritual initiation that fuses an individual's aspiration to join the community of professional re-ligious, known as the sangha, with public recognition by members of that community of the sincerity of that expressed aspiration. However symbolic tree-ordination may be in Thailand, the disconnect between what may be nothing more than political theater and the religious importance of the ordi-nation of monks (for whom this means abiding by 227 precepts) for maintain-ing Buddhism itself is jolting and worth further scrutiny.

What does it mean for a tree to join the sangha? The very notion cries out for a reconsideration of context, for in the traditional Buddhist context, including the Thai Buddhist context, trees are not considered to be part of sentient life as defined by the term *sattva* (Pāli: *satta*). While this action was taken by monks who had banded together specifically to pursue environmental activism and thus one could understand this as more of a political act than a religious one, the sheer radicalness of the conception nevertheless raises many questions, such as: Is there intentionality in plants? Under what doctrinal tradition or historical precedent can one classify such rituals as Buddhist?

Of course, as Darlington has pointed out, the Thai environmentalist monks recognize that the "ordained" trees are not actually becoming monks. Indeed, in at least one case, the ceremony was based on an adapted version of a Buddha image consecration ceremony, not a monastic ordination at all! Nevertheless, it is clear that the local villagers whose forests are at risk *do* regard—and speak of—the ritual as an ordination. While they may not recognize the distinctions between ordination and consecration rituals, they do recognize the "ordained" trees, now swathed in orange robes, as sacred, and they stop in passing to bow to them just as they would to a (human) monk.

In an attempt to situate this and similar events in a plausible context within the history of ideas, I would like to propose the thesis that it is one particular evolution of Buddhist culture in the West—among the American Transcendentalists—that has provided the conceptual framework that has made these environmentalist monks a possibility in Thailand and in contemporary Buddhist Asia as a whole. In other words, the ordaining of trees by Buddhist monks in Thailand could only have happened at the end of the twentieth century, first, because of the maturation of Buddhist discourse within the American religious tradition of Transcendentalism, and second, because of the subsequent spread of this rhetoric to Thailand. But by saying there is no earlier tradition for this sort of ritual behavior in Buddhism (or Transcendentalism), I am not taking the position that such acts can never be considered Buddhist or sacred in general and therefore do not deserve our respect and support. The destruction of the forests of Thailand, and indeed all of Southeast Asia, is a huge problem and an important environmental concern for everyone. If by performing such rituals the activist monks are able to garner greater public awareness of the problem, these people should be praised. But sympathizing with bold environmental activism does not change the fact that ordaining trees is inconceivable within ancient, medieval, and even premodern forms of Asian Buddhist orthodoxy or orthopraxy. We are thus led to ask, *what* form of Buddhism is this? What we see in such forms of Buddhist-inflected environmental activism—what we might call ecoBuddhism—is, in short, something new, and as such it is much too early to pass historical judgment on whether it will be accommodated by one or more of the Buddhist traditions.

There are many issues involved here, and it may be helpful to frame those most central in terms of what I would like to call "dichotomies of concern." First is the tension between the differing roles that a member of the sangha inevitably plays internally in pursuit of personal liberation and externally in care of the community. By the term *community*, I include both professional monastics and lay supporters. In this context it is worth noting that the monks identified in Darlington's study of Thai "ecology monks" are typically "village monks" from rural areas. As they are generally not considered "scholar-monks," they are therefore less restricted by what are termed "abstract" doctrinal problems inherent within Buddhist doctrine that might not support their activism. What is intriguing about the monks who ordain trees is what she describes as "their responsibility as monks and as Buddhists to become engaged in this manner" (Darlington 1998, 4). That monks should feel inclined to help their surrounding lay community is not particularly surprising, as there are many mentions in the Vinaya literature of interactions between the sangha and secular society, but this stance expresses a rather strong sense of protectionism not toward people in their surroundings but toward the natural, physical environment, and this is not attested to in any of the canonical Theravādin literature that I am aware of.

How is the sangha to balance its concern or responsibility to itself with its responsibility to the outside world? This dichotomy is particularly important insofar as the sangha's responsibility to maintain its own population, the discipline within its ranks, and the rigor of its active engagement with its own tradition must be of primary importance. Otherwise the sangha would cease to exist, and the consequences for Buddhism in any given culture are such that while lay populations may complain about specific cases of lax discipline or wealthy monasteries, they are by and large supportive of this presumption of responsibility to self-preservation within the sangha. The consequences for the sangha in China during the Cultural Revolution, when the authorities did everything they could to eliminate it as an institution from society, have been dire, and the reflowering of Buddhism in China today is often measured by the numbers of monastics. Given that the modern world has been devastating to the sangha in every Buddhist country, we are compelled to ask how much room is there for professional Buddhist involvement in the modern environmentalist movement?

In the United States, the so-called ecoBuddhism movement has "solved" this dilemma by following two innovative hermeneutic moves of the late twentieth century made by poet Gary Snyder and deep ecology founder Arne Naess.

Taking an East Asian approach suffused with *tathāgatagarbha* doctrine, Snyder took the notion of the *dharmadhātu* from the Gandavyūha tradition, wherein the phenomenal world is viewed as inherently sacred, and declared that this should be "our" meaning of sangha. This has proved extremely influential within American ecoBuddhism and arguably among convert Buddhists in the West as a whole. But while it rhetorically resolves this particular dichotomy by eliminating the inside/outside distinction for the sangha, one could argue that this approach works in American convert Buddhism precisely because there is no institutional sangha tradition in the Asian sense. Since the founding of the San Francisco Zen Center, the number of American Buddhist communities dominated or run entirely by non-immigrant Buddhists has grown dramatically, but this has never resulted in a clearly defined monastic sangha.

Unlike Snyder, Spinoza scholar and avid outdoorsman Naess did not receive Buddhist training in an Asian monastery. But Naess took the rhetorical link between the Huayan mutual identification doctrine and the belief that nature is sacred or holy one step further in promoting his vision of environmental activism as itself a process that should result in self-transformation, and ultimately in a revolution of human consciousness as a whole.

This has led ecoBuddhists to two doctrines not seen in the history of Buddhist thought prior to the modern era. First is the identification of the self with the natural world as a religious attainment. Picking up on the Chan/Zen tradition of a "true self" or a "great self" based on another influential *tathāgatagarbha* text, *The Nirvāṇa Sūtra* (that is, the Mahāyāna version of the *Mahāparinirvāṇa-sūtra*). Joanna Macy distinguishes a conventional, even dysfunctional, "empirical" self from a spiritually exalted "wider ecological self" that either identifies with nature's creatures, both seen and unseen, or regards them somehow as lovers (1990, 1991). Second is the presumption that the natural world that this deeper, "true" self identifies with is, a priori, not only sacred but *liberated* or *enlightened*. That is, if one can awaken to their internal ecoself, he or she will be liberated because the identification with Nature is, in essence, a mystical union with the Sacred. Looked at in another way, this redefines practice for the Buddhist; the Earth itself becomes both the "sacred platform" for the performance of ritual meditation (*dōjō, bodhimaṇḍa*) and icon (*honzon*) that serves as the object of the ritual meditation as well. Nature thus stands as Buddha for us, preaching the way to truth and liberation, as a kind of eternal *nirmāṇakāya*. But when Elizabeth Roberts states that "Earth is infused with meaning, awareness, and a creative evolutionary drive" (1990), she has gone beyond the given notion of sacrality in nature that we find even in the *tathāgatagarbha* doctrines of Mahāyāna Buddhism to something that suggests a teleology entirely absent from traditional Buddhist discourse. I would argue that regarding trees as suitable objects of ordination is of a piece with seeing in nature some kind of "awareness" (of what?), and we cannot understand this gestalt without resorting to another religious paradigm that has entered the mix of what is essentially a form of "world Buddhism." In other words, is ecoBuddhism a new form of Buddhism? It certainly looks something like a Protestant Buddhism in the prominence of its social activism. But whatever name or label is used, the notion of seeking the liberating truth in the physical, material world of *rūpa* requires a non-Buddhist conception of earth or nature as the embodiment of the sacred.

In exploring the likelihood that the American Transcendentalism movement is a more plausible source for the religious impetus to ordain trees, I do not seek to challenge the appreciation of this as heroic or even the judgment of it as "Buddhist" within today's context of American Buddhism or Western Buddhism, such as it is. While it would be disingenuous to speak with authority about the relationship between humanity and nature in American Transcendentalism, traditional Buddhism, or even American Buddhism, if we limit ourselves to canonical statements within the first two categories—we cannot yet speak of a canon in the context of the third—a clarification of these two positions may be instructive.

A third question worthy of consideration is precisely what Buddhist thought was available to or had an impact on people such as Emerson and Thoreau. Here one must look at the specific ways in which Buddhist thought can be detected in their discourse, taking care to identify *which* of the many forms of Buddhism they understood or thought they understood, and what was it about their particular understanding that may be seen in the discourse of ecoBuddhism. Were there sufficient space, we could mark a divide in American Transcendentalist thinking on religion around 1860. The initial Transcendentalist period of religious exploration prior to 1860 was represented by Emerson and Thoreau, as seen in such works as Emerson's *Nature* in 1836, his public lecture entitled *The Transcendentalist* of 1842, Thoreau's *Walden* published in 1854, and the initial run of the experimental quarterly *The Dial*, published between 1840 and 1844. After 1860, the journals *The Radical* (1865–1872) and *The Index* (1881–1886) seem to mark a second phase, one that progressed further toward the idealized conception of what was variously enunciated as "American religion," "free religion," "absolute religion," or "universal religion," in the writing of people such as Samuel Johnson, John Weiss, Thomas Wentworth Higginson, and Lydia Maria Child, a group more openly struggling to find a way to recognize the validity of other religious traditions without assailing the unassailable—namely, the a priori status of Christianity as authoritative.

But there is enough in the religious thought of Emerson and Thoreau that is suggestive of an outlook that set the groundwork for the religious view of nature that is so prevalent in ecoBuddhist thought today, that the discussion of American Transcendentalism here will be limited to these two early figures.

But first let us begin by clarifying the Buddhist perspective in terms of its traditional doctrine. As there are many Buddhisms, we will restrict discussion to the two traditions of Buddhist thought that dominate the ecoBuddhist discourse today: Abhidharma in India and medieval thought in Japan.

Nature in Early Buddhist Thought and the Abhidharma

The relationship between humanity and nature in traditional Buddhist religious culture as seen in a Theravādin society such as Thailand is most easily known through the Indian doctrinal tradition known as Abhidharma, for this is the cultural milieu within which Theravādin monks have traditionally lived and thought. There has been some influence of both Indian and Chinese Mahāyāna ideas in Thailand, but these have been subjugated to the more dominant Abhidharma or Abhidhamma (Pāli) since the establishment of the Theravādin tradition.

The first point to be made, one that hardly needs mentioning to Buddhologists but may not be well known to ecoBuddhists without doctrinal training, is that the ideology of *tathāgatagarbha* and *dharmadhātu* that impacted Chinese and Japanese Buddhist attitudes toward nature so significantly is essentially missing from Theravādin Buddhist thought. These are relatively late Mahāyāna notions. This is not to say that Theravādins do not have religious sentiments toward nature; they do, but not in the way we see in Japan, where *tathāgatagarbha* thought is pervasive.

Although there is some ambiguity as to the limits or borders of what these terms include, one must distinguish between *sattva,* living beings (generally excluding plants), and *rūpa,* which designates matter or the physical. This only follows tradition and is especially pertinent for Thailand, or Theravādin Buddhism in general, because it was only in late sixth- or early seventh-century China that some Buddhist philosophers began to argue for erasing this distinction. The environmental movement often points to the Buddhist sense of the "interconnectedness of all life," which seems to be a reference to the *pratītyasamutpāda,* or dependent origination, the core Buddhist doctrine of causality as it relates to organic matter. The ability to imagine that one could be reborn as a hungry-ghost in the next life, or that one was an animal in a previous life, these are typical discussions in the canon of how one relates to other *sattva*. But when it comes to physical matter, and, with only few exceptions, to non-sentient, that is, non-animal, life, the professional monks who wrote the sutra and Abhidharmic literature may have developed skillful theories about its nature, but their motivation for doing so was certainly not to *identify* with it. To quote Edward Conze's remarks in a book review of Y. Karunadasa's *Buddhist Analysis of Matter* (1967), a study of *rūpa* in the Theravāda tradition: "The last chapter investigates the motives which induced these Yogins to work out a fairly complicated theory of matter, and shows that they were *in every way motivated by the religious and ethical purpose of removing craving for and attachment to rūpa*" (emphasis added) (Conze 1970).

In other words, at least for the Theravādin tradition, the physical world—and of course the same sentiment would hold toward a great deal of human culture—was perceived from the point of view of a monk to be primarily a potential source of suffering. This is why *rūpa* is so frequently discussed in the context of the other four *skandhas* (which are all psychological). This position does not see the physical world as inherently evil, corrupt, or illusory, but it does not see it as sacred either. The physical world is neutral, but it holds such enormous potential for causing attraction, revulsion, and attachment in every affective response we have to it, that it is generally viewed with cold objectivity rather than as an object of awe and beauty. The only thing sacred in nature were spirits who lived in trees, but the fact that a spirit will move to a different tree when the one it has been residing in becomes uninhabitable shows that the locale of the power is in the spirit, not the tree.

The core concern in early Buddhist references to nature, or what is in the natural world, is essentially karmic. That is, how the individual *reacts* toward what is in one's physical environment is what the suttas discuss. Thus even in the cosmological myth of the *Aggacus suttanta* (Dīgha N. 27), which contains perhaps the only clear statement in the early literature about how humanity affects its environment and the environment affects humanity, constructs its narrative as a moral argument against the evils of greed. The text makes no reference to anything smacking of the presumed mutual dependence of humanity and nature. The trope is that after humans become attached or covetous of the sustenance provided to them by the natural world, that sustenance disappears, as Schmithausen has pointed out (2000). So, while today's environmental activists may also be *motivated by religious and ethical purpose,* it is useful to remember that the yogin-scholars who were the authors of the canonical Theravādin treatises that discussed the physical world had a *religious and ethical purpose* defined not by a desire to embrace, revere, or ordain nature, but to remove any and all personal *craving for and attachment to* nature within themselves so as to become aloof or indifferent (*upekṣa*).

Another presumption of karma theory among Buddhists and other Indian religious traditions that is often overlooked in the West is the fact that it is inherently hierarchical. Of the original five realms of existence (later expanded to six), the world of humans and gods is distinctly superior. Animals are traditionally grouped along with hungry ghosts and hell-beings as being one of the three "unfortunate" realms (*durgati*) where living creatures are reborn after doing evil. In other words, to be reborn as an animal is a form of punishment. As Schmithausen has pointed out, animals are presumed to be unhappy and eager to leave their state. From a traditional Indian Buddhist point of view, the ideal world would have few, if any, animals in it.

It is worth repeating here that the disdain for the physical promoted within the Theravādin sangha does not imply any demonization of nature any more than it implies a demonization of the householder's life similarly rejected. Again, as a category of reality, *rūpa* denotes everything physical—both the physical world and one's own physical body. But in this "elder" tradition neither is the practitioner's own body regarded as sacred, nor is the natural world something a monk is drawn toward as a source of the sacred or even described as a place sought for spiritual comfort (that is, a place of refuge that stands in opposition to human society). In fact, the highest plane of meditation "heaven," called *ārūpya,* is without any *rūpa* at all. Not only is "nature" not one of the three refuges, it does not even exist as a concept; and if there is one thing Abhidharmic Buddhism is rich in, it is concepts. To see nature objectified as a source of the sacred we must move to East Asia, where a paradigm based on *tathāgatagarbha* doctrines extolling universal buddha-nature was, after some five hundred years, extended to the physical world, a topic to be discussed next.

Nature in Japanese Buddhism

Given the invisibility of nature in early, Abhidharmic, Buddhism, it is not surprising to see so many ecoBuddhist writers draw upon traditions of Daoist escapism and, even more commonly, medieval Japan. The premodern Japanese relationship to nature is unquestionably one of intimacy, awe, and reverence. While this kind of animism or pantheism is common in many ancient cultures, in Japan's medieval period there is also a poetic-religious discourse that looks to nature as a source of spiritual inspiration and, as some interpret it, as the Absolute itself offering salvation. This view was famously extolled by the noted Japanese historian Ienaga Saburō (1913–2002) in a 1944 publication entitled *Nihon shisōshi ni okeru shūkyōteki shizenkan no tenkai* (The Development of a Religious View of Nature in the History of Japanese Thought), and more recently discussed in some detail in the context of Buddhist notions of the phenomenal world as sacred by William LaFleur, who has contributed to the ecoBuddhism discussion with an essay on poetics and the universality of the term *sattva* (LaFleur 1990, 2001). Inasmuch as the Japanese view, or shall I say "the Japanese Buddhist" view, of nature as sacred object continues to play a significant role in Western ecoBuddhist discourse, it is worth summarizing here.

Arguably the most novel ideological event in the history of Buddhism in East Asia was the thesis first put forward in the sixth century by Jizang (549–623) that plants and trees also have buddha-nature, and by extension are therefore part of the universal reality of truth expressed in *tathāgatagarbha* doctrines.[1] According to the *Nirvāṇa Sūtra*, that is, the Mahāyāna version of the *Mahāparinirvāṇasūtra*, Emptiness (*śūnyatā*) is not the only absolute—both empty (*śūnya*) and nonempty (*aśūnya*) aspects of reality are equally sacred. Putting aside the question as to whether this is an ontological or epistemological statement, LaFleur quotes Fung Yu-lan's interpretation that when Jizang extended the *Nirvāṇa Sūtra*'s claim of universal buddha-nature to insentient plants, he was only expanding upon the hermeneutic precedent of Daosheng (360–434) who insisted buddha-nature include even *icchantika* (those who lack faith or ethical responsibility) before he actually saw this expounded in Dharmakṣema's full translation of the sutra. But while the approach of Jizang's argument may seem similar to Daosheng's, the question for Daosheng pertained to the standing of *icchantika* within the rubric of *sattva*. He did not attempt, as Jizang was doing, to redefine the boundaries of *sattva* itself, a far more radical endeavor. It is ironic that Jizang's view actually reflects an ancient, pre-Buddhist Indian religious paradigm that original Buddhism explicitly rejects (Schmithausen 1991).

The Nirvāṇa Sūtra was admittedly not accepted by everyone in East Asia, for the Yogācāra schools continued to assert a five-*gotra* scheme that included a category for *sattva* incapable of realizing *bodhi* and attaining liberation.[2] But by the early seventh century, *Nirvāṇa Sūtra* doctrines had deeply permeated all other schools of Chinese Buddhism. By the end of the eighth century, the ninth patriarch of the Tiantai school, Zhanran (711–782), had laid out a skillful argument that not only maintained Jizang's buddha-nature in plants but extended it to the inorganic physical world as well. By Zhanran's time, Vajrayāna thought had entered China in a major way, and he may have been influenced by the new conception of the *dharmakāya* that added a manifest aspect to its traditional definition as unmanifest essence. In the Vajrayāna worldview, the affirmation of nonemptiness in the *Nirvāṇa Sūtra* is expanded to where the Absolute, labeled alternatively as buddha, emptiness, suchness (*tathatā*), or "dharma-ness" (*dharmatā*), is equally present in all phenomena.

This doctrine shows up explicitly in the writings of the Japanese monks Kūkai (774–835) and Dōgen (1200–1253) but also resonates in the writings of many other medieval Buddhists in Japan. It takes a millenarian, even nationalistic, turn with Nichiren (1222–1282), for example, who regards the *Lotus Sūtra* metaphor of bodhisattvas "welling up out of the earth" as a prediction for the future of Japan as the physical locale where the full glory of the Buddha's truth will be realized in history. Ienaga's study infers that the rejection of an urban lifestyle in the poets Kamo no Chōmei (1155–1216), Saigyō (1118–1190), and Matsuo Bashō (1644–1694) reflects their search for salvation in nature. This argument has been reproduced by writers such as LaFleur, Graham Parkes, Deane Curtin, and the Sri Lankan–Australian scholar Padmasiri de Silva, to name but a few, in their efforts to discern a Buddhist basis for environmental activism.

But this approach has brought on confusion and the misunderstanding that often occurs when ideas are removed from context. For example, consider this famous poem by Saigyō remembering Kūkai as he looks out upon the island-dotted Inland Sea, as translated by LaFleur (2001, 202):

Cloud-free mountains	*kumori naki*
Encircle the sea, which holds	*yama nite umi no*
The reflected moon	*tsuki mireba*
A view of it there changes the islands	*shima zo kōri no*
Into holes of emptiness in a sea of ice	*taema narikeri*

LaFleur sees a conception of "nature as mandala" here, and draws out the poem's religious implications both by translating *taema* as "holes of emptiness" and interpreting that word choice to reflect Saigyō's intention to signal that "the island there is really Emptiness itself." If this is indeed a poem about emptiness and nature as a mandala, it certainly supports the Ienaga thesis. While LaFleur, to his credit, points out that the poem "does not mean that religious value is attributed to the concept of nature or to 'Nature' *as something abstracted from the phenomena that compose it*," his reading nonetheless implies an affirmation of the Ienaga thesis that in nature Saigyō saw Buddhist expressions of truth as mandala and within the mandala representations of emptiness. Thomas Rohlich in chapter 6 discusses Saigyō's actual religious sensibility, but I would suggest that LaFleur's reading is more in the interpretation, especially the English translation, than the poem itself. The key religious references here, "encircle" and "emptiness," are words that are in fact not in the poem; a more literal reading would yield something like "to see the moon on the sea amidst cloud-free mountains, the islands are now breaks in the ice." Without taking anything away from the poetic achievement of the LaFleur translation, I merely wish to point out that its use of religiously charged images such as "mountains encircle the sea" and "holes of emptiness" do create associations with mandalas and emptiness, and do indeed suggest a statement about "nature as sacred expression of Buddhist truth." But insofar as there is neither "encircling" nor "emptiness" in the original, such a reading requires a significant interpretive leap.

Given this modern hermeneutic of portraying ancient and medieval Japanese Buddhist thinkers as embodying not merely a sense of awe toward nature but genuine religious reverence, it is not surprising to see many of the new and rather free interpretations of Buddhism and environmental concerns linked to traditional Japanese Buddhist soteriology. But canonical statements about the buddha-nature of plants, trees, rocks, and mountains from medieval China or Japan display no concern whatsoever for a deteriorating environment and its geological and cultural implications. A typical comment in premodern Chinese and Japanese poetry about a house abandoned to the natural elements is that it has been rendered decrepit by natural forces and lost. When Ienaga Saburō proffered his thesis about Japanese views of nature as savior, not only did he not conclude with any ecological imperative but he was explicit that the Japanese religious view of nature only happened after Japanese culture left behind its animistic identification with nature, "when nature is seen as something *different* from human life" (Bellah 1965, 390). Ienaga concluded that this abandonment of human environs for natural environs did not solve in itself the spiritual crises of the individuals who sought it but only brought on new crises of loneliness (Bellah 1965, 392–93). In other words, even in the ancient and premodern contexts, nature did not succeed in achieving Ienaga's own category of absolute savior.

Contributions to ecoBuddhist discourse also come from creative translations of Buddhist doctrinal concepts. The ecoBuddhist writer Padmasiri de Silva, for example, likes to cite an essay by Daisaku Ikeda on the environment in which Ikeda selects the Buddhist term *eshō funi* to be representative of the Buddhist viewpoint on humanity and nature: "The Buddhist doctrine of the oneness of the living entity and its environment (*eshofumi*) [*sic*] focuses on the human being as part of the vast physical universe" (Ikeda n.d., 32).[3] But while *funi* does mean nondual, the term *eshō*, an abbreviation of *ehō-shōhō*, is traditionally used to denote one's state of existence defined karmically: namely, one's body, mind, and the particular locale where one is born are all the results of previous karma. The term *eshō funi* is a doctrinal statement on the inescapable impact of past karma on present conditions *for the individual;* it has nothing to do with humanity's impact on the environment. Ikeda, however, has creatively redefined the term in an ecologically appealing way such that when de Silva and others understand that "the Japanese word *eshofumi* [*sic*] is one word referring both to nature and humans" they are not wrong, but when someone says "the import of esho funi is that, since we shape our environment, we have to take action to change it"[4] we have moved beyond Buddhism.

To Ikeda's dictum, de Silva adds: "In the Sinhala language the term *svābhava dharma* captures the lawful nature of the universe within which humans and nature live." A reference to Abhidharma theories of dependent origination based on the notion of discrete dharmas as the product of karma, the *traditional* context for talking about the self-nature of dharmas is moral and psychological, not ecological. Statements like these from Ikeda and de Silva, Asian Buddhists well trained in their own traditions, are thoughtful responses to the need for new, creative thinking about the fundamental problem of humanity and nature. But their ecological implications objectify nature in a way wholly unnatural to Buddhist thought. Their statements are more of a piece with notions of mystical identification with nature that one finds in pre-Buddhist India and in phrases like "think like a mountain" associated with contemporary writers such as Aldo Leopold, John Seed, and Bill Devall. Rather than anything from the Buddhist tradition, even in Japan, this viewpoint is more reminiscent of nature as a prime source of spiritual truth as seen in American Transcendentalist thinkers, who were influenced themselves somewhat by non-Buddhist Indian thought. Let us turn now to consider how that tradition came to view nature as religious object, beginning with the Unitarian movement.

Transcendentalism, Eastern Religion, and Nature I: Unitarianism

Transcendentalism, at least the form of it expounded by Emerson and Thoreau, was something like a Protestantism of Nature in that it saw nature as a given medium between humanity and the Creator God, much as Rudolph Otto viewed Christ in that role. Given Transcendentalism's origins in Unitarianism's assertion of the authority of reason and scientific inquiry, this may seem somewhat paradoxical, but neither spoke with only one voice. As there are Transcendentalists in Europe as well, in this chapter I am specifically referring to views of nature in early American Transcendentalism, a movement that arose in New England with little influence from Europe. American Transcendentalism was born from, and therefore shared with, Unitarian and other liberal Congregationalist churches, a standpoint that consciously moved away from the Puritan doctrine of humanity's nature as "total depravity," recognizing the value of human agency in all religious matters. Unitarians and Transcendentalists are known for encouraging the personal cultivation of religious virtues also held sacred by Puritan culture but rejected as a means to salvation, namely self-reliance, frugality, morality, and the avoidance of materialism.

The Unitarian movement traces its origins to the sixteenth-century Protestant Reformation with communities first forming in Poland, Hungary, and England. But it was English Unitarianism, flourishing in late eighteenth and early nineteenth centuries despite legal restrictions, that was transplanted to America. Although there has never been a fixed creed of the Unitarian church, it has consistently distinguished itself by denying the doctrine of the trinity in order to direct faith toward only the Creator, and by asserting universal access to the noumenal (extra-empirical) realm through human beings' exercise of their rational faculties to uncover the truths in "natural religion." The timing of the establishment of the Unitarian churches in England and America coincides precisely with the American Revolution,[5] and in the United States the Unitarians became notably successful among elite intellectuals at this time, where among their adherents can be counted John Adams, Alexander Hamilton, and Daniel Webster.

The British thinker Joseph Priestley (1733–1804) is a key figure in this story. Credited with bringing the Unitarian faith from Britain to the United States in 1794, he also may have been the first church figure in the United States to publish on Asian religion with his 1799 monograph entitled *A Comparison of the Institutes of Moses with those of the Hindoo and other ancient nations; with remarks on Mr. Dupuis's "Origin of All Religions"* and his more fully developed *The Doctrines of Heathen Philosophy Compared with Those of Revelation*, written at the request of Thomas Jefferson and published posthumously in 1804. But Priestley also wrote *A Grammar of the English Language* and *The History of Electricity* after meeting Benjamin Franklin. Priestley is considered one of the founders of modern chemistry because he was the first person to isolate oxygen, ammonia, and carbon monoxide; discover the function of blood in respiration; and create artificially carbonated water. He also took an openly enthusiastic position in support of both the American and French revolutions, a stance that led to the torching of his house in England and eventual emigration to the United States, where he became friends with Jefferson and John Adams. Priestley is a defining figure for the first phase of American Unitarianism prior to it yielding to the Transcendentalist values outlined by Emerson. Reference books cite Priestley for defining the creed of Unitarian faith as one that emphasized "scriptural rationalism, materialist determinism, and . . . a humanitarian Christology."[6] But for all his modernism, for all his devotion to scientific inquiry and investigation of other faiths, what the reference books do not mention is that Priestley was intensely dogmatic in asserting that Christianity was the only true religion, a point about which he was unabashedly polemic. Only Christianity was inspired by divine revelation, all other religions were created by humanity; only Christianity produced rational doctrines; and only Christianity produced rational humans to appreciate them. That is how it was known that Western societies were superior. Scientific inquiry into the Bible among these early Unitarians was restricted to arguments that proved its divine origins by virtue of the miracles attested to therein. The core contradiction in early Unitarian doctrine, then, lies in its assertion of the imperative to use humanity's rational powers to discern the truth of the Creator in the Bible and the natural world but its abhorrence of applying those same powers to examine the irrational assumption that among the world's many religions only Christian narratives of truth could be genuine.

But in the early nineteenth century, when much of America was still under the sway of church revivals inspired by the legacy of Jonathan Edwards (1703–1758) known as the Great Awakening, the paradox of Unitarian scientific Protestantism was not keenly felt. More significant for our discussion is that the Unitarian movement growing out of the liberal wing of the Congregationalist churches in New England rejected the emotional faith of Edwards that, in its reassertion of the Puritan assumption of humanity's wicked depravity, had resurrected the Calvinist doctrine of predestination wherein only the elect were saved. By contrast, under the influence of theologians such as William Ellery Channing (1780–1842), Unitarianism developed a rationalist faith that asserted that all people possessed an element of divinity, a "fact" that reflected God's desire for people to progress through their own efforts and through that progress come to know Him and the goodness He has placed in the world.

Transcendentalism, Eastern Religion, and Nature II: Emerson

Ralph Waldo Emerson (1803–1882) was born in Boston to a Unitarian minister with an interest in the arts, and thus grew up in a "progressive" religious environment. Harvard College had been ideologically taken over by Unitarian thinkers by 1810, and they dominated the intellectual environment when Emerson matriculated there in 1817. He went on to its Divinity School, but by the 1830s his views had begun to shift. His diaries speak of a deep spiritual crisis that resulted from the death of his first wife two years after their marriage in 1829. But we should also look to Europe for possible causes of a shift in thinking, for his older brother William had then returned from Germany with the new biblical criticism wherein miracles were questioned and human agency was speculated in biblical authorship.[7] His brother might also have brought back something of contemporary German interest in India, already explicit in the works of Schopenhauer, Schlegel, Novalis (Friedrich von Hardenberg), and Schleiermacher.

By 1832 Emerson had resigned his ministry. After a trip to Europe in which he met Coleridge and Wordsworth and established a lifelong friendship with Thomas Carlyle, he returned to settle in Concord, Massachusetts, where he began a new career as author and lecturer and where he remained, except for one other trip to Britain, until his death. From a lecture delivered in 1835, *Defects in Historical Christianity,* and his first book, *Nature,* published in 1836, the core ideas that continued over most of his career are made clear. The publication of *Nature* is considered by many to mark the beginning of Transcendentalism in the United States, even though he himself disavowed the name. In July 1838, he delivered a lecture to the Harvard Divinity School later published as the *Divinity School Address*, an event that caused an uproar, alienating him from the leaders of that institution while attracting a group of like-minded followers from among its students.

Going beyond mere questioning of the miracles in the Bible, in these works Emerson took issue with the entire biblical tradition that looked to an utterly transcendent Other as the only source for salvation and to logic as the best means to find one's way to Truth. No doubt influenced by the Romanticism and Kantian idealism of Coleridge and Carlyle, Emerson's expansion of the Unitarian belief in the presence of divinity in all men also reflected a reaction against what he saw as the evisceration of free will implied in rationalist thinkers such as Locke, for whom reason was the only way to understand the scriptures, and Newton, for whom the world functioned in wholly mechanistic fashion. Instead Emerson stressed the value of spiritual knowledge through intuition, and that redemption was to be sought within. Jesus indeed manifested or incarnated the divine, but the real meaning of his story was as an ideal example of how a universal principle in everyone is fully realized. Emerson also stressed the importance of realizing the continuity between the natural world and the mind of the individual, for God's presence is in all living things. Toward the end of *Nature* he weighs in with a passionate plea to embrace nature so as to let the eternal spirit inside oneself run free:

> The foundations of man are not in matter, but in spirit. But the element of spirit is eternity. . . . We distrust and deny inwardly our sympathy with nature. We own and disown our relation to it. We are, like Nebuchadnezzar, dethroned, bereft of reason, and eating grass like an ox. But who can set limits to the remedial forests of spirit? (Sealts and Ferguson 1969, 33)

Although this implies in some sense that nature's value to humanity is metaphorical or even instrumental, in another sense nature is the designated, authoritative object of the spiritually seeking mind. For Emerson, a basic, primordial relationship exists between humanity, nature, and God as something that can be known and experienced. In *Nature,* Emerson famously describes a mystical experience of unity with nature that completely erased his sense of individuality, as if he were a "transparent eye-ball" wherein he sensed the universal just as his personal vantage point disappeared. In his words, "I am nothing, I see all." As mentioned above, this notion of mystical union with nature or earth, which is identified as the source of all that is sacred, is a common sentiment in the discourse of deep ecology and ecoBuddhism specifically.

Another critical aspect of Emerson's thought that one finds echoed in ecoBuddhism is the idea that there is an aspect of divinity in all people. Akin to the Mahāyāna doctrine of universal *buddha-nature,* when Emerson proclaimed this position in the *Divinity School Address* given at Harvard in 1838 it caused an estrangement between him and that institution, one that continued for more than thirty years. Despite the nature of a Harvard dominated by what were progressive Unitarians at that time, Emerson in effect attacked the assumed truth, as seen in the work of Priestley, for example, of the singularity of Jesus as the only immanent source of what is truly sacred, the only link between God and humanity in the known world. But from his journals we can see that Emerson understands this as the flip side of *maya,* or illusion. Thus the source for this radically new perspective was Hindu, not Buddhist (Versluis 1993, 54–55, 66).[8]

Another aspect of Emerson's thought in *Nature* that resonates well with deep ecology is his critique of humanity as "fallen" by virtue of its estrangement from nature rather than the usual view of humanity as fallen from events in Eden. All beings in nature carry individual souls that are "imbedded in" or "mingle" with what he called "the One Universal Mind." Later, apparently after reading in the Purāṇas, in 1841 he would publish an essay entitled "The Over-Soul" in which he put forth this same notion but expressed using only examples of mystic experiences from the Western tradition. What is critical here and what develops more explicitly after his study of the Upaniṣads is the idea that humanity does have the ability to unite with this Over-Soul if we can only return to our original state of unity, and the natural world is where this path is best found.

Where Channing applied himself in defense of reason to develop principles of interpretation for discerning "the last and perfect revelation of [God's] will by Jesus Christ," explaining that "all Christians are compelled to use [rational principles] in their controversies with infidels" (Channing 1957), Emerson sought to develop his intuition to sense God's presence both in the individual and in the natural world. And unlike Channing, Emerson was happy to hear suggestions from other religious traditions. Emerson's religious sensitivity in effect shoved hard against the boundaries of Unitarianism, reminding us that despite its efforts to define itself as the anti-Calvinist alternative through its valorization of human rationality, Unitarianism in the nineteenth century still shared an unshakeable faith that religious truth can be found only in a proper reading of the New Testament. In 1886, some fifty years after *Nature* appeared and three years after Emerson's death, fellow Unitarian James Freeman Clarke (1810–1888) published *Vexed Questions in Theology,* in which he described five points of a "theology of the future," wherein many of Emerson's ideas were still treated as radical. Most vexing of all, according to Clarke, was whether one could reject the core Calvinist doctrines of original sin and "atonement by Christ for the elect only" (Clarke 1886).[9] The latter dogma is overturned by what Clarke describes as belief in "salvation by character," meaning salvation can be earned by anyone on the basis of how he or she lives his or her life. This is pure Emerson or what might be called Emersonian Transcendentalism. But this means not only a new, rather exciting religious optimism but also a concomitant devotion to self-discipline and morality as the key to personal salvation, virtues ironically in sync with the Puritan/Calvinist religious culture of his native Massachusetts.

Transcendentalism, Eastern Religion, and Nature III: Thoreau

Henry David Thoreau (1817–1862) was born and lived almost his entire life in Concord, Massachusetts. He met the elder Emerson while a student at Harvard, and the two became good friends. It is often said that while Emerson dreamed up an ideal lifestyle of seeing God in the natural world and living a life that rejoiced in this, Thoreau was the person who actually lived this way, or at least tried to.

Both men were clearly affected by Asian ways of thought. As Arthur Versluis puts it, "Both Emerson and Thoreau were profoundly interested in the Vedanta, Confucianism, Buddhism, and without question more than anyone else in mid-nineteenth century New England" (Versluis 1993, 79). Thoreau thus walked in step with Emerson as pioneers in blending Asian notions of spirituality with progressive Unitarian thought.

Unlike Emerson, however, Thoreau was overtly antimaterialistic and antisocial; he abandoned any pretense to an academic or ecclesiastical life and shunned the public eye. Thoreau was known for an extreme bluntness that at times waxed into a decided coldness to people, a quality not evident in the public intellectual Emerson. Although Emerson is arguably more responsible for pushing American religiosity to accept the presence of sacred truth in places outside the legacy of Christ and Christianity, today when that issue is no longer publicly debated it is Thoreau who far more Americans find inspirational and thought-provoking. Like their neighbors in Massachusetts, Melville and Hawthorne, Thoreau and Emerson both fall within the tradition of literary romanticism; and while Emerson's sense of philosophic inquiry never waned, our image of the poetic, ideologically searching and idealizing Thoreau is only apropos of the young Thoreau, for as he aged he became less interested in philosophy and more interested in the physical laws of nature. That is, Thoreau, man of letters, gave way to Thoreau, scientist (Versluis 1993).[10]

The period of Thoreau's life when both his religious attitudes and his interests in Asian thought are most clearly expressed is the decade of the 1840s. In 1840, Thoreau, Emerson, and the other Transcendentalists started a journal called *The Dial* to publish their views and to produce some income.[11] Thoreau is featured in the very first issue. Around 1840 he is introduced to Asian thought through Gerando's *Histoire comparée des systèmes des philosophie*, and soon afterward *The Dial* begins a mini-series called "Ethnical Scriptures." Unlike Emerson, we can confirm Thoreau's direct knowledge of Buddhism because in 1854 one chapter of the *Lotus Sūtra* (*Saddharmapuṇḍarīka-sūtra*) appears in *The Dial* under Thoreau's name as translator, the first appearance of any part of that important scripture in English. Thoreau was in no position to read such a difficult Buddhist sutra in Sanskrit, Chinese, or Tibetan—what appeared in *The Dial* was translated from Eugene Burnouf's (1801–1852) French translation of a Sanskrit text. Burnouf's work had come out only in 1852, which means that within two years Thoreau and those who ran the journal had managed to learn of the importance of Burnouf's achievement, had obtained a copy from France, had become familiar enough to have chosen a chapter of personal interest ("Medicinal Plants"), and had published a partial translation when there was in fact no literary precedent in English for Mahāyāna language. Although it is accepted today that the *Dial* translation was actually made by Elizabeth Palmer Peabody (1804–1887) (Piez 1993, 10–11; Tweed 2000, 82; Marshall 2005, 425), editor of the journal at that time, this does not take away from the significance of this achievement or what we may infer was Thoreau's strong interest in Buddhist thought; it only broadens the scope of that interest in Buddhism to that intellectual circle as a whole.

In his 1849 book, *A Week on the Concord and Merrimack Rivers,* Thoreau reveals how taken he was with Buddhism:

> I trust that some may be as near and dear to Buddha, or Christ, or Swedenborg, who are without the pale of their churches. . . . I know that some will have hard thoughts of me, when they hear their Christ named beside my Buddha, yet I am sure that I am willing they should love their Christ more

than my Buddha, for the love is the main thing, and I like him too. . . . Why need Christians be still intolerant and superstitious? (Thoreau 1849, 55)

As pointed out above, this was a time in America when Christ was still assumed to be the only avenue to truth and salvation, even among the most progressive Unitarian theologians at the Harvard Divinity School. Thus, for Thoreau to refer to Christ as situated "beside my Buddha," that is, in a secondary role to "my Buddha," was scandalous, though it may have elicited cheers among a few friends in the fledgling Transcendentalist movement.

Yet for all this bravado, this remains the one and only clear statement of anything like reverence for Buddhism in Thoreau. In addition to Gerando, we know that much later he received Hardy's *Manual of Budhism* [*sic*] (see Snodgrass, chapter 1), but this came long after his seminal "Eastern" essays *Walden* and *A Week on the Concord and Merrimack Rivers* were published.[12] Aside from the translated chapter of the *Lotus Sūtra* and the above reference to the figure of Buddha as an exalted being, Thoreau does not mention Buddhism again. And although there does appear to be somewhat more knowledge of Buddhism in Thoreau than in Emerson, whether hindered by a lack of sound scholarship available to him or his own deep-seated Christian leanings, these scant references suggest only superficial understanding. Similar to Emerson, Thoreau therefore cannot be considered a "Buddhist thinker." And despite similarities of expression, it is also a misnomer to label his ideas or leanings Zen or Daoist, given that these religions had not yet been introduced to the West.

So, what was Thoreau's religious perspective? It may be summed up in the phrase "self-transcendence in nature" (Versluis 1993, 94). Wary of any organized religion, Western or Eastern, in *Walden* Thoreau displays a yearning for transcending the limitations of who he is by losing his consciousness of self. If one interprets this to be a kind of mystical urge, then clearly nature is the medium and God is the object. And if we analyze the way in which Thoreau expresses this yearning, there are two clear themes, neither of which are particularly Buddhist: reverence for the wild and savage, and faith in the absolute value of self-discipline. While the influence of Brahmanic thought should be recognized in the latter, the former bespeaks pure German and English romanticism. Notice in the following passage from *Walden* how Thoreau contrasts not good with evil, but good with wild, and in locating his religious identity in both good *and* wild, he implies an acknowledgment of the sacred in both civilized discourse and nature in all its ferocity.

Once or twice, however, while I lived at the pond, I found myself ranging the woods, like a half-starved hound, with a strange abandonment, seeking some kind of venison which I might devour, and no morsel could have been too savage for me. The wildest scenes had become unaccountably familiar. I found in myself, and still find, an instinct toward a higher, or, as it is named, spiritual life, as do most men, and another toward a primitive rank and savage one, and I reverence them both. I love the wild not less than the good. (Stern 1970, 339)

At the heart of the "good" we find self-discipline, expressed in a kind of blending of Puritanism and Brahmanism/Hinduism. We know he and Emerson frequently read together and discussed the *Laws of Manu* ("nothing was trivial to the Hindoo lawgiver"), and his discussion of the value of vegetarianism in *Walden* makes direct reference to Hinduism (ibid., 345). They were impressed with the fact that they found rules in the Indian tradition, as no heathen culture was thought capable of such rational structures. And there is undoubtedly some overlay of Indian asceticism onto the unmistakable presence of Puritan radical self-denial in Thoreau when he decries the enjoyment of liquor, coffee, tea, and music as evil indulgences with serious consequences.

I believe that water is the only drink for a wise man; wine is not so noble a liquor; and think of dashing the hopes of a morning with a cup of warm coffee, or of an evening with a dish of tea! Ah, how low I fall when I am tempted by them! Even music may be intoxicating. Such apparently slight causes destroyed Greece and Rome, and will destroy England and America. (Stern 1970)

This assertion of Puritan values is all the more remarkable in that Thoreau can also display rather vituperative anger toward even the progressive Unitarian church.

What great interval is there between him who is caught in Africa and made a plantation slave of in the South, and him who is caught in New England and made a Unitarian minister? In course of time they will abolish the one form of servitude, and, not long after, the other. I do not see the necessity for a man's getting into a hogshead and so narrowing his sphere, nor for his putting his head into a halter. . . .

All genuine goodness is original and as free from cant and tradition as the air. The accepted or established church is in alliance with the graveyard. (Torrey and Allen 1984, 284, 424–25)

In other words, Thoreau has internalized the self-denying lifestyle of Puritanism but disdained its self-righteous theology of humanity as reactionary and in danger of falling back into that state without constant religious guidance. He writes, "Our whole life is startlingly moral. There is never an instant's truce between vice and virtue. Goodness is the only investment that never fails." Thoreau's concern for doing the right thing combined with his belief in humanity's innate nature as good ("all genuine goodness is original and free from cant") is strikingly anti-Puritan. While his impetus to self-discipline is reinforced by Indian thought, his belief in humanity's natural goodness is most likely based on the Confucian philosopher Mencius, whom he quotes in both *A Week on the Concord and Merrimack Rivers* and *Walden*. One is thus not surprised that when it comes to locating the sacred, Thoreau has long since left the church: "It would imply the regeneration of mankind, if they were to become elevated enough to truly worship sticks and stones" (ibid., 45).

The later Thoreau's stance on education and literacy reflects a similar orientation: "Talk about learning our *letters*, and being *literate!* Why, the roots of *letters* are *things*. Natural objects and phenomena are the original symbols or types which express our thoughts and feelings" (ibid., 389). To say Thoreau finds God in nature not only signifies communing with animals, plants, and rocks but doing so in a place where human society is either minimally present or, ideally, totally absent. In a statement uncannily close to the motivation for the anchorite lifestyle of the "forest monks" of the Theravādin tradition, he is explicit about the tension between nature and society: "I am sure that if I call for a companion in my walk I have relinquished in my design some closeness of communion with Nature. The walk will surely be more commonplace. The inclination for society indicates a distance from Nature" (ibid., 262).

Despite the image of Thoreau as someone who discovered his spirituality "naturally" or "in nature," he in fact held a belief system with very specific notions about himself and the world. This may be summed up as follows. Like Emerson, his "Oriental" influence was almost entirely Hindu, Brahmanic, and Confucian. He revered the Buddha of the *Lotus Sūtra* but appears to have viewed Sakyamuni through a Hindu lens, leaving nothing to indicate he understood how Buddhism differs from Hinduism. (Note that publication of the series *Sacred Books of the East* does not commence until 1879, and the Pāli Text Society is not founded until 1881, both more than a decade after Thoreau's death.) He seems to have absorbed a notion of karma and rebirth from India, an idea that human law should be based on divine origins from both the Hebrew bible and the *Laws of Manu*, and a strict personal imperative to moral action that fused New England Protestantism with Mencius-based Confucianism. Here it might be instructional to put Thoreau's disdain for intrusive government, even voting, in *Civil Disobedience* next to his rant in *Walden* against the use of alcohol, coffee, and tea; together they express a rather extreme confidence in what amounts to his personal sense of morality. Religiously speaking, this anti-societal sense of morality directed him to seek a multifaceted, multi-aspected God as an immanent presence in the natural environment. On all these points Thoreau's religious outlook seems close to Emerson's, as was his deep-seated reverence for the wild, even violent aspect of nature, a view that characterizes the romantic movement in eighteenth- and early nineteenth-century literature and painting. It is not difficult therefore to see many elements in Emerson and Thoreau common to the ecoBuddhist outlook: seeing the natural environment as sacred and even seeking God or Truth in nature, regarding nature and human society as being at counter-purposes, belief in the intrinsic value of antimaterialism, a sense of personal commitment to proper moral action, and the conviction that one knows what the morally correct choice is.

Calling out the Ghost: Incorporating Transcendentalism into EcoBuddhist Discourse

It is often overlooked that while interest in Buddhism was steadily growing in Europe by the mid-nineteenth century, there is little evidence of this in North America. Scholars of Buddhism today all know of the historical importance of the work of Burnouf in bringing Sanskrit-based Mahāyāna materials into Western languages for the first time, but he was hardly a major figure in Europe, much less the United States. Hence, the English rendering in the *Dial* of one chapter of Burnouf's translation of the *Lotus Sūtra* —a work extolling universal liberation through faith and insight—was completely unprecedented on the American side of the Atlantic. Through various writings over a twenty-five year period after Thoreau's death, James Freeman Clarke, mentioned above as a progressive Unitarian, became one of the most widely read interpreters of Buddhism in the United States. Clarke avidly studied the European writings on Buddhism by Burnouf and Burnouf's student Müller, among others, and wrote one of the most well-read descriptions of Buddhism of the time in an essay in the June 1869 edition of the *Atlantic Monthly*, called "Buddhism or, the Protestantism of the East." Clarke sought to discredit those who saw Buddhism as overtly Catholic in tone (what Clarke called "Romanism") by arguing that "it established a doctrine of individual salvation based on personal character" and even more astonishingly, that "in Protestantism and Buddhism sermons are the main instrument by which souls are saved" (Clarke 1869, 715).

It is in this post–Civil War era that the discourse of the intellectual leaders of Transcendentalism begins to turn away from Christian exclusivity in an more explicit way, though Emerson and Thoreau wrote of this in the 1840s. This shift can be seen in the launching of the journal *The Radical* in 1865, in which Transcendentalist inquiry into comparative religion, ironically intended initially to bolster the ancient claim of Christianity as God's only true revelation, instead leads many to assert the reality of a *universal religion* in which truth could be found in a myriad of places. From its inception, the pages of *The Radical* featured a debate between two Transcendentalists: the nondenominational minister Samuel Johnson (1822–1882), who argued for the universal religion position, and Clarke, who insisted on the unique authority of the Bible and Jesus.[13]

Despite the many links between this mid- to late-nineteenth-century American Transcendentalism and postwar American Buddhism, it is striking how the Transcendentalist ideas are often understood by the devotees of deep ecology and American Zen in very different ways. Emerson and Thoreau are, of course, no exception. For example, in *Zen and American Thought* Van Meter Ames writes, "Emerson thinks of men of science as spokesmen for the realms of Nature, representing them and so bringing them into the discourse"; and "[Emerson] saw science enabling man to be a more effective reformer and remaker of his being" (Ames 1962, 71, 75). Compare Ames's view with the following statement by Stephen Whicher, a renowned Emerson scholar:

> Emerson was on the whole unsympathetic with the patient experimentation of which scientific achievement is based and prescribed instead of a moral and spiritual reformation in the scientist. Scientists will never understand nature, he wrote in *Nature,* using Swedenborgian language, until they approach her in the fire of holiest affections, and not simply with the intellect. . . . The Idea of nature Emerson desired, needless to say, was not forthcoming. . . . Man could not immerse himself in the unconsciousness of nature, nor could he conquer her through consciousness, by achieving her explanation. . . . Nature was an enchanted circle, which he was forbidden to enter. (Whicher 1985, 26–27; also Whicher 1953)

Here we see how the 1960s American Zen-inspired view transforms the romantic Emerson who distrusts scientists for their inability to see the religious dimension of nature into the modern Emerson who embraces scientists as noble reformers. It is worth remembering that the word "science" in Emerson's time did not exclude philosophy. In Ames we see an ideological fusion that expresses the prototype of what is found in many of the writers on deep ecology today: a faith in scientific inquiry into the mechanisms of nature coupled with a deeply romantic, even mystical, view of nature that believes in its healing powers. Can the truths uncovered by scientific inquiry into nature become, in Ames's words, the vanguard "enabling man to be a more effective reformer and remaker of his being"? In this view, the scientist is the new priest and nature is his or her revealed text. Whicher's depiction of Emerson's search for a "moral and spiritual reformation of science" has become anachronistic in a postmodern setting where the only truths are those "documented" by scientists. This rejection of postmodern cynicism for a nostalgic return to romanticism bolstered by faith in science is not uncommon in twenty-first century discourse, and points to the expressly religious nature of ecoBuddhism and other deep ecology discourses.

I have remarked above my surprise to the ascription in ecoBuddhism of "meaning, awareness, and an evolutionary drive" to nature or the earth. Even in the most extreme examples where nature is viewed as a sacred teacher—Thoreau's or Ienaga's theory of Japan's "nature religion"—we do not see anything like this. To say that the earth has awareness is to ascribe to the earth a discreet identity, a mind capable of knowing, agency, or even personality. While there is agency in gods who live in nature or who manifest certain aspects of nature, such as fire or wind, there is nothing in any canonical Buddhist discourse, even in medieval Japan, that remotely suggests agency in nature as a whole.

This kind of oddity is of a piece with another curious sentiment in postmodern Western writings on Buddhism: religious identification with nature. It is not uncommon to encounter this "ideal" among ecoBuddhist writers or ecology-minded people who publish in Buddhist books on environmentalism. This, too, is clearly a reification of Buddhist, especially Japanese Buddhist, reverence for nature as something conceptually Transcendentalist. For example, Jeremy Hayward, a nuclear physicist associated with (Buddhist-founded) Naropa University in Colorado, gives this description:

> Rarely is one able to identify with other more distant members of the human species, and even more rarely with members of other species. Yet all spiritual growth is based in the experience that such broader identification is possible. The growing into maturity of a human is experienced as an ever widening sense of self, from identification with the individual bodymind, to self as family, self as circle of friends, as nation, as human race, as all living beings, and perhaps to self as all there is. Buddhists emphasize the obstacle that arises at each step on the way of this gradually widening circle of identification, namely the belief that there is a separate self at all. (Hayward 1990, 64–65)

Following Gregory Bateson, Hayward wants to see the self made bigger, locating it outside the mundane "individual bodymind," which we may take as a reference to *namarūpa* in the Buddhist doctrine of *pratītyasamutpāda*. Like the apotheosis of Earth as a deity with agency, in this view "self" has become the *dharmadhātu*. Maturity is thus defined as an ever-expanding capacity for *identifying*, or what we might refer to as *selving*. This view has been labeled by Freya Mathews as the *identification thesis* (1988, 350).

But one would be hard-pressed to find a discourse like this in the traditional canon of any Buddhist school. The problem of self, and the various ways in which self is deconstructed, reconstructed, emptied, and so forth in traditional Buddhist discourse simply does not flow in the direction of valorizing the process of identification, regardless of scale. Instead, it is the very process of identification, *ahamkāra*, or *manaskāra,* that lies at the karmic origins of *duḥkha,* the core Buddhist problematic of suffering. When the *Diamond Sūtra* states that the Buddha leads all sentient beings to Nirvāṇa but will never lead any sentient beings to Nirvāṇa, this is not an expansion of self but a radical removal or deconstruction of self. More concrete is a long section in the fifth fascicle of the *Nirvāṇa Sūtra* on what liberation is and is not. There I have examined eighty-five metaphorical or analogous statements on the nature of liberation and found nothing remotely close to any notion of the expansion of self through a process of identification with the world. Instead of an ever-widening identification of the natural world, even a world-affirming Mahāyāna sutra like the *Nirvāṇa Sūtra* teaches that liberation is without any physical form, indefinable, without any home or location, impossible to hold in your hand, invisible, without limits, and so forth. This is a rhetoric of nonidentification. It is worth noting here that the locus classicus for the teaching of *buddha-nature* as a universal in East Asian Buddhism—the very doctrine that Jizang, Zhanran, and others extended to the natural world—is the *Nirvāṇa Sūtra* itself.

But if the world is not the embodiment of liberation, then why would Dōgen speak of non-sentient phenomena preaching the dharma? I would suggest that we need to interpret this kind of statement ontologically, akin to what he is saying in his essay "Being and Time" (*Uji*). Whereas some have read this to be suggesting that we immerse ourselves in the out-of-doors in order to learn the language of rocks, rather than an inveterate outdoorsman like Thoreau, Dōgen was a strong proponent of monastic discipline practiced in monasteries. Such statements, like his comment that the concept of sutra should encompass the entire universe, the self and others because all take meals and wear clothes and so forth, are surely his attempt to express his awakening to the immanence of the sacred in the world. Dōgen's statements affirming the sacrality of the world must be read in terms of, or at least alongside, his critical statements about the more central issue of how to liberate the self, such as "to lay out the self is to exhaust [all] worlds" (*ware wo hairetsu shi-okite, jinkai to seri*),[14] or "when talking about the passage of time, if you imagine your field of perception to be outside yourself . . . your study of the Buddhist path is not fully focused" (*kyōreki wo iu ni, kyō wa getō ni shite . . . butsudō no sangaku, kore nomi wo sen'ichi ni sezaru nari*).[15] Dōgen's affirmation of the environment as sacred when considered in the context of the above statements directing his students to drop their focus on the external world strongly suggests that Dōgen did not urge his students to seek liberation by identifying with the physical world. The confusion seems to lie in postwar American Buddhists confusing *nonduality* with *identity*. When Dōgen says "body and mind drop off," this is about the perceiving self and perceived object merging, but in a cosmic, nonspecific sense. It is not that this or that *topos* is sacred, it is that sacred awareness arises when such discriminations cease.

If we infer from this that we should be ordaining trees to express our respect for them as expressions of the sacred, then we should be ordaining pencils and streetlamps as well. Clearly such ritual directed at trees reflects an ordering—a decidedly discriminatory ordering—of priorities, rather than the indiscriminateness that is at the heart of Dōgen's message. When Dōgen says to study the dharma is to study the self and to study the self is to forget the self, he is referring again to an *internal* process of heightened awareness in meditation where the self can no longer be located, and thereby location *no longer matters*.

But there need be no shame, no excuses given, for a discriminatory ordering of priorities; a nondiscriminatory set of priorities would be an oxymoron, and as discussed above, the Buddhist notion of *saṃsāra* includes its own discriminatory ordering of different life forms. Setting ecologically sound priorities toward the natural world that are not only very different from but at cross-purposes to someone else's exploitative priorities is reasonable, plausible, and ethical, but it need not be *religious* to have meaning and power. As I have tried to show, however clear the occasional reference to an aspect of the natural world as sacred might be in Buddhist literature, when current ecological discourse takes what are essentially poetic expressions as statements of doctrine it inevitably raises serious historical and cultural problems. If we have no evidence that Dōgen's speech community took his statement literally when he claimed that plants and trees take meals and wear clothes, then for us to read in Dōgen's words a recognition of agency in nature says more about our perspective than Dōgen's.

I argue, moreover, that when personality or agency is ascribed to nature we are no longer in the realm of Buddhism as an Asian cultural form, but in something of a Buddhist-inspired new American religion, one that appears to draw on the legacy of Emerson and Thoreau as much as Jizang and Dōgen. Today the principle of "biocentric equality" that asserts the "equal right to live" of all organic forms is central to the writings of deep ecology.[16] One may find this a profound notion, but it does not reflect Buddhist doctrines of dependent origination, *dharmadhātu, dharmakāya,* or buddha-nature, for none of these affirm any biological values per se, and there is no notion of "rights" of any kind. Biological values in some form can be inferred in the notions of *saṃsāra* and *sattva,* but those of the former are inherently unequal and those of the latter exclude plant life. Indeed one is often dismayed at the confusion in these writers regarding what is Hindu, Buddhist, and Daoist in origin, a century and a half after Emerson and Thoreau had the same problem. This only illustrates how secondary these religious systems ultimately are to the ecology movement, and indeed we are now seeing the assertion that deep ecology should be recognized as a religion itself. One wonders how many who delight in the idea that there is buddha-nature in all phenomena know that the *Nirvāṇa Sūtra* also advocates murder in defense of religion. If we take every idea, every notion that has ever occurred in a tradition to be of equal religious or cultural value, in other words if we applied a hermeneutic of "biocentric equality" to religious scriptures, we may have ideational richness but we will also have religious chaos. Even strict fundamentalists do not aver that all the injunctions in the bible are of equal value. There are reasons why certain notions within a religious tradition are more salient or weighty than others and this kind of prioritization is precisely what gives a particular heritage or school its identity.

Buddhist references to the human-nature relationship at various points in its history do indeed reflect a value system less exploitative than God's granting dominion over nature to humanity. Though animals are perceived in the Buddhist tradition as the victims of punishment, the Buddhist reaction to this fact calls for compassion toward them; there is no figure in Buddhist history like Descartes, who argued that animals have no soul and therefore no feelings. For that reason, Buddhism echoes something closer to a healthy respect for other life forms so dear to the ecology movement. But just as the move to redefine the biblical dominion as "stewardship" has functioned to give God a new role as protector of the earth, so too do we need to recognize that the absence of any implication of ethical imperative toward the physical world other than respect and compassion for living beings in Buddhism means that redefining postmodern Buddhism as ecoBuddhism is tantamount to giving the religion a new role and a new set of priorities. This is not necessarily a bad thing, but in the process we need to be careful not to lose the core ideational structure that makes Buddhism work as a religion, at least in the intellectual, meditative tradition. I am referring to its traditionally internal focus on how the mind processes experience, both in normal consciousness and in the meditative states of *dhyāna* and *samādhi.* And while many forms of the sacred have been identified, one's *loka* or physical world of existence has no special claim in this area. In India, Buddhism was born and flourished at a time when the pollution of nature by humans simply did not warrant any concern. Even in the later cultural traditions of Buddhism, pollution is more a cultural problem than a physical one. And where nature is held sacred, humanity is never embodied with a felt need either to protect or identify with its environment.

Individuals and institutions today who are devoted to halting the needless destruction of our habitat deserve our respect and support. This includes many in the Buddhist clergy as well as lay men and women with deeply held Buddhist beliefs. But we should also be prudent about identifying a particular ecological value as Buddhist or reflective of Buddhist tradition. Buddhist understandings of causality are based on principles of dependence and interdependence. And though humanity's relationship with its physical environment may not be a traditional theme within that discourse, the principle is certainly applicable to the cause of increasing environmental awareness and even activism to protect it, for it not only presumes that we are influenced by the environment, it also holds us responsible for influencing the environment. But when our sense of ecological responsibility takes a religious turn, we have to be careful about identifying that sensibility in terms of established religious traditions. To see the natural world as sacred and thereby to seek personal liberation through identification with it reflects the thinking of American Transcendentalism and probably its incorporation of some aspects of Vedic/Upaniṣadic thought, but not Buddhism. To view our intimacy with the environment affectively, as a relationship between lovers, is the language of Hindu *bhakti* devotionalism, not Buddhism. These views of nature come out of the Unitarian-Transcendentalist struggle to bring God down into the world to make the sacred accessible to anyone anywhere, a theological movement that asserted the presence of God in each individual and in the phenomenal world, and accessible in both realms through intuition and scientific investigation. There is something here in common with the Mahāyāna doctrines of buddha-nature and *dharmadhātu*, but there is scant evidence of any Mahāyāna influence in Transcendentalist thought in Europe or North America. However relevant to the problem of environmental responsibility the Buddhist doctrines of *pratītyasamutpāda, dharmadhātu, dharmatā,* and universal buddha-nature may seem, those doctrines were never applied to ecological issues until the last thirty years. This is not to say that because this application is new, I think it is improper. Rather, I am calling for a better understanding of the complexity of what those doctrines have meant over time so that we can be more precise about how they may be used in the future most appropriately; and I am calling for a willingness to recognize the Transcendentalist roots of religious environmentalism. After all, those roots run very deep in American culture and reflect a similarly remarkable story of people on the margins struggling to overcome the prejudices of mainstream cultural values.

Notes

This is a revised version of a paper titled "Baptizing Nature: Environmentalism, Buddhism, and Transcendentalism" in *Bukkyō to Shizen* (Buddhism and Nature). Kyoto: Research Institute of Bukkyo University, 2005.

1. Although Miyamoto Shōson and others have pointed to Jizang 吉藏 (549–623) as the first scholiast to proffer this perspective, quotations from certain recensions of the *Zhongyin jing* 中陰經 (Antarābhava sūtra), translated in the late fourth century, brought to Japan in the Nara period express the same notion.

2. The term *gotra* refers to a kind of religious lineage in the sense that one is understood to be born into different "families" of spiritual potential. This explains why religious understanding varies so much within societies, and this view was argued to be a more realistic teaching than the universal "potential" of buddha-nature, which will be realized by only a few.

3. De Silva mistakenly rendered this as *eshofumi,* but as I am unable to access Ikeda's study, I cannot ascertain where the mistake originates.

4. Ted Morino, SGI-USA Study Department Chief, at http://etherbods.com/study/q-and-a/question16.shtml.

5. The first legally sanctioned Unitarian denomination in England was formed by Theophilus Lindsey in 1773 and in the United States in 1785 at King's Chapel in Boston. See Robert Handy, *A History of the Churches in the United States and Canada,* 160.

6. Encyclopedia Britannica, 15th edition (1973), vol. 26, 264. Priestley's religious views are also characterized as "emphasizing Jesus' humanity, God's omnipotence, and the rational faculty of man" in vol. 12, 137. For a general biography, see vol. 9, 696–698.

7. Emerson must have seen the first English translation of Friedrich Schleiermacher's (1768–1834) seminal statement of Biblical criticism *Über die Schriften des Lukas* (A Critical Essay on the Gospel of St. Luke) when it appeared in 1817.

8. See also Carpenter 1930, 123. Versluis quotes Emerson *Journals,* vol. IV, 426: "In the history of intellect no more important fact than the Hindu theology teaching that the beatitude of Supreme Good is to be attained through science; namely, by perception of the real and unreal, setting aside matter and qualities, and affectations or emotions and persons and actions as Maias or illusions."

9. See Versluis 1993, 13n9. Versluis also cites Robinson 1985, 104ff.

10. See also Eiseley 1987, 57. Although one need not accept the popularly conceived Thoreau as a kind of "nature yogi," this is more due to his self-admitted lack of discipline than any lack of intimacy with nature.

11. The Transcendentalists were continually short of money and tried bookstores, subscription libraries, paint stores, and so forth, hoping to find a steady source of income. The *Dial* was primarily aimed at spreading their ideas, but they also hoped it

might produce revenue. Unfortunately, this was not to be the case, as even at the height of its popularity it found only three hundred subscribers (Marshall 2005, 424).

12. Thoreau received the Hardy book as part of a collection of books on Indian thought given to him in 1855 by Thomas Cholmodeley; the others mostly translations of non-Buddhist texts such as the *Ṛg Veda*, *Laws of Manu*, *Bhagavadgītā*. and various Upaniṣads and Puraṇas. By this time he had little interest in studying religion. Cholmodeley was English, and many believe that his gift gave Thoreau the largest personal collection of books on Indian thought in America.

13. Johnson had argued that since Hindu scriptures were traditionally subject to interpretation within that tradition as was the Bible in the West, it showed that all scriptures were merely guidelines to a universal truth as understood within each culture. Clarke responded by pointing out the Johnson had erred in (1) considering the Bible to be fallible, and (2) denying the fact that Christ was the unique "mediator of Divine truth" (Versluis 1993, 203).

14. われを排列しおきて盡界とせけ.

15. 經歴をいふに、境は外頭にして、〜 佛道の參學、これのみを專一にせざるなり.

16. For some, the organic as well as the inorganic, thus more appropriately an "equal right to exist." See http://www.envirolink.org/.

REFERENCES

Almond, Phillip. 1985. *The British Discovery of Buddhism*. Cambridge: Cambridge University Press.

Ames, Van Meter. 1962. *Zen and American Thought*. Honolulu: University of Hawai'i Press.

Appadurai, Arjun. 1990. "Disjuncture and Difference in the Global Cultural Economy." *Public Culture* 2 (2): 1–24.

Arnold, Edwin. 1906. *The Light of Asia*. London: Kegan Paul, Trench, Trubner.

Bar-On, D. 1993. "Indeterminacy of Theory and Practice." *Philosophy and Phenomenological Research* 53:781–810.

Batchelor, Stephen. 1994. *The Awakening of the West: The Encounter of Buddhism and Western Culture*. Berkeley: Parallax Press.

Baumann, Martin. 2002. "Protective Amulets and Awareness Techniques, or How to Make Sense of Buddhism in the West." In *Westward Dharma: Buddhism beyond Asia,* ed. Charles S. Prebish and Martin Baumann, 51–65. Berkeley: University of California Press, Berkeley Publishing Group.

Bellah, Robert. 1965. "Ienaga Saburō and the Search for Meaning in Modern Japan." In *Changing Japanese Attitudes toward Modernization*, ed. Marius B. Jansen, 369–423. Princeton: Princeton University Press.

Bestrom, Craig, Lisa Furlong, and Caroline Stetler. 2007. "Golf Digest's Athlete-Golfer Rankings." *Golf Digest*, May 2. http://sports.espn.go.com/golf/news/story?id=2857062.

Bishop, Scott. 2002. "What Do We Really Know about Mindfulness-Based Stress Reduction?" *Psychosomatic Medicine* 64:71–83.

Bjerklie, David. 2003. "A Shopper's Guide to Meditation." *Time* 162 (5): 56.

Blum, Mark L. 2009. "The Transcendentalist Ghost in EcoBuddhism." In *Trans-Buddhism: Transmission, Translation, Transformation*, ed. Nalini Bhushan, Jay L. Garfield, and Abraham Zablocki. Amherst: University of Massachusetts Press.

Blumenthal, James. 2002. *The Ornament of the Middle Way: A Study of the Madhyamaka Thought of Santaraksita*. Ithaca, NY: Snow Lion Publications.

Bowie, Katherine A. 1997. *Rituals of National Loyalty: An Anthropology of the State and the Village Scout Movement in Thailand*. New York: Columbia University Press.

Buddhist Peace Fellowship. 1992. *Turning Wheel: The Journal of Socially Engaged Buddhism* (winter).

Buddhist Peace Fellowship. 1993. *Turning Wheel: The Journal of Socially Engaged Buddhism* (summer).

Burlingame, Eugene Watson. 1969. *Buddhist Legends*. Translated from the Pali text of the Dhammapada Commentary. Books 3 to 12. Great Britain: Luzac.

Caddyshack. 1980. A Jon Peters Production. Directed by Harold Ramis. Warner Bros. Home Video.

Callahan, Tom. 2003. "'My Heart Is Thai': A Window to Tiger's Soul Through His Mother." *Golf Digest*, April, 167–71.

Candrakirti with Commentary by Ju Mipham. 2002. *Introduction to the Middle Way*. Boston: Shambhala Publications.

Carpenter, Frederic Ives. 1930. *Emerson and Asia*. Cambridge: Harvard University Press.

Chandler, Stuart. 1998. "Chinese Buddhism in America: Identity and Practice." In *The Faces of Buddhism in America*, ed. Charles S. Prebish and Kenneth K. Tanaka, 13–30. Berkeley: University of California Press.

Chang, Christie Yu-ling. 2008. "The Name of the Nun: Towards the Use of Inclusive Language and True Equality in the Buddhist Community." In Karma Lekshe Tsomo, *Buddhist Women in a Global Multicultural Community,* ed. Karma Lekshe Tsomo, 260–66. Kuala Lumpur: Sukhi Hotu Press.

Channing, William Ellery, ed. 1957. *Unitarian Christianity and Other Essays*. Introduction by Irving Bartlett. New York: Liberal Arts Press.

Chayant Pholpoke. 1998. "The Chiang Mai Cable-Car Project: Local Controversy over Cultural and Eco-tourism." In *The Politics of Environment in Southeast Asia: Resources and Resistance*, ed. Philip Hirsch and Carol Warren, 262–77. London: Routledge.

Chopra, Deepak. 2003. *Golf for Enlightenment: The Seven Lessons for the Game of Life*. New York: Harmony Books.

Christy, Arthur. 1963. *The Orient in American Transcendentalism*. New York: Columbia University Press.

Clarke, James Freeman. 1869. "Buddhism, or, the Protestantism of the East." *Atlantic Monthly* 23, 713–29.

Clarke, James Freeman. 1886. *Vexed Questions in Theology: A Series of Essays*. Boston: George H. Ellis.

Clasquin, Michel. 2002. "Buddhism in South Africa." In *Westward Dharma: Buddhism beyond Asia,* ed. Charles S. Prebish and Martin Baumann, 152–62. Berkeley: University of California Press.

Cleary, Thomas. 2005. *Soul of the Samurai*. North Clarendon, VT: Tuttle Publishing.

Cole, C. L. 2002. "The Place of Golf in U.S. Imperialism." *Journal of Sport and Social Issues* 26 (4): 331–36.

Coleman, James William. 2001. *The New Buddhism: The Western Transformation of an Ancient Tradition*. Oxford: Oxford University Press.

Conover, Sarah. 2001. *Kindness: A Treasury of Buddhist Wisdom for Children and Parents*. Spokane: Eastern Washington University Press.

Conze, Edward. 1970. "Review of Y. Karunadasa: Buddhist Analysis of Matter." *Bulletin of the School of Oriental and African Studies*, University of London 33 (2).

Conze, Edward. 1975. "Problems of Buddhist History." In *Further Buddhist Studies*, ed. Bruno Cassirer, 144–49.

Csikszentmihalyi, Mihaly. 1990. *Flow: The Psychology of Optimal Experience*. New York: Harper and Row.

Darlington, Susan M. 1990. *Buddhism, Morality and Change: The Local Response to Development in Thailand*. Ph.D. dissertation, University of Michigan.

Darlington, Susan M. 1998. "The Ordination of a Tree: The Buddhist Ecology Movement in Thailand." *Ethnology* 37 (1): 1–15.

Darlington, Susan M. 2003. "The Spirit(s) of Conservation in Buddhist Thailand." In *Nature Across Cultures*, ed. Helaine Selin, 129–45. Dordrecht: Kluwer Academic Publishers.

Das, Lama Surya. 2003. "Practicing with Loss." *Tricycle: The Buddhist Review* (fall): 82–84.

David Donnenfield Productions and the University of California. 1998. *Changing from Inside*. University of California Extension Center for Media-Dependent Learning.

DeBary, William Theodore, Donald Keene, George Tanabe, and Paul Varley, eds. 2001. *Sources of Japanese Tradition*. Volume One, *from Earliest Times to 1600*. Second edition. New York: Columbia University Press.

Deford, Frank. 1998. "Hooked on Golf." *Sports Illustrated*, September 7, 93–102.

Derrida, Jacques. 1982. *Margins of Philosophy*. Cambridge: Harvard University Press.

Desmond, Lisa. 2004. *Baby Buddhas: A Guide for Teaching Meditation to Children*. Kansas City, MO: Andrews McMeel Publishing.

De Silva, Kingsley M. 1965. *Social Policy and Missionary Organizations in Ceylon, 1854–1855*. London: Longmans.

De Silva, Ranjani. 2004. "Reclaiming the Robe: Reviving the Bhikkhun Order in Sri Lanka." In *Buddhist Women and Social Justice: Ideals, Challenges, and Achievements*, ed. Karma Lekshe Tsomo, 119–35. Albany: State University of New York Press.

Devall, Bill. 2000. "Deep Ecology and Political Activism." In *Dharma Rain: Sources of Buddhist Environmentalism*, ed. Stephanie Kaza and Kenneth Kraft, 379–92. Boston: Shambhala Publications.

Diaz, Jaime. 2004. "Finding the Zone." *Golf Digest* 55 (7), 134–45, 178.

Doyle, Arthur Conan. 1984. *The Illustrated Sherlock Holmes Treasury*. New York: Avenel Books.

Droit, Roger-Pol. 2003. *The Cult of Nothingness: The Philosophers and the Buddha*. Chapel Hill: University of North Carolina Press.

Eck, Diana L. 2001. *A New Religious America*. San Francisco: Harper Collins.

Eiseley, Loren. 1987. "Thoreau's Vision of the Natural World." In *Henry David Thoreau (Modern Critical Views)*, ed. Harold Bloom, 51–61. New York: Chelsea House Publishers.

Emerson, Ralph Waldo. 1883. *Nature, Addresses and Lectures*. Boston: Houghton Mifflin.

Emerson, Ralph Waldo. 1890. *The Divinity School Address*. Boston: American Unitarian Association.

Emerson, Ralph Waldo. 1909. *Journals of Ralph Waldo Emerson*. Cambridge: Harvard University Press.

England, Philippa. 1996. "UNCED and the Implementation of Forest Policy in Thailand." In *Seeing Forests for Trees: Environment and Environmentalism in Thailand*, ed. Philip Hirsch, 53–71. Chiang Mai: Silkworm Books.

Ericsson, Karl Anders, and Neil Charness. 1994. "Expert Performance: Its Structure and Acquisition." *American Psychologist* 49 (8): 725–47.

Fahn, James David. 2003. *A Land on Fire: The Environmental Consequences of the Southeast Asian Boom*. Chiang Mai: Silkworm Books.

Fields, Rick. 1992. *How the Swans Came to the Lake: A Narrative History of Buddhism in America*. Boston: Shambhala Publications.

Freud, Sigmund. 1917. "Mourning and Melancholia." *Standard Edition* 14:73–102.

Fromm, Erich. 1978 (1950). *Psychoanalysis and Religion*. New Haven: Yale University Press.

Gallwey, W. Timothy. 1998. *The Inner Game of Golf*. New York: Random House.

Garfield, Jay. 1995. *The Fundamental Wisdom of the Middle Way: Nāgārjuna's Mūlamadhyamakakārikā*. New York: Oxford University Press.

Garfield, Jay. 2006. "Buddhist Ethics." http://www.smith.edu/philosophy/jgarfield .html#RecentPapers (accessed September 16, 2008).

Gellner, David L. 2004. "Buddhism, Women, and Caste: The Case of the Newar Buddhists of the Kathmandu Valley." In *Buddhist Women and Social Justice,* ed. Karma Lekshe Tsomo, 155–60. Albany: State University of New York Press.

Glass, Newman Robert. 1995. *Working Emptiness: Toward a Third Reading of Emptiness in Buddhism and Postmodern Thought*. Atlanta: Scholars Press.

Goleman, Daniel. 1995. *Emotional Intelligence: Why it Can Matter More Than IQ*. New York: Bantam Books.

Gómez, Luis O. 1999. "The Way of the Translators: Three Recent Translations of Śāntideva's Bodhicaryāvatāra." *Buddhist Literature I*, 262–354.

Goonatilake, Hema. 2006. "Women Regaining a Lost Legacy: The Restoration of the Bhikkhunī Sagha in Sri Lanka." In *Out of the Shadows: Socially Engaged Buddhist Women in the Global Community*, ed. Karma Lekshe Tsomo, 42–47. Delhi: Sri Satguru Publications.

Gotō, Shigeo, ed. 1982. *Sankashū Shinchō Nihon Koten Shūsei 49*. Tokyo: Shinchōsha.

Gregory, Peter N., and Lesley J. Weaver. 2004. *The Gate of Sweet Nectar: Feeding Hungry Spirits in an American Zen Community* (video). Northampton: Smith College.

Griffiths, Paul J. 1999. *Religious Reading: The Place of Reading in the Practice of Religion*. New York: Oxford University Press.

Gross, Amy. 1999. "An Interview with Joseph Goldstein." *Tricycle Magazine: The Buddhist Review* (summer).

Gross, Rita M. 1993. *Buddhism after Patriarchy: A Feminist History, Analysis, and Reconstruction of Buddhism*. Albany: State University of New York Press.

Gutting, Gary. 1999. "MacIntyre, Alasdair." In *The Cambridge Dictionary of Philosophy*, ed. Robert Audi, 526–27. New York: Cambridge University Press.

Halifax, Joan. 1990. "The Third Body: Buddhism, Shamanism, and Deep Ecology." In *Dharma Gaia: A Harvest of Essays in Buddhism and Ecology*, ed. Allan Hunt Badiner, 20–38. Berkeley, CA: Parallax Press.

Hall, Stephen S. 2003. "Is Buddhism Good for Your Health?" *New York Times*, September 14. http://www.nytimes.com (accessed September 16, 2008).

Hallisey, Charles. 1995. "Roads Taken and Not Taken in the Study of Theravāda Buddhism." In *Curators of the Buddha: Buddhism under Colonialism*, ed. Donald Lopez Jr., 31–61. Chicago: University of Chicago Press.

Hallisey, Charles. 1996. "Ethical Particularism in Theravada Buddhism." *Journal of Buddhist Ethics* 3:32–43.

Hallisey, Charles, and Anne Hansen. 1996. "Narrative, Sub-Ethics, and the Moral Life: Some Evidence from Theravada Buddhism." *Religious Ethics* 24 (2): 305–28.

Handy, Robert. 1976. *A History of the Churches in the United States and Canada*. Oxford: Oxford University Press.

Hardy, Robert Spence. 1841. *British Government and the Idolatry of Ceylon*. London: Crofts and Blenkarn.

Hardy, Robert Spence. 1850. *Eastern Monachism*. London: Williams and Norgate.

Hardy, Robert Spence. 1853. *Manual of Budhism* [*sic*]. London: Partridge and Oakey.

Harris, Ian. 1991. "How Environmentalist Is Buddhism?" *Religion* 21:101–14.

Harris, Ian. 1995. "Getting to Grips with Buddhist Environmentalism: A Provisional Typology." *Journal of Buddhist Ethics* 2:173–90. http://www.buddhistethics.org/2/harris2.html (accessed September 16, 2008).

Harris, Ian. 1996. "Environment and Environmentalism in Thailand: Material and Ideological Bases." In *Seeing Forests for Trees: Environment and Environmentalism in Thailand*, ed. Philip Hirsch, 15–36. Chiang Mai: Silkworm Books.

Harris, Ian. 1997. "Buddhism and the Discourse of Environmental Concern: Some Methodological Problems Considered." In *Buddhism and Ecology: The Interconnection of Dharma and Deeds*, ed. Mary Evelyn Tucker and Duncan Ryuken Williams, 377–402. Cambridge, MA: Harvard University Center for the Study of World Religions Publications.

Harris, Ian. 2002. "A 'Commodius Vicus of Recirculation': Buddhism, Art and Modernity." In *Westward Dharma: Buddhism beyond Asia,* ed. Charles S. Prebish and Martin Baumann, 365–82. Berkeley: University of California Press.

Hayes, Richard P. 1999. *The Land of No Buddha*. Barnett: Windhorse Press.

Hayes, Richard P. 1999. "The Internet as Window onto American Buddhism." In *American Buddhism: Methods and Findings in Recent Scholarship*, ed. Duncan Ryuken Williams and Christopher S. Queen, 168–79. Surrey, UK: Curzon Press.

Hayward, Jeremy. 1990. "Ecology and the Experience of Sacredness." In *Dharma Gaia*, ed. Allan Hunt Badiner. Berkeley: Parallax Press.

Hebron, Michael. 1990. *The Art and Zen of Learning Golf.* St. James, NY: Learning Golf, Inc.

Hendricks, Gay. 2003. *Conscious Golf: The Three Secrets of Success in Business, Life and Golf.* New York: Rodale Books.

Herrigel, Eugen. 1953. *Zen in the Art of Archery.* New York: Vintage Books.

Hilton, James. *Lost Horizon.* New York: William Morrow.

Hirsch, Philip. 1993. *Political Economy of Environment in Thailand.* Manila: Journal of Contemporary Asia Publishers.

Hirsch, Philip. 1996. "Environment and Environmentalism in Thailand: Material and Ideological Bases." In *Seeing Forests for Trees: Environment and Environmentalism in Thailand,* ed. Philip Hirsch, 15–36. Chiang Mai: Silkworm Books.

Hori, G. Victor Sogen. 1998. "Japanese Zen in America: Americanizing the Face in the Mirror." In *The Faces of Buddhism in America,* ed. Charles S. Prebish and Kenneth K. Tanaka, 49–78. Berkeley: University of California Press.

Hurst, G. Cameron III. 1990. "Death, Honor, and Loyalty: The Bushidō Ideal." *Philosophy East and West* 40 (4): 511–27.

Hurst, Philip. 1990. *Rainforest Politics: Ecological Destruction in Southeast Asia.* New York: St. Martin's Press.

Ienaga, Saburō. 1944. 家永三郎著, *Nihon shisoshi ni okeru shukyoteki shizenkan no tenkai* 日本思想史に於ける宗教的自然観の展開 (The Development of a Religious View of Nature in the History of Japanese Thought). Tokyo: Sogensha 創元社.

Ikeda, Daisaku. 1998. *The Environmental Problem and Buddhism* (Tokyo: Institute of Oriental Philosophy, n.d.), as quoted in Padmasiri de Silva, *Environmental Philosophy and Ethics in Buddhism.* Houndsmills, London: Macmillan.

Ishii, Yoneo. 1986. *Sangha, State and Society: Thai Buddhism in History.* Trans. Peter Hawkes. Honolulu: University of Hawai'i Press.

Jackson, P. 1995. *Sacred Hoops: Spiritual Lessons of a Hardwood Warrior.* New York: Hyperion.

James, William. 1987 (1902). *The Varieties of Religious Experience.* In *William James: Writings 1902–1910,* ed. Bruce Kuklick. New York: Library of America.

Jarmusch, Jim. 1999. *Ghost Dog: The Way of the Samurai.* Written and directed by Jim Jarmusch. Plywood Productions. DVD distributed by Artisan Home Entertainment.

Jeen-Fong. n.d. "Can Meditation Solve the Crime Problems in Prisons?" *The Supreme Master Ching Hai News* 98. http://www.godsdirectcontact.org.tw/eng/news/98/ (accessed May 1, 2008).

Jodorowsky, Bess. 2000. *The White Lama.* Trans. Geoffrey Finch and Justin Kelly. Los Angeles: Humanoids Publishing.

Jones, Charlie, and Kim Doren. 2000. *Be the Ball: A Golf Instruction Book for the Mind.* Kansas City: Andrews McMeel Publishing.

Jones, Ken. 2003. *The New Social Face of Buddhism: A Call to Action*. Somerville, MA: Wisdom Publications.

Kabat-Zinn, Jon, and University of Massachusetts Medical Center/Worcester. 1991. *Full Catastrophe Living: Using the Wisdom of Your Body and Mind to Stress, Pain, and Illness*. New York: Dell Publications.

Kamala Tiyavanich. 1997. *Forest Recollections: Wandering Monks in Twentieth-Century Thailand*. Honolulu: University of Hawai'i Press.

Kamens, Edward. 1990. *The Buddhist Poetry of the Great Kamo Priestess*. Ann Arbor: University of Michigan, Center for Japanese Studies.

Kassor, Constance. 2003. "Prison Meditation Groups. The Buddhist Peace Fellowship." http://www.bpf.org/html/current_projects/transformative_justice/pdfs/Star taPMG.pdf (accessed September 16, 2008).

Kaza, Stephanie, and Kenneth Kraft, eds. 2000. *Dharma Rain: Sources of Buddhist Environmentalism*. Boston: Shambhala Publications.

Keenan, John P. 1989. "Spontaneity in Western Martial Arts: A Yogācāra Critique of *Mushin* (No-Mind)." *Japanese Journal of Religious Studies* 16 (4): 285–98.

Keown, Damien V., Charles S. Prebish, and Wayne R. Husted, eds. 1998. *Buddhism and Human Rights*. London: Curzon Press.

Keyes, Charles F. 1971. "Buddhism and National Integration in Thailand." *Journal of Asian Studies* 30 (3): 551–67.

Kirsch, A. Thomas. 1977. "Complexity in the Thai Religious System: An Interpretation." *Journal of Asian Studies* 36 (2): 241–66.

Koyasan Buddhist Temple, 1912–1962 (a commemorative book for the temple's fiftieth anniversary).

Krucoff, Carol. 2003. "Insight from Injury." *Yoga Journal*, May/June, 120–24, 203.

Kusuma, Bhikkhuni. 2000. "Inaccuracies in Buddhist Women's History." In *Innovative Buddhist Women: Swimming against the Stream*, ed. Karma Lekshe Tsomo, 5–12. Surrey, UK: Curzon Press.

LaFleur, William R. 1990. "Sattva: Enlightenment for Plants and Trees." In *Dharma Gaia*, ed. Allan Hunt Badiner, 136–44. Berkeley: Parallax Press.

LaFleur, William R. 2001. "Saigyō and the Buddhist Value of Nature." In *Nature in Asian Traditions of Thought*, ed. John Baird Callicott and Roger T. Ames, 183–208. Albany: State University of New York Press.

Laird, John. 2000. *Money Politics, Globalisation, and Crisis: The Case of Thailand*. Singapore: Graham Brash Pte.

Lamotte, Étienne. 1983/1984 (1947). "The Assessment of Textual Authenticity in Buddhism." Trans. Sara Boin-Webb. *Buddhist Studies Review* 1 (1): 4–15.

Lamotte, Étienne. 1988 (1949). "Assessment of Textual Interpretation in Buddhism." In *Buddhist Hermeneutics*, ed. Donald S. Lopez Jr., 11–27. Trans. Sara Boin-Webb. Honolulu: University of Hawai'i Press.

Lavine, Amy. 1998. "Tibetan Buddhism in America: The Development of American Vajrayāna." In *The Faces of Buddhism in America,* ed. Charles S. Prebish and Kenneth K. Tanaka, 99–115. Berkeley: University of California Press.

Lawrence, Ian. 2005. "The Emergence of 'Sport and Spirituality' in Popular Culture." *Sport Journal* 8 (2). http://www.thesportjournal.org/article/emergence-sport-and-spirituality-popular-culture (accessed October 28, 2008).

Learman, Linda. 2005. *Buddhist Missionaries in the Era of Globalization*. Honolulu: University of Hawai'i Press.

Lee, Cyndi, and David Nichtern. 2007. "Yoga Body, Buddha Mind." *Shambhala Sun*, March, 50–57.

LeVine, Sarah, and David N. Gellner. 2005. *Rebuilding Buddhism: The Theravada Movement in Twentieth-Century Nepal*. Cambridge: Harvard University Press, 76–85.

Li Yuchen. 2000. "Ordination, Legitimacy, and Sisterhood: The International Full Ordination Ceremony in Bodhgaya." In *Innovative Buddhist Women: Swimming against the Stream*, ed. Karma Lekshe Tsomo, 168–98. Surrey, UK: Curzon Press.

Lohmann, Larry. 1991. "Peasants, Plantations and Pulp: The Politics of Eucalyptus in Thailand." *Bulletin of Concerned Asian Scholars* 23 (4): 3–17.

Lopez, Donald S., Jr. 1998. *Prisoners of Shangri-La: Tibetan Buddhism and the West*. Chicago: University of Chicago Press.

Lopez, Donald S., Jr. 2002. *A Modern Buddhist Bible: Essential Readings from East and West*. Boston: Beacon Press.

Lopez, Donald S., Jr., ed. 2005. *Critical Terms for the Study of Buddhism*. Chicago: University of Chicago Press.

Loy, David R. 2003. *The Great Awakening: Buddhism and Social Theory*. Boston: Wisdom Publications.

Lozoff, Bo. 1985. *We're All Doing Time: A Guide to Getting Free*. Rev. ed. Durham, NC: Human Kindness Foundation.

MacIntyre, Alasdair. 1990. *Three Rival Versions of Moral Enquiry: Encyclopaedia, Genealogy, and Tradition*. Notre Dame: University of Notre Dame Press.

Mackenzie, Vicki. 1988. *The Boy Lama*. San Francisco: Harper & Row.

Mackenzie, Vicki. 1996. *Reborn in the West: The Reincarnation Masters*. New York: Marlowe & Company.

Macy, Joanna. 1990. "The Greening of the Self." In *Dharma Gaia: A Harvest of Essays in Buddhism and Ecology*, ed. Allan Hunt Badiner, 53–63. Berkeley: Parallax Press.

Macy, Joanna. 1991. *World as Lover; World as Self*. Berkeley: Parallax Press.

Macy, Joanna. 2000. "The Third Turning of the Wheel." In *Dharma Rain: Sources of Buddhist Environmentalism*, ed. Stephanie Kaza and Kenneth Kraft, 150–60. Boston: Shambhala Publications.

Maisel, Ivan. 2006. "Mickelson's Win Defined by Dominance." http://espn.com (accessed April 12, 2008).

Marshall, Megan. 2005. *The Peabody Sisters*. Boston: Houghton Mifflin.

Masters, Jarvis Jay. 1997. *Finding Freedom: Writings from Death Row*. Junction City, CA: Padma Publishing.

Mathews, Freya. 1988. "Conservation and Self-Realization: A Deep Ecology Perspective." *Environmental Ethics* 10 (winter).

Matthews, Bruce. 2002. "Buddhism in Canada." In *Westward Dharma: Buddhism beyond Asia,* ed. Charles S. Prebish and Martin Baumann, 120–38. Berkeley: University of California Press.

Maull, Fleet. 2004. *Tricycle: The Buddhist Review* (spring).

McCreddie, Laura. 2003. "It's Just Not Cricket." *Yoga,* June, 94.

McCullough, William H., and Helen Craig McCullough, trans. 1980. *A Tale of Flowering Fortunes.* Stanford: Stanford University Press.

McFarlane, Stewart. 1990. "*Mushin,* Morals, and Martial Arts: A Discussion of Keenan's Yogācāra Critique." *Japanese Journal of Religious Studies* 17 (4): 397–420.

McKinney, Meredith, trans. 1998. *The Tale of Saigyō (Saigyō Monogatari).* Ann Arbor: Michigan Papers in Japanese Studies, Number 25, Center for Japanese Studies, The University of Michigan.

McMahan, David L. 2002. "Repackaging Zen for the West." In *Westward Dharma: Buddhism beyond Asia,* ed. Charles S. Prebish and Martin Baumann, 218–29. Berkeley: University of California Press.

McMahan, David L. 2008. *The Making of Buddhist Modernism.* Oxford: Oxford University Press.

Merullo, Roland. 2005. *Golfing with God: A Novel of Heaven and Earth.* Chapel Hill: Algonquin Press.

Meston, Daja Wangchuk with Clare Ansberry. 2007. *Comes the Peace: My Journey to Forgiveness.* New York: Free Press.

Metcalf, Franz Aubrey. 2002. "The Encounter of Buddhism and Psychology." In *Westward Dharma: Buddhism beyond Asia,* ed. Charles S. Prebish and Martin Baumann, 348–64. Berkeley: University of California Press.

Miller, Karen Maezen. 2006. *Momma Zen: Walking the Crooked Path of Motherhood.* Boston: Trumpeter.

Miyata, Taisen. 2002. *Koyasan Buddhist Temple of Los Angeles* (pamphlet), October 20.

Miyata, Taisen. n.d. *Oregon Shinnoin Temple (Koyasan Shingon Mission).*

Moran, Peter. 2004. *Buddhism Observed: Travelers, Exiles and Tibetan Dharma in Kathmandu.* London: RoutledgeCurzon.

Murphy, Michael. 1972. *Golf in the Kingdom.* New York: Penguin Books.

Naess, Arne. 1989. *Ecology, Community, and Lifestyle: An Outline of Ecosophy.* Cambridge: Cambridge University Press.

Napthali, Sarah. 2008. *Buddhism for Mothers of Young Children: Becoming a Mindful Parent.* Chicago: Allen & Unwin.

Nattier, Jan. 1995. "Visible and Invisible: Jan Nattier on the Politics of Representation in Buddhist America." *Tricycle: The Buddhist Review* (fall), 42–49.

Nattier, Jan. 1998. "Who Is a Buddhist? Charting the Landscape of Buddhist America." In *The Faces of Buddhism in America,* ed. Charles S. Prebish and Kenneth K. Tanaka, 183–95. Berkeley: University of California Press.

Norbu, Jamyang. 1999. *Sherlock Holmes: The Missing Years.* New York: Bloomsbury Publishing.

Numrich, Paul David. 1998. "Theravāda Buddhism in America: Prospects for the *Sangha.*" In *The Faces of Buddhism in America,* ed. Charles S. Prebish and Kenneth K. Tanaka, 147–62. Berkeley: University of California Press.

Owen, David. 2001. *The Chosen One.* New York: Simon and Schuster.

Padgett, Douglas M. 2002. "The Translating Temple: Diasporic Buddhism in Florida." In *Westward Dharma: Buddhism beyond Asia,* ed. Charles S. Prebish and Martin Baumann, 201–17. Berkeley: University of California Press.

Pandey, Rajyashree. 1998.*Writing and Renunciation in Medieval Japan, The Works of the Poet-Priest Kamo no Chōmei.* Ann Arbor: Michigan Monograph Series in Japanese Studies, Number 21, Center for Japanese Studies, University of Michigan.

Parent, Joseph. 2002. *Zen Golf: Mastering the Mental Game.* New York: Doubleday.

Paul, Diana. 1985. *Women in Buddhism: Images of the Feminine in Mahayana Tradition.* Berkeley: University of California Press.

Payne, Richard K. 2005. "Hiding in Plain Sight: The Invisibility of the Shingon Mission in the United States." In *Buddhist Missionaries in the Era of Globalization,* ed. Linda Learman, 101–22. Honolulu: University of Hawai'i Press.

Peck, M. Scott. 1999. *Golf and the Spirit: Lesson for the Journey.* New York: Three Rivers Press.

Penick, Harvey, and Bud Shrake. 1992. *Harvey Penick's Little Red Book.* New York: Simon and Schuster.

Penor Rinpoche. 1999. "Statement by H.H. Penor Rinpoche Regarding the Recognition of Steven Seagal as a Reincarnation of the Treasure Revealer Chungdrag Dorje of Palyul Monastery." http://www.palyul.org/docs/statement.html (accessed December 16, 2007).

Piez, Wendell. 1993. "Anonymous Was a Woman—Again." *Tricycle: The Buddhist Review* 3 (1) (fall).

Pinkaew Leungaramsri, and Noel Rajesh, eds. 1992. *The Future of People and Forests in Thailand after the Logging Ban.* Bangkok: Project for Ecological Recovery.

Prebish, Charles S. 1999. *Luminous Passage: The Practice and Study of Buddhism in America.* Berkeley: University of California Press.

Prebish, Charles S. 2002. "Studying the Spread and Histories of Buddhism in the West: The Emergence of Western Buddhism as a New Subdiscipline within Buddhist Studies." In *Westward Dharma: Buddhism beyond Asia,* ed. Charles S. Prebish and Martin Baumann, 66–84. Berkeley: University of California Press.

Prebish, Charles S., and Kenneth K. Tanaka, eds. 1998. *The Faces of Buddhism in America.* Berkeley: University of California Press.

Prebish, Charles S., and Martin Baumann. 2002. *Westward Dharma: Buddhism beyond Asia.* Berkeley: University of California Press.

Pronger, Brian. 2002. *Body Fascism: Salvation in the Technology of Physical Fitness.* Toronto: University of Toronto Press.

Reynolds, Frank E. 1994. "Dhamma in Dispute: The Interactions of Religion and Law in Thailand." *Law and Society Review* 28 (3): 433–52.

Rhys Davids, Thomas William. 1878. *Buddhism: A Sketch of the Life and Teachings of Gautama the Buddha*. London: Society for Promoting Christian Knowledge.

Rhys Davids, Thomas William. 1881. "The Foundation of the Kingdom of Righteousness (Dhanna-Kakka-Ppavattana-sutta)." In *Buddhist Suttas (Sacred Books of the East)*, Volume 11, ed. F. Max Muller, Oxford University Press. Reprinted Delhi: Motilal Banarsidas, 1980.

Rieff, Philip, ed. 1963. *Psychological Theory: Papers on Metapsychology*. New York: Collier Books.

Roberts, Elizabeth. 1990. "Gaian Buddhism." In *Dharma Gaia: A Harvest of Essays in Buddhism and Ecology*, ed. Allan Hunt Badiner, 147–54. Berkeley: Parallax Press.

Roberts, Katherine, and Deborah Moss. 2004. "Pre-round Poses." *Golf for Women*, May/June, 46.

Robinson, David. 1985. *The Unitarians and the Universalists*. Westport, CT: Greenwood.

Rohlich, Thomas H. 1997. "In Search of Critical Space: The Path of *Monogatari* Criticism in the *Mumyōzōshi*." *Harvard Journal of Asiatic Studies* 57:1.

Rohlich, Thomas H. 2003. "Mountain Villages in the *Tale of Genji*." In *Gengo to Kyōiku: Nihongo o Taishō toshite*, ed. Satoru Koyama, Kanoko Ōtomo, and Miwako Nohara, 121–47. Tokyo: Kuroshio Shuppan.

Roth, Gustav, ed. 1970. *Vinaya: Manual of Discipline for Buddhist Nuns*. Patna: K. P. Jayaswal Research Institute, 224.

Sabol, William, Todd Minton, and Paige Harrison. 2007. "Bureau of Justice Statistics Bulletin: Prison and Jail Inmates at Midyear 2006." http://www.ojp.usdoj .gov/bjs/abstract/pjim06.htm (accessed September 16, 2008).

Saddhatissa, Hammalawa. 1997. *Buddhist Ethics*. 2nd ed. Boston: Wisdom Publications.

Safran, Jeremy, ed. 2003. *Psychoanalysis and Buddhism: An Unfolding Dialogue*. Boston: Wisdom Publications.

Saint-Hilaire, Barthelémy. 1860. *The Buddha and His Religion*. London: Routledge.

Śāntideva. 1997. *The Way of the Bodhisattva*. Boston: Shambhala Publications.

Schmithausen, Lambert. 1991. *Buddhism and Nature: The Lecture Delivered on the Occasion of the Expo 1990; An Enlarged Version with Notes*. Volume 7 of Studia Philologica Buddhica Occasional Paper Series. Tokyo: The International Institute for Buddhist Studies.

Schmithausen, Lambert. 2000. "Buddhism and the Ethics of Nature—Some Remarks." *Eastern Buddhist* 32:2.

Seager, Richard Hughes. 1999. "Buddhist Worlds in the U.S.A.: A Survey of the Territory." In *American Buddhism: Methods and Findings in Recent Scholarship*, ed. Duncan Ryuken Williams and Christopher S. Queen, 238–61. Surrey, UK: Curzon Press.

Seager, Richard Hughes. 2002. "American Buddhism in the Making." In *Westward Dharma: Buddhism beyond Asia*, ed. Charles S. Prebish and Martin Baumann, 106–19. Berkeley: University of California Press.

Sealts, Merton, Jr., and Alfred R. Ferguson 1969. *Emerson's Nature*. New York: Dodd, Mead & Company.

Sens, Josh. 2002. "Good Karma, Bad Golf." *Golf Digest,* November, NE-1–NE-4.

Sherrill, Martha. 2000. *The Buddha from Brooklyn*. New York: Random House.

Shoemaker, Fred, and Pete Shoemaker. 1996. *Extraordinary Golf: The Art of the Possible*. New York: Perigee Trade.

Snellgrove, David L. 1978. *The Image of the Buddha*. Paris: Serindia Publications.

Snodgrass, Judith. 2003. *Presenting Japanese Buddhism to the West: Orientalism, Occidentalism and the Columbian Exposition*. Chapel Hill: University of North Carolina Press.

Snodgrass, Judith. 2007. "Defining Modern Buddhism: Mr and Mrs Rhys Davids and the Pāli Text Society." *Comparative Studies of South Asia, Africa and the Middle East* 27 (1):186–202.

Snodgrass, Judith. 2009. "Publishing Eastern Buddhism: D. T. Suzuki's Journey to the West," in Thomas DuBois, ed., *Casting Faiths: Imperialism and the Transformation of Religion in East and Southeast Asia*. New York: Palgrave Macmillan.

Sogyal Rinpoche. 1992. *The Tibetan Book of Living and Dying*. San Francisco: HarperOne.

Somboon Suksamran. 1977. *Political Buddhism in Southeast Asia: The Role of the Sangha in the Modernization of Thailand*. London: C. Hurst.

Somboon Suksamran. 1982. *Buddhism and Politics in Thailand*. Singapore: Institute of Southeast Asian Studies.

Spletzer, Andy. 2000. "Gun-Toting Samurai: An Interview with Jim Jarmusch." *The Stranger* (Seattle), March 16–22.

Sports Illustrated. 2006. "The Crack-Up," June 26, cover.

Spuler, Michelle. 2002. "The Development of Buddhism in Australia and New Zealand." In *Westward Dharma: Buddhism beyond Asia,* ed. Charles S. Prebish and Martin Baumann, 139–51. Berkeley: University of California Press.

Stein, Joel. 2003. "Just Say Om." *Time* 162, 5.

Stern, Philip Van Doren, ed. 1970. *The Annotated Walden by Henry D. Thoreau*. New York: Clarkson N. Potter.

Stoddard, Brian. 1994. "Golf International: Considerations of Sport in the Global Marketplace." In *Sport in the Global Village*, ed. R. Wilcox, 21–34. Morgantown, VA: Fitness Technology.

Strong, John S. 2001. *The Buddha: A Short Biography*. Oxford: Oneworld Publications.

Sulak Sivaraksa. 2004. *Trans Thai Buddhism and Envisioning Social Resistance: The Engaged Buddhism of Sulak Sivaraksa*. Bangkok: Suksit Siam.

Swearer, Donald K. 1997. "The Hermeneutics of Buddhist Ecology in Contemporary Thailand: Buddhadasa and Dhammapitaka." In *Buddhism and Ecology: The Interconnection of Dharma and Deeds*, ed. Mary Evelyn Tucker and Duncan Ryuken Williams, 21–44. Cambridge, MA: Harvard University Center for the Study of World Religions Publications.

Swearer, Donald K., Sommai Premchit, and Phaithoon Dokbuakaew. 2004. *Sacred Mountains of Northern Thailand*. Chiang Mai: Silkworm Books.

Tambiah, Stanley J. 1976. *World Conqueror and World Renouncer: A Study of Buddhism and Polity in Thailand against a Historical Background*. Cambridge: Cambridge University Press.

Taylor, Jim. 1993a. *Forest Monks and the Nation-State: An Anthropological and Historical Study in Northeastern Thailand*. Singapore: Institute for Southeast Asian Studies.

Taylor, Jim. 1993b. "Social Activism and Resistance on the Thai Frontier: The Case of Phra Prajak Khuttajitto." *Bulletin of Concerned Asian Scholars* 25 (2): 3–16.

Tennent, Sir James Emerson. 1850. *Christianity in Ceylon*. London: John Murray.

Thompson, Annette. 1997. "Talk to Yourself . . . the Right Way." *Golf for Women*, May/June, 84–86.

Thoreau, Henry David. 1849. *A Week on the Concord and Merrimack Rivers*. Boston: James Munroe.

Thurman, Robert. 1994. *The Tibetan Book of the Dead*. New York: Bantam Books.

Time. 2003. "How Your Mind Can Heal Your Body." *Time* 161 (3).

Time. 2003. "The Science of Meditation." *Time* 162 (5) August 4.

Torrey, Bradford, and Francis Allen, eds. 1984. *The Journal of Henry David Thoreau*. 14 volumes, vol. 9. Salt Lake City: G.M. Smith.

Trébuil, Guy. 1995. "Pioneer Agriculture, Green Revolution and Environmental Degradation in Thailand." In *Counting the Costs: Economic Growth and Environmental Change in Thailand*, ed. Jonathan Rigg, 67–89. Singapore: Institute of Southeast Asian Studies.

Tricycle. 2006. "The Enlightened Body." *Tricycle: The Buddhist Review* (spring).

Tsai, Kathryn Ann. 1994. *Lives of the Nuns: Biographies of Chinese Buddhist Nuns from the Fourth to Sixth Centuries*. Honolulu: University of Hawai'i Press.

Tsomo, Karma Lekshe. 2002. "Buddhist Nuns: Changes and Challenges." In *Westward Dharma: Buddhism beyond Asia,* ed. Charles S. Prebish and Martin Baumann, 255–74. Berkeley: University of California Press.

Tsomo, Karma Lekshe, ed. 2004. *Buddhist Women and Social Justice: Ideals, Challenges, and Achievements*. Albany: State University of New York Press.

Tsong khapa. 2005. *Ocean of Reasoning: A Great Commentary on* Nāgārjuna's Mūlamadhyamakakārikā. Trans. Geshe Ngawang Samten and Jay L. Garfield. New York: Oxford University Press.

Tucker, Mary Evelyn, and Duncan Ryuken Williams, eds. 1997. *Buddhism and Ecology: The Interconnection of Dharma and Deeds*. Cambridge, MA: Harvard University Center for the Study of World Religions Publications.

Turnbull, Stephen. 2006. *The Samurai and the Sacred*. New York: Osprey Publishing.

Tweed, Thomas A. 2000. *The American Encounter with Buddhism, 1844–1912: Victorian Culture and the Limits of Dissent*. Chapel Hill: University of North Caroline Press.

Venturino, Steven J. 2008. "Placing Tibetan Fiction in a World of Literary Studies: Jamyang Norbu's *The Mandala of Sherlock Holmes.*" In *Modern Tibetan Literature and Social Change,* ed. Lauran R. Hartley and Patricia Schiaffini-Vedani, 301–26. Durham: Duke University Press.

Versluis, Arthur. 1993. *American Transcendentalism and Asian Religions.* New York: Oxford University Press.

Vickers, Joan. 2004. "The Quiet Eye." *Golf Digest,* January, 96–101.

Wallace, B. Alan. 2002. "The Spectrum of Buddhist Practice in the West." In *Westward Dharma: Buddhism beyond Asia,* ed. Charles S. Prebish and Martin Baumann, 34–50. Berkeley: University of California Press.

Wallace, B. Alan. 2006. *The Attention Revolution: Unlocking the Power of the Focused Mind.* Boston: Wisdom Publications.

Wallace, B. Alan, and Vesna A. Wallace. 1997. *A Guide to the Bodhisattva's Way of Life:* Śāntideva's Bodhicaryāvatāra. Ithaca, NY: Snow Lion.

Wallach, Jeff. 1995. *Beyond The Fairway: Zen Lessons, Insights, And Inner Attitudes of Golf.* New York: Bantam Books.

Weld, Eric Sean. 2004. "Mind Body Books: A Healthful Balance." *NewsSmith* (winter).

Wetzel, Sylvia. 2002. "Neither Monk nor Nun: Western Buddhists as Full-Time Practitioners." In *Westward Dharma: Buddhism beyond Asia,* ed. Charles S. Prebish and Martin Baumann, 275–84. Berkeley: University of California Press.

Whicher, Stephen. 1953. *Freedom and Fate: An Inner Life of Ralph Waldo Emerson.* Philadelphia: University of Pennsylvania Press.

Whicher, Stephen. 1985. "The Question of Means." In *Ralph Waldo Emerson, Modern Critical Views,* ed. Harold Bloom. New York: Chelsea House Publishers.

White, Dana. 2003. "Canyon Ranch Cure." *Golf for Women,* November/December, 82, 85–89.

Whitney, Kobai Scott. 2003. *Sitting Inside: Buddhist Practice in America's Prisons.* Boulder, CO: Prison Dharma Network.

Wickremaratne, Ananda. 1984. *Genesis of an Orientalist.* Delhi: Motilal Banarsidas.

Wijayasundara, Senarat. 1999. "Restoring the Order of Nuns to the Theravadin Tradition." In *Buddhist Women across Cultures: Realizations,* ed. Karma Lekshe Tsomo, 79–87. Albany: State University of New York Press.

Williams, Duncan Ryuken, and Christopher S. Queen, eds. 1999. *American Buddhism: Methods and Findings in Recent Scholarship.* Surrey, UK: Curzon Press.

Wilson, Horace H. 1854. "On Buddha and Buddhism." *Journal of the Royal Asiatic Society of Great Britain and Ireland* 16 (1): 229–65.

Winklemann, Carole. 2009. "The Language of Tibetan Nuns in the Indian Himalayas: Continuities as Change." In *Buddhist Women in a Global Multicultural Community,* ed. Karma Lekshe Tsomo, 274–81. Kuala Lumpur: Sukhi Hotu Press.

Yamamoto Tsunetomo. 2002 (1716). *Hagakure: The Book of the Samurai.* Trans. William Scott Wilson. Tokyo: Kodansha International.

Ziff, Bruce H., and Pratima V. Rao. 1997. *Borrowed Power Essays on Cultural Appropriation.* New Brunswick, NJ: Rutgers University Press.

Žižek, Slavoj. 2001. *On Belief.* New York: Routledge.

CONTRIBUTORS

NALINI BHUSHAN is professor of philosophy at Smith College.

MARK L. BLUM is professor of East Asian studies at The University at Albany.

MARIO D'AMATO is associate professor of religious studies at Rollins College.

SUSAN M. DARLINGTON is professor of anthropology at Hampshire College.

ELIZABETH EASTMAN is a graduate of Smith College 2004.

JAY L. GARFIELD is Doris Silbert Professor in the Humanities and professor of philosophy at Smith College, professor of philosophy at Melbourne University, and professor of philosophy at the Central University of Tibetan Studies.

CONSTANCE KASSOR is a graduate student in religious studies at Emory University.

JUDITH SNODGRASS is professor at the Centre for Cultural Research at the University of Western Sydney.

JANE M. STANGL is instructor in the Department of Exercise and Sports Studies at Smith College.

THOMAS H. ROHLICH is professor of East Asian languages and literatures at Smith College.

MERIDEL RUBENSTEIN is an independent artist. Her most recent book is *Belonging: From Los Alamos to Vietnam. Photoworks and Installations.*

KARMA LEKSHE TSOMO is associate professor of religious studies at University of San Diego.

ABRAHAM ZABLOCKI is assistant professor of religious studies at Agnes Scott College.

NOTE ON THE IMAGES

Photoworks from the *Millennial Forest Project* (2000–2004) by Meridel Rubenstein are made with vegetable inks printed digitally on tree bark paper hand coated with ground mica and gum arabic, each 46×23".

Cover: *New Growth Tapestry*, 60×46" in 3 sections. (Dinh Q. Le, Southern California artist living in Saigon, with 4 trees from Angkor Wat).

Introduction: *Spong Tree,* Ta Prohm, Siem Riep, Cambodia.

Chapter 1: *Village Tree*, Tien Lac village, Giang Province, Vietnam, 1,000 yrs old.

Chapter 2: *Bald Cypress*, Bayou de View, E. Arkansas, between 800 and 1,000 years old.

Chapter 3: *Tree at Old Chiang Mai,* excavation Wat E-Kang, Thailand.

Chapter 4: *Fire Pine*, S Site, Los Alamos National Laboratory, New Mexico.

Chapter 5: *Bodhi Tree*, Botanical Gardens Temple, Saigon.

Chapter 6: *Bristlecone Pine*, cousin of "Methuselah," over 4,700 years old. Methuselah is recognized as the oldest dated tree in the world. Both trees are tagged and located in the Ancient Bristlecone Pine Forest at Inyo National Forest near Bishop, California.

Chapter 7: *Temple Tree*, at Hien Lam Pavilion, Imperial City Hue.

Chapter 8: *Pinchot Sycamore*, circumference 23'7", located in Simsbury, Connecticut, the largest tree in the state. Approximately 425 years old. It is the only known tree of its age and species in the United States.

Chapter 9: *Queen Tree*, Cuc Phuong National Forest, Vietnam, over 1,000 years old.

Chapter 10: *Piñon Pine*, Capulin Volcanic Monument, near Clayton, New Mexico, 600 years old.

Chapter 11: *Tree at Chedi Luang*, Chiang Mai, Thailand.

Chapter 12: *Post Oak*, S. Osage County, Oklahoma. Between 300 and 500 years old. Located in Cross Timbers ancient forest along the eastern flank of the southern Great Plains, dividing the deciduous eastern forests from the Great Plains.

INDEX